# Exposed

# Exposed

## WHY OUR HEALTH INSURANCE IS INCOMPLETE AND WHAT CAN BE DONE ABOUT IT

Christopher T. Robertson

WITHDRAWN

Harvard University Press

Cambridge, Massachusetts, and London, England   2019

First printing

*Library of Congress Cataloging-in-Publication Data*

Names: Robertson, Christopher T., 1975– author.
Title: Exposed : why our health insurance is incomplete and
    what can be done about it / Christopher T. Robertson.
Description: Cambridge, Massachusetts : Harvard University Press, 2019.
Identifiers: LCCN 2019016987 | ISBN 9780674972162
Subjects: LCSH: Health insurance—United States. | Medical care,
    Cost of—United States. | Health care reform—United States.
Classification: LCC HG9396 .R63 2019 | DDC 368.38/200973—dc23
LC record available at https://lccn.loc.gov/2019016987

For those suffering with illness or injury

# CONTENTS

# INTRODUCTION

The U.S. healthcare system has been the battleground for some of the most trenchant political disputes of our time, challenging Americans to think in life-or-death terms about the meaning of their political union. The key battles have raged over whether all Americans should have health insurance.

This stark disagreement occludes a more fundamental consensus. For most of the last fifty years, there has been a broad bipartisan agreement that, regardless of whether it is a government program or a private insurance plan, the coverage should be incomplete. Liberals and conservatives alike seem to have agreed on the cost-exposure consensus—that sizable deductibles, copays, and coinsurance should cause patients to individually bear a large portion of the costs for the healthcare they consume. This point has seemed about as controversial as the idea that banks should have locks on their doors. To do otherwise—to have a system of altogether "free" (i.e., fully insured) healthcare—would be imprudent, irresponsible, and wasteful. This book exposes the ideological roots of the cost-exposure consensus and reassesses those foundational commitments, normatively and empirically.

Deductibles, copays, and coinsurance are all called "out-of-pocket payments." In 1950, it may have made sense for a patient in a Norman Rockwell painting to pull out his wallet to pay for a doctor's visit, and maybe likewise pay for a course of penicillin at the local drug store. Today, aggregate healthcare spending is driven by proton beams, biologic drugs grown with proprietary cell lines, and organ transplantations—all of which can cost multiples of an entire year of patient income. Half of all health spending in the United States is driven by the one-twentieth of us who unluckily get sick enough to need these high-tech and very expensive treatments, spending on average over $50,000 each during that year.[1] For middle-class patients to somehow afford these health technologies, the vast majority of these monies must come from insurance and the rest often comes from elsewhere, such as debt. Indeed, as of 2017, healthcare is the leading category of the $78.5 billion in consumer debt collected each year, which is more than forty times the size of credit-card debt in contrast.[2] Today, it is only a quaint euphemism to suppose that substantial deductibles, copays, and coinsurance are paid "out-of-pocket."

Often, the mere exposure to costs can deter a patient from ever even consuming healthcare in the first place—and that's often the point of imposing such costs. According to a 2019 poll, three in ten (29%) of adults reported that costs caused them not to take their medicines as prescribed in the past year.[3] And of course, failing to take prescribed medicines can have adverse health consequences; for example, a recent paper found that financial barriers to care were associated with worse recovery after coronary heart disease.[4] Thus, as a policy mechanism we should think about the *exposure* to costs itself. We can then attend realistically to whether the care is consumed and whether exposed cost is paid and, if so, how.

Elsewhere in the world, these are known as "user fees," because the user of the healthcare is made to pay herself. Another way to think about cost exposure is to define it as the absence of insurance for some portion of a patient's healthcare expenses. For these costs, the patient is effectively uninsured, just like a person who has no insurance coverage at all. Indeed, in research published in the *New England Journal of Medicine,* scholars have shown that children with insurance but huge cost exposures in relation to their family incomes have difficulties accessing healthcare similar to kids with no insurance at all.[5]

Although the term "cost-sharing" is commonly used to refer to deductibles and copays, it is a misleading label, because those exposed costs are precisely the ones that are *not shared* with others in the insurance pool. Because the individual patient (and perhaps her family) must pay the costs alone, they would be better understood as *"unshared costs."* To what degree *should* those costs be borne individually or shared collectively is a primary question of this book.

To be sure, cost exposure is growing. In recent decades, even as we have reduced the number of Americans who altogether lack insurance coverage, we have made coverage less and less complete for those that have it. In the last decade alone, Figure I.1 shows that deductibles have increased 212%, which is ten times the rate of inflation or wage growth.[6] Even under the progressive 2010 Affordable Care Act (ACA), which expanded coverage to millions more Americans, those with insurance could still be exposed to devastating levels of copayments, up to $15,000 per year for a family. In this sense, we are trading the problem of uninsurance for another problem of underinsurance.

Americans have noticed. Every American has received a befuddling "explanation of benefits" document in the mail from an insurer weeks after he or she made treatment choices, showing absurdly high prices, which are then negotiated down by insurers, and then a portion assigned to the patient. This practice demonstrates the fallacy of any theory that would depend on consumers to factor prices into their healthcare decisions. Imagine trying to buy a television, and, instead of a set sticker price, you get the price in the mail weeks *after* buying the television.

While only about one in six Americans are uninsured, everyone else is concerned about the quality of their health insurance coverage.[7] When polled, only a third of Americans describe their coverage as excellent or good.[8] Two-thirds of Americans say they want to lower their healthcare costs but don't know how; over half say they have received a medical bill that they could not afford.[9] In the 2018 election, healthcare was the single most important issue for voters (with nearly 75% saying it was very important to them), and when asked what they meant, "healthcare costs" arose as the most common focal point for their interest.[10]

In the U.S. healthcare system, cost exposure serves two distinct functions: one distributional, one behavioral. First, someone must pay for the costs of our healthcare, and insurance is one way of doing so. An insurance plan transfers costs from individuals to the larger insurance pool so that the costs can be borne collectively through premiums (and through taxes). Half of all Americans receive health insurance from their employer.[11] In the typical employer-sponsored plan, the employees individually bear about 18% of the cost of their healthcare; the remaining 82% is borne collectively by the insurer—which means it is paid through direct premiums; through implicit premiums from employees who forgo higher wages in exchange for them; through some portion by the employer; and by the federal government, which forgoes income taxes on such employer-based insurance, to the tune of $300 billion per year.[12] As convoluted as these insurance mechanisms may be, the point is that they cause the costs of healthcare to be borne collectively. Cost exposure, on the other hand, imposes costs on the individual.

Cost exposure also has a behavioral function, because it can affect whether the patient chooses to consume versus decline the healthcare offered. Since we lack infinite resources to spend on healthcare, somebody must decide whether any particular healthcare option is worth its price. This behavioral function of cost exposure is a form of rationing, spread across the population of healthcare consumers rather than centralized in an authoritative source. Through cost exposure, patients must determine whether the healthcare in question is worth the cost they will potentially bear. If cost exposure can reduce consumption of healthcare or shift patients toward less expensive forms of healthcare, it might then reduce the cost of insurance premiums ex ante. It may also make the economy more efficient, as individuals trade for other types of healthcare or other forms of non-healthcare consumption that deliver higher value to them.

Or cost exposure might distract patients and increase their fear of bad outcomes. It might cause patients to decline valuable healthcare and thereby exacerbate health problems that could have been cheaply treated if caught early. Under cost exposure, patients may spread untreated contagious disease, experience stress and lost work, and lose their homes and access to credit— ultimately increasing the social burden of illness and driving healthcare costs higher. Even more, cost exposure can change the meaning of the treatment relationship and debase our fellow citizens, who are left to beg on social media for crowdsourced donations to meet their basic healthcare needs.

To understand cost exposure, one can look to the world of academic scholarship, but the debate over health insurance has been fragmented. Economists have approached the questions from a particular theory of rational decision making and the related theory of "moral hazard," buttressed by large-scale quantitative approaches using administrative data about healthcare purchases. Another academic field, health services research, has relied more heavily on surveys of patients and physicians and tracked healthcare outcomes. Public health scholars worry about access to healthcare and disparities for certain groups. Psychologists and business school professors have pursued related questions about choice and credit in laboratory experiments. Philosophers have been plowing in other fields altogether, as they sought to understand what we owe each other and why. Legal scholars have approached these questions in subfields as disparate as tax, employee benefits, consumer protection, bankruptcy, and contract law. This book is a project of synthesis, recovering all that we know about cost exposure from these many different perspectives to tell a coherent story about cost exposure and its implications for reform.

## HEALTHCARE SPENDING, NEW TECHNOLOGIES, AND WASTE

In 2017, U.S. spending on healthcare reached $3.5 trillion, or $10,739 per person.[13] Consider that the median family income in the United States is about $61,372.[14]

It was not always this way. Historically, Americans spent only one-twentieth of the economy on healthcare—it was 5% of gross domestic product (GDP) in 1960.[15] By the mid-1980s, one in every ten dollars was spent on healthcare. During the 2020s the rate will double again, as we approach the point of allocating one-fifth of the entire U.S. economy to healthcare spending (we rolled past 17.8% in 2016).[16] In 2008, the U.S. Congressional Budget Office (CBO) projected that health spending could grow to half of all U.S. spending.[17] Of course, that depends on technological develop-ments, market developments, and policy reforms that may or may not happen in the interim. But one former Secretary of the U.S. Department of Health and Human Services called this the "healthcare inflation mon-ster" that is eating our economy.[18]

To say that we spend a lot on healthcare is not to say that this spending is irrational. Once a family has a home, two cars, and plenty of home appli-ances and other amenities, perhaps it is perfectly sensible to direct more and more discretionary income to extending the length of our lives and the quality of our living. An additional good year of life could be worth immea-surably more than just another gizmo, gadget, or even an extravagant two-week vacation. And, indeed, life expectancy has risen and disease burdens have fallen during this period of growth in healthcare costs.

On this theory, as countries become wealthier, we should not be surprised to see them shift more spending to healthcare. Comparisons to other highly developed countries suggest, however, that something is peculiar about the United States. Countries such as the United Kingdom (where health spending is 9.7% of GDP), Australia (9.6%), New Zealand (9.2%), and Canada

(10.6%) have found ways to capture longer lifespans and less morbidity, at about half the spending compared to the United States.[19] Indeed, statistical comparisons bear this out: as countries become richer, their healthcare spending remains relatively flat as a proportion of GDP.[20] The United States is truly an outlier—no other developed country spends anywhere near as much.

Although the aging of the baby boomer population and the expanding waistlines of Americans suggest demographic and lifestyle factors are driving this growth in U.S. healthcare spending, they are not the primary culprits. Analysts estimate that aging of the population accounts for only about 2% of growth in healthcare spending, and increasing obesity may account for about 4% of the total growth.[21] In contrast, according to the CBO, "most analysts have concluded that the bulk of the long-term rise resulted from the healthcare system's use of new medical services that were made possible by technological advances," including new drugs and devices specifically.[22] The United States has led the world in pioneering exciting new medical technologies, mastering both the innovation and the marketing to ensure that they are broadly adopted, and in return we have paid for these new technologies with breathtakingly high prices.

This point is important, because it shows how our level of health spending is not inevitable; it is based on our choices about what healthcare to consume, how much, and at what prices. Even more, healthcare cost growth is determined by our laws and policies regulating health insurance as those policies affect our consumption choices.

## A PRIMER ON COST EXPOSURE

Policymakers and insurance designers have created a range of mechanisms to try to stymie healthcare spending, and cost exposure has been a primary tool. To define and illustrate the primary forms of cost exposure, let's consider how they are experienced by the patient, whose spending on healthcare grows during a given year. In effect, these most common cost-exposure schemas cause an individual's degree of insurance coverage to change twice, as she moves through three different "zones" of insurance—from no insurance, to partial insurance, and finally to full insurance. Yet all the way through this process, patients are also exposed to a "twilight zone" of additional costs, which require our attention as well.

## Zone 1—No Insurance

An annual deductible sets a threshold for health spending, say $1,000, which gives the patient complete exposure to the first health expenditures in a year. Until the patient reaches that threshold, she pays everything out-of-pocket. (In fact, patients can be exposed to separate deductibles for medical care and prescriptions, but I simplify here.) In a 2018 survey of employers, 85% of covered workers have a general deductible, and the health plans had average annual deductibles of $1,600.[23]

As Figure I.1 reflects, one of the biggest policy trends in recent decades has been to expand deductibles, keeping patients in the no-insurance range during more and more of each year, but also setting up special tax-preferred savings accounts, so they have designated money to spend for their own health expenses. About one-third of American workers are in such "high-deductible health plans"—a more than doubling of the proportion since 2010—and their average deductible is about $2,245.[24] Federal law caps deductibles from being more than about $7,000 for families (an amount that grows each year), but few employer plans reach that level anyway.

Federal law requires that these high-deductible health plans are paired with "health savings accounts" which allow patients to sock away untaxed funds for future health expenditures, not unlike the way people sock away money in retirement accounts. About twenty to thirty million Americans have such health accounts, but the average balance is only $2,700, which could barely carry the beneficiary through the deductible in a single bad year, before being wiped out.[25] A recent survey of Americans found that the higher their deductible was, the more likely the individual was to have negative views of their health plan, and the more likely they are to experience problems affording their care or to put off care due to cost."[26] Three quarters of those in the highest deductible plans with chronic conditions say that they have had to skip or delay medical care for cost reasons.

Roughly fifteen million patients buy insurance on the individual market exchanges that arose from the ACA. In this market, health plans are "tiered," and named for precious metals, to reflect different levels of coverage. In 2019, the average deductible was $6,258 for bronze plans and $4,375 for silver plans.[27] So even the silver plans are about double what would be considered the typical "high-deductible" plan in the employer market, and these levels have been trending upward as well.

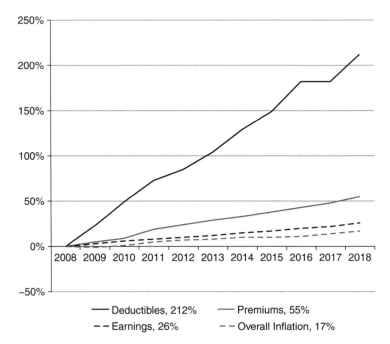

*Figure I.1* Cumulative Increases in General Annual Deductibles, Family Coverage Premiums, Workers' Earnings, and Inflation 2008–2018 (Data source: Kaiser Family Foundation)

In Medicare, the program for the elderly and disabled, deductibles are more modest, though the program divides them into three categories. Patients pay the first $1,364 for ("Part A") hospital inpatient expenses during a benefit period, along with another $135.50 for the first medical care ("Part B") in a year.[28] The prescription drug benefit program ("Part D") has deductibles that vary by plan.

Medicaid is the federal / state insurance program for roughly the poorest fifth of Americans. There deductibles are uncommon, or if present, nominal.[29]

### Zone 2—Some Insurance

Next, there is a middle range in which patients have insurance, but are also exposed to costs through copays, coinsurance, or reference pricing. About two-thirds of workers face copays when they visit a doctor, and about a quarter face coinsurance.[30]

A copay is a flat fee paid at a doctor's office, hospital, or pharmacy. Among employer-based plans, the average copay is $25 for a primary care visit, $151 for outpatient surgery, and $284 for hospital admission.[31] For prescription drugs, employer plans often implement tiers, from generic drugs as low as $11 to as much as $105 for specialty drugs, on average.[32]

Coinsurance is a percentage of the healthcare providers' charges for goods and services, often about 18% for care within the network of providers, which the patient reimburses to the health plan.[33] Some plans (PPOs, or preferred provider organizations) have substantially higher coinsurance, say 40% of billed costs, for patients who consume healthcare outside the plan (regardless of whether they do so intentionally, inadvertently, or in an emergency situation).

In Medicare, patients typically pay 20% of medical expenses after their deductible is met (the rules are different and more complicated for prescription drugs).[34] However, about 85% of Medicare patients also purchase supplemental insurance, which offsets some or all of their cost exposure.[35]

In Medicaid (the program for the poor), cost-exposure profiles vary, and the poorest patients pay little or none. While in some states, coinsurance can be as high as 50% of the amount that the state Medicaid agency pays for the first day of care in an institution, more commonly the coinsurance is 10% to 20% of charges.[36]

Unlike coinsurance, copays have the advantage of simplicity and predictability. It is relatively easy for a patient to predict that she will owe $50 if she walks into a physician's office. For the health-policy designer on the other hand, coinsurance has the advantage of scaling with the patient's consumption decisions. While a copay may give patients an incentive to go to the doctor less often, it does nothing to encourage the patient to figure out whether some doctors may be less expensive than others or to get less expensive care once at the doctor.

Under a "reference price," an insurer pays the basic charges for a service and the beneficiary pays all additional charges beyond that level. In the United States, reference prices have been used, with some success, in the domain of orthopedic surgery.[37] For example, an insurer may pay $28,000 for a hip surgery, if that is the lowest cost available in a region, but patients are free to pay the $6,000 difference for a $34,000 surgery, if it is more convenient or otherwise preferable. A primary advantage of reference prices is that the patient/consumer is guaranteed access to the healthcare (at the reference price), but has discretion to choose other options she may be able to afford, which also has the effect of driving down the prices of other providers, who seek market share.

## Zone 3—Full Insurance

Finally, there is a zone in which patients have no exposure to healthcare costs. The Affordable Care Act requires that certain preventative services must be covered without cost exposure at all. So these are always in Zone 3.

More generally, even for services that normally have cost exposure, the ACA requires that (non-grandfathered) health insurance coverage have a cap on patient cost exposure, and as of 2018, virtually all (99%) of employer-sponsored plans had such a maximum limit.[38] The amounts of these "catastrophic caps" vary widely by employer, but they are almost always below the $15,800 maximum allowed by the ACA in 2019.[39] Eighty-six percent of these workers are in a plan with an annual cost-exposure maximum for single coverage of more than $2,000, while 20% are in a plan with a maximum of $6,000 or more.[40] The median employer-based plan is in the $3,000–$3,999 range.[41]

Oddly, Medicare does not have catastrophic caps in its fee-for-service program, which covers most enrollees. However, Medicare Advantage is required to provide a catastrophic cap on cost exposure, even if they have flexibility in structuring other cost-exposure requirements. In general, cost-exposure profiles in Medicare Advantage plans more closely resemble private insurance plans.

For the individual market, the ACA requires that insurers lower the cost-exposure levels for lower-income families. For example, a family at 100% of the Federal Poverty Level (FPL) has cost exposure capped at $2,600, while those above 250% may by exposed to up to $7,900 in costs before entering Zone 3 of full insurance.[42] To compensate the insurer for these reductions, the ACA allocated funds from the U.S. Treasury, but one federal district court has held that Congress never actually appropriated the funds. Although the Trump administration stopped making those payments, the insurers have nonetheless been required to maintain the cost-sharing reductions for their beneficiaries, and they have simply raised premiums (and garnered larger federal subsidies on that front).[43]

Regardless of which insurance system applies a cost-exposure cap, it is useful to illustrate how these caps can work. Imagine Ms. Mildred Median, a patient in a plan with a $1,500 deductible, an 18% coinsurance burden, and a $3,500 cost-exposure maximum, and assume that the plan counts the deductible toward the cost-exposure maximum as most plans do. Suppose that this year, Ms. Median will spend tens of thousands of dollars on a heart stent or a chemotherapy drug. After spending her $1,500 deductible, Ms. Median will be exposed to up to $2,000 more in costs ($3,500 cap minus the $1,500 deductible). Given her 18% coinsurance rate, that $2,000 will be consumed after the next $11,111 in healthcare expenses. Thus, Ms. Median has reached Zone 3, the range of full insurance, after consuming $12,611 in health expenses, $3,500 of which she paid out-of-pocket.[44]

Notwithstanding this example, there is, in fact, wide variability in how plans apply these caps, making it difficult to generalize across plans. One study of insurance policies in Massachusetts gave the example of two policies that had the same $5,000 cost-exposure limit but counted different expenses toward that limit. The authors explain that a breast cancer patient would pay $7,641 in cost exposure under one plan and $12,907 in cost exposure under the other.[45] Key differences included whether there was a separate deductible for prescription drugs, and whether the out-of-pocket limit included copays.

### The Twilight Zone

The forgoing cost-exposure mechanisms take a given healthcare product or service and then divide its cost between the insurer and the patient. But insurance policies also leave patients exposed to costs by simply excluding certain types of expenses from health insurance coverage altogether. I call this the "twilight zone," because these costs typically do not appear in the denominator of such analyses, and they are not typically considered for the sake of deductibles or caps. Yet, for patients these costs are quite real, and for policymakers they are essential for understanding patients' real financial risk.

Most generally, health plans tend to cover only "medically necessary" care, which in the first instance depends on whether your physician says that you need the care to treat a recognized disease or other medical problem. For example, although the insurer covers childbirth, it may not cover an upgrade to a private hospital room. But "medical necessity" may also be used to deny a patient a new insulin pump for her type-1 diabetes, even though her physician recommends the care as a way to help stabilize her blood sugars and protect her against dangerous lows overnight. As a spokesman for a nurses' association argues, "Insurers employ warehouses full of claims adjusters who, as a primary function, scrutinize claims for pretexts to deny care, saying it is 'experimental' or 'not medically necessary' even when the medical treatment, prescription medication, diagnostic procedure or referral to a specialist is recommended by doctors."[46]

Even if a physician says a certain expense is medically necessary, most health plans also have other specific exclusions of coverage. They typically do not cover experimental treatments, such as drugs not approved by the Food and Drug Administration, or various alternative sorts of care, such as acupuncture, chelation therapy, or midwifery. On the other hand, a hodge-podge of 2,000 state laws have imposed coverage mandates for whatever disease or treatment may have caught the interest of legislators (e.g., forty-six states require coverage for autism).[47] Insurers also maintain formularies, which limit reimbursements to certain pharmaceuticals, and thereby gives insurers leverage to haggle with the drug makers about prices charged. One recent study found that insurers in the individual markets included only 78% of available drugs on their formularies for reimbursement.[48]

Next, there are a range of uncovered expenses that are so common-place that they are almost hard to notice. For example, in the U.S. health-care system, over-the-counter drugs are generally not covered by health insurance, even if there is an equivalent drug available by prescription. Nor are needed disposable products, such as diapers for incontinence. Nor travel to the hospital or the time it takes for a spouse or parent to take off work.

Many health plans also limit the range of providers that will be reimbursed, so that a patient who receives care from an "out-of-network" physician would have to pay more or all of those costs "out-of-pocket," if at all. "Balance billing" is the related phenomenon of a healthcare provider demanding that the patient pay whatever the insurer does not. A 2011 survey found that 8% of consumers had used an out-of-network physician, and this most commonly occurred in emergency departments (40% of the time).[49] Patients can also face large-balance bills due to ambulance services and even air evacuation. But it can also arise for elective healthcare. In one notorious example discussed later, a patient carefully chose a hospital in his network, expecting to pay the $3,000 annual cap on cost exposure for his surgery, but he later also received a $117,000 bill from an assistant surgeon, who was not in the patient's network. This sort of bill, sometimes called "drive-by doctoring," makes the patient's $3,000 cap trivial to the real financial risks facing patients. About a quarter of state governments have passed laws regulating these practices; however, the laws are often quite specific, for example, only applying to ambulance care.[50]

Cutting across these areas of uncovered healthcare, the ACA required that all insurance plans cover ten categories of "essential health benefits" (EHBs), including emergency care, prescription drugs, maternity and pediatric care, and mental healthcare. One goal of this law is to eliminate some heterogeneity in the health insurance market, allowing consumers to make apples-to-apples comparisons across plans, gaining some reassurance that they all cover the core risks.

Prior to the ACA, some health insurance plans covered some of these EHBs but capped how much the insurer would pay either annually or during the patient's lifetime. This sort of provision effectively created a fourth zone of noninsurance. Individuals who spent more than the cap lost insurance coverage for additional costs above those caps. The ACA made these sorts of insurance plans illegal, thereby reducing the realistic out-of-pocket exposure to patients facing these catastrophic risks.

## THE ARC OF THE ARGUMENT

With this overview of the U.S. health system's ubiquitous use of cost exposure in a menagerie of forms, we can now preview the argument of this book, which spans six chapters. I show why U.S. health policy has systematically embraced cost exposure as a solution to one particular economic problem, which turns out to be insubstantial compared to the rampant monopolies, lack of investment in the production of knowledge, and conflicts of interest that together drive real healthcare waste in the United States. Once we understand the function of insurance to provide access to otherwise unaffordable care, we see the problems of using cost exposure as a rationing mechanism, given both the limits of human decision-making capacity and the limits of American pocketbooks. Finally, as we think about what we owe to fellow citizens, we can try, at the very least, to use the cost-exposure tool more intelligently, with the benefit of several innovative reforms that tailor exposure to the value of care and the patient's ability to pay for it. Ultimately, we should simply reject the American cost-exposure consensus and instead pursue the real drivers of wasteful healthcare spending.

More specifically, Chapter 1 explains how we have found ourselves in this peculiar situation, having fought for universal health insurance coverage but ending up with incomplete insurance that leaves us exposed to huge costs. This chapter reviews five decades of economic theory about how insurance allows patients to spend "other people's money," which is known as the theory of moral hazard. This doctrine has driven U.S. health policy to resist universal and complete coverage. Looking under the hood of this theory, we see that to understand the effects of insurance on spending, traditional economic analysis has compared insured persons to those with less or no insurance. Sure enough—people with insurance spend more. However, this form of counterfactual analysis confuses healthcare waste with healthcare access. People without complete insurance decline care because they cannot afford it, not because it is valueless! A closer look at the evidence shows that cost exposure reduces spending indiscriminately—cutting good and bad healthcare alike—and imposes negative health effects on those with lower incomes and chronic illnesses. Rather than the uninsurance counterfactual, I show that a better analytical comparison for traditional health insurance is insurance paid in cash, which is known as an indemnity. Although these policies do not presently exist for healthcare, we can simulate them, and when we do so we find that moral hazard turns out to be quite minimal. Decades of health policy have been chasing a bugaboo.

The second chapter reviews the phenomenology and behavioral science of cost exposure. We see that cost exposure changes the experience of healthcare, making healing harder rather than easier to achieve. Weighing treatment options and thinking about the cost of care may itself change the experience and meaning of healthcare, increasing complexity, stress, and fear. It may commodify our bodies in ways that feel demeaning, and it can also alter the doctor-patient relationship, changing it from a sacred healing relationship to one of quid pro quo exchange. For these reasons we see that cost exposure may actually contribute to healthcare waste, worsen consumption choices, and, overall, undermine patient welfare in this range of ways.

Chapter 3 evaluates whether and how substantial cost exposure is feasible as a means for financing modern healthcare. A sober look at the scale of contemporary spending—often multiples of median U.S. income—and at the levels of income and assets held by Americans, shows a profound mismatch. The predicament is exacerbated when one considers that health problems are also associated with income loss and many other incidental expenses that are typically not insured in the U.S. Thus cost exposure is inevitably not "out-of-pocket" but "on credit" instead. This is an important reconceptualization of cost exposure, because it has behavioral implications for healthcare consumers. We proceed to explore economic and psychological evidence about how credit changes consumer behavior. Ironically, debt and the risk of bankruptcy (or death) create another dissociation between consuming at one time and (maybe) paying at a future time, which is not unlike the moral hazard of health insurance. We also see that the use of debt to finance healthcare has a range of downstream effects on mental health, families, and the economy more generally. The evidence shows that medical debt can stand in the way of sound treatment, and even make us sick.

It is time to evaluate this national experiment of large cost exposures in the healthcare system. Evaluation requires a framework of values. In Chapter 4, I take up that task, grappling with some of our implicit notions of responsibility and laying out a normative argument for what we owe to fellow citizens in terms of healthcare access. I will suggest that health insurance policy can and should be approached from a neutral position, not presuming that individuals would be responsible for their own healthcare expenses or presuming that they would *not* be so responsible. Instead, we can see individual and collective aspects of health and healthcare and decide how to construct social policy on this dimension of healthcare financing. Thin theories of democratic equality provide an account of the minimum responsibilities we owe to fellow citizens as citizens—guaranteeing access to a middle-class level of healthcare to protect the dignity and security of fellow citizens. This analysis shows the injustice and folly of current cost-exposure profiles, which treat wildly different situations as if they were the same.

Chapter 5 draws together many of the prior threads to argue for a range of reforms. If we are to evaluate cost exposure as a policy mechanism, let us consider not just its currently existing forms, but also the potential revisions that could have the greatest chance of making it really work to achieve its goals and minimize harm. Specifically, the law should push healthcare providers to be much more transparent in their pricing—and that means more than just a data avalanche of numbers and codes. Providers must guide patients in making healthcare choices in light of their cost exposure, which should be material to any informed consent process. I also suggest a much broader agenda of scaling cost exposure to value, using systematic reviews of the biomedical literature and national practice guidelines. Cost exposure need not be so indiscriminate in its effects. To solve access problems, I propose income-scaling of cost exposure, and, for large healthcare expenses, the use of partial indemnities, which would become a novel form of cost exposure that does not impinge on access or patient choice.

These plausible reforms are something of a test. They are a sketch of what it would take to make cost exposure really up to the task of aligning healthcare consumption with health, rather than merely discriminating on wealth. Yet, I am not confident that the champions of the cost-exposure consensus will reengineer this mechanism to make it really work for all Americans. And even if we accomplished this entire slate of reforms to cost exposure, we still would be left with rampant waste in our healthcare system.

In Chapter 6, we see that real healthcare waste is driven by three causes. First, our healthcare providers enjoy virtual monopolies and no regulation of prices. Second, we suffer from institutionalized ignorance about efficacy and safety of healthcare interventions because we lack public investments in knowledge production. Third, our healthcare is driven by providers with misaligned incentives—they too often pursue their own wealth rather than our health. This analysis shows the limits of cost exposure as a panacea for all that ails our healthcare system. Even while it undermines the core function of insurance to guarantee access to care, cost exposure simply does not target the real drivers of healthcare waste. It has been a fifty-year failed experiment.

We can do better. And we can do better without cost exposure.

# CHAPTER 1

# YOUR HEALTHCARE, THEIR MONEY

What explains the cost-exposure consensus? Why does the U.S. healthcare system depend so heavily on deductibles, copays, and coinsurance? One reason is that a generation of policymakers have been taught a certain story, an economic doctrine, in which cost exposure is necessary to avoid the pernicious effect of health insurance: "moral hazard." This story provides that, if individuals instead pay (some of) their own costs, they will be less likely to consume wasteful health-care. In this chapter, I explore the intellectual history of this idea, along with the theory and evidence as it developed and was written into U.S. policy. It is true that with less insurance people consume less healthcare, but it is not clear how we should evaluate that change in behavior. The evidence shows that the reductions in care are indiscriminate, cutting good and bad healthcare alike, without tracking the value of care. More fundamentally, this half-century economic-policy agenda has misconceived the appropriate comparison for measuring moral hazard. It's not about more or less insurance, but about the type of insurance. When properly analyzed, we find that insurance is not the cause of substantial wasteful spending. Our policy fixation on cost exposure turns out to be misguided.

## THE TEXTBOOK ECONOMICS VIEW OF INSURANCE

"There is nothing like doing things with other people's money," says President Donald Trump.[1] Before turning to politics, Trump famously used investors' money to build the real estate empire he is known for, as well as a casino empire, a mail-order steak company, an airline, and even a vodka company. As his investors know well, the problem with spending other people's money is that the costs and risks might not seem as salient to the one doing the spending.

Health insurance is another of the many ways in which people can spend other people's money, when fully-insured patients consume care, the larger insurance pool pays those costs. Accordingly, some policymakers have seen health insurance as a problem, and complete health insurance is the worst kind of problem. President Trump has thus worked to dismantle the Affordable Care Act (ACA), which had expanded insurance coverage to tens of millions of people who would otherwise have been uninsured.[2]

But this view that health insurance is the problem is not some sort of aberrant political hack. It is quite respectable. According to textbook economic theory, because insurance allows people to purchase care that the insurer pays for, it causes people to consume more healthcare than they need, even more than a rational person spending her own money would even want. Thus, much of that additional consumption is wasteful, that is, not worth its cost. On this theory, insurance can do more harm than good.

It is useful to see how this textbook notion developed in the academic field of economics during the last half-century. Even more, it is valuable to see how political and policymaking elites have incorporated a simplified understanding of this economic reasoning, degrading it into what James Kwak calls "economism." He explains that "economism is influential because of its seductive elegance and explanatory power. It presents a model of the world in which policy outcomes are determined by theoretical axioms as inevitably as mathematical proofs from their assumptions."[3]

### The Early Theory of the 1960s

This story starts with a teleological question. Why do people want health insurance in the first place? What purpose does it serve?

In an influential 1963 paper, building on prior work by Daniel Bernoulli, Milton Friedman, and J. L. Savage, the economist Kenneth Arrow argued that people buy health insurance largely to offset risk.[4] In any given year, a person is likely to have little or no healthcare costs, but if it turns out to be a bad year, they will incur thousands of dollars of medical bills, which may then start to impinge on other spending priorities, such as leisure activities or fancy food. Accordingly, Arrow argued that it is rational to pay relatively small premiums every year, because the forgone money in good years would have little effect on a person's welfare. If the bad year materializes, the security of receiving insurance payouts could be profoundly important for a person's welfare and well-being. The insurance transaction could make sense, even if the total of such payouts is somewhat less than the premiums paid in (as it must be, because the insurer will have administrative costs and may seek profits). This theory turns on the concept of "diminishing marginal utility of money," meaning that the more money you have, the less important additional dollars are. In a very bad year, money is precious, and that is when the insurance kicks in.

Arrow thought that the risk-protection function of health insurance was so important and indisputable that if for any reason the market failed to efficiently provide insurance, the government should do so, perhaps even compulsorily. Arrow would go on to win the 1972 Nobel Memorial Prize in Economic Science, and his analysis was a central part of the national debate around the 1965 establishment of Medicare and Medicaid.

At the same time, Arrow foreshadowed a problem created by insurance. While patients and doctors choose what to consume, the insurer pays for it. He did not develop this point, however. That would be left to a young economist named Mark Pauly in his 1968 seminal article on the economics of moral hazard.[5]

If health insurance is the medicine to treat the disease of risk, it brings along a nasty side effect. Pauly described the problem in terms of "elastic" demand, a fundamental economic concept meaning that the amounts consumed are linked to the prices charged. In a regular market, if low prices drive more consumption, that is great, because it means that more people are enjoying more goods and services. We can assume that each such trade improves overall social welfare, because the buyer ostensibly prefers the product to the cash in her hand, and vice versa for the seller. In a regular market, prices can go down because of technological advances or other increases in productivity, allowing sellers to make more sales even if prices are lower. So, everybody is better off. But the healthcare market is irregular and the relationships among prices, value, and efficiency in this marketplace are unique.

At the point of sale, health insurance has the effect of driving down prices for consumers, and, as such, insured people predictably will consume more healthcare. However, Pauly warned that health insurance drives down the consumer's price in an artificial way. The healthcare still costs just as much, but it is paid by someone else—the insurer. Consumers insulated from the true price will thus consume more, even if the trade does not create consummate value. Thus, with insurance a patient may spend $2,000 (of the insurer's money) on healthcare services that only deliver $50 of value to the patient, an exchange that harms overall welfare. The world would be better off without that extra consumption.

Economists call this underlying dynamic "moral hazard."[6] The "hazard" is that, with insurance, people spend more than they otherwise would. The tinge of "morality" comes from the fact that insurance pools the money of many people together, whether through premiums or taxes. Thus, one person's choice can waste a collective resource belonging to everyone in the insurance pool. As Pauly explains, "Each individual may well recognize that 'excess' use of medical care makes the premium he must pay rise. No individual will be motivated to restrain his own use, however, since the incremental benefit to him for excess use is great, while the additional cost of his use is largely spread over other insurance holders, and so he bears only a tiny fraction of the cost of his use."[7]

Law professor Tom Baker has traced how the concept of moral hazard has been used to signal "the perverse consequences of well-intentioned efforts to share the burdens of life, and [the concept] also helps deny that refusing to share those burdens is mean-spirited or self-interested."[8] In short, the theory of moral hazard advises that we make health insurance stingy in order to prevent social waste. Indeed, Pauly speculated that the welfare loss due to moral hazard could be larger than the welfare benefits of insurance: "the net change in utility from a compulsory purchase of this 'insurance' could well be negative."[9] Contrary to Arrow's suggestion for universal coverage, Pauly implies that if Americans decline to buy health insurance, it is a wise move, recognizing that insurance is a bad deal.

The theory of moral hazard became a core ideological commitment—some might say a preoccupation—of U.S. economists, and it has influenced and reinforced similar trends in U.S. political discourse. At the birth of Medicare, in a 1966 meeting with hospital leaders, Democratic President Lyndon Johnson worried that the newly insured would "abuse" their insurance and "demand unnecessary treatment."[10] Johnson appealed to those at the "grassroots" level to "stand firm against these abuses."[11] Insurance was already conceived as a potential problem; but the solution had not yet crystalized.

### Cost Exposure as a Solution: The 1970s

In a seminal 1970 paper, the Harvard economist Richard Zeckhauser darkly suggested that "no practicable market structure will simultaneously produce optimal risk-spreading and appropriate incentives for individual action."[12] That is, the more that insurance provides risk protection, the more it induces wasteful spending—it's a zero-sum game. Still Zeckhauser set out to define an economic compromise to secure "some risk-spreading and some incentive."[13] This is the theory of cost exposure: if we make insurance incomplete, we can give patients *some* skin-in-the-game. Accordingly, when President Nixon embraced healthcare reform in 1972, he proposed a package that "would include certain deductibles and coinsurance features, which would help keep costs down by encouraging the use of more efficient health care procedures."[14]

Marty Feldstein would later chair Ronald Reagan's Council of Economic Advisors, but in 1973 he first published an important paper revealing a pernicious feedback loop in health insurance. As insurance caused decision makers to ignore the actual price of the healthcare they consumed, the producers and providers of that care (e.g., hospitals and drug companies) could freely raise their prices. Nobody is minding the till. However, "the more insurance increases the price of care, [the] higher price of care [then] increases the demand for insurance."[15] In the modern world, where an episode of care can cost double or triple the median income, it would be altogether foolish to go without insurance. In this way, Feldstein raised the stakes, showing how health insurance can be both the problem and the solution.

Nonetheless, Feldstein's bottom line was to scale back insurance, as he argued that "American families are in general overinsured against health expenses," meaning that they could bear more risk themselves.[16] Feldstein agreed that comprehensive health insurance policies arguably do more harm than good, just as Pauly had suggested. Feldstein proposed a 66% coinsurance rate as a solution, a move that would dramatically shift costs back to individual patients.[17] In other work in the early 1970s, Feldstein argued for a government-sponsored health insurance system, which would include "an annual direct expense limit (i.e., deductible) that increased with family income," an idea that he has occasionally revisited with coauthors.[18] This idea of income-scaled cost exposure is remarkable for both its progressivity, and its utter lack of uptake by those advocating for cost-exposure in the real world. (We return to the idea in Chapter 5.)

In a 1976 message to Congress about reforming Medicare, Republican President Gerald Ford echoed this emerging cost-exposure consensus, calling for "additional cost sharing provisions . . . to encourage economical use of the hospital and medical services."[19] Nonetheless, the zero-sum nature of this approach was beginning to become apparent—additional cost exposure would undermine the risk-protection function of insurance. In his National Health Plan, Democratic President Jimmy Carter emphasized the need to protect all Americans from "catastrophic expenses," so that "no American should live in fear that a serious illness or accident will mean bankruptcy or a lifetime of debt."[20] To this end, he proposed general caps on cost exposure and for further curtailment for the most vulnerable populations.[21]

All of this economic thought and political movement was largely based on theory and anecdote. However, scholars began to test these theories rigorously in the 1970s, with a landmark study called the RAND Health Insurance Experiment (HIE), the results of which were published in several articles through the early and mid-1980s and ultimately in a 1993 book.[22] Remarkably, social scientists were allowed to actually manipulate health insurance coverage for thousands of Americans, randomly assigning some patients into a "free care" condition, with no cost exposure, and other patients into several conditions with increasing levels of cost exposure.

Among academics, this study has achieved almost mythical status, both for its unprecedented manipulation of real people in the field and for its findings, which confirmed so much that economists had predicted. In a retrospective paper, the MIT economist Jonathan Gruber summarized the key finding: "higher co-insurance rates, with an out-of-pocket limit, can significantly reduce health care use without sacrificing health outcomes for the typical person."[23] The effect was large: in experimental conditions with nearly full insurance, the health expenses were 50% greater than in plans with large but bearable deductibles. Notably, the reduction of consumption had no detectable adverse impact on the health outcomes of the median- and higher-income beneficiaries. Cost exposure seemed to be a powerful tool to reduce waste in the healthcare system.

The HIE included a $1,000 "stop-loss" cap on cost-sharing burdens in all their plans (equal to $4,368 adjusting from 1977 to 2019) but—just as Feldstein recommended—scaled that cap downward for lower-income participants (at 5–15% of annual income, depending on experimental condition).[24] While the study has been a cornerstone of health policy research for decades, this particular feature of scaling has been forgotten.[25] It is hard to know if we should extrapolate the HIE findings to real-world insurance that typically does not scale according to income. In the real world, as we see in Chapter 3, cost exposure can be much larger as a proportion of income, thus possibly having greater adverse effects.

### The Political Convenience of Economic Ideology: The 1980s and Beyond

In a 1983 address to Congress, Republican President Ronald Reagan proposed to increase cost sharing in Medicare to "encourage beneficiary cost consciousness and the efficient use of health resources."[26] With Feldstein now on board, Reagan's speeches channeled academic economists: "First-dollar insurance coverage, such as that which Medicaid provides, leaves the consumer with virtually no financial incentive to question the need for services. Services that are totally free are likely to be over utilized. If patients share in some of the costs, they and their physicians will reduce unnecessary or marginal utilization."[27] Unfortunately, the Republican approach never seemed to pick up Feldstein's idea of scaling cost exposure to income.

The empirical evidence also continued to mount. A 1989 study documented a health maintenance organization's (HMO's) introduction of a $5 copayment for office visits among 51,000 enrollees. The researchers estimated that the cost exposure caused a 10.9% drop in primary care visits.[28] Like many research papers that simply use insurance claims databases, the researchers were unable to observe whether the reductions in healthcare harmed patient health or disproportionately affected the poor. Instead, the researchers cranked the wheel of textbook economic theory, to infer that the decline in usage "suggests that one in every nine primary care visits made in the absence of cost sharing have low marginal value to enrollees."[29] The care was apparently not worth even the $5 fraction of its total cost (most of which was still borne by the insurer).

The drumbeat against full insurance continued in a 1991 paper by Minnesota economists Roger Feldman and Bryan Dowd. The authors charitably acknowledged that "consumers are considerably more risk-averse than Feldstein assumed," yet even on that accounting, "this gain [from insurance's risk protection] is not large enough to outweigh the loss due to excess consumption of medical care."[30] If risk protection is the only purpose for insurance, as economists assumed, it is not enough to make it worthwhile.

President Bill Clinton's 1993 Health Security Act proposed six key principles, including "responsibility." According to him, "Too many of us have not taken responsibility for our own health care and for our own relations to the health care system. Many of us who have had fully paid health care plans have used the system whether we needed it or not without thinking what the costs were."[31] President Clinton said, "There can't be any something for nothing. . . . Even small contributions, as small as the $10 co-payment when you visit a doctor, illustrate that this is something of value. There is a cost to it. It is not free."[32]

In a 1995 survey by health economist Victor Fuchs, economists resoundingly endorsed the moral hazard theory and many opposed the creation of national health insurance coverage.[33] These are the economists who trained an entire generation of undergraduate and graduate students.

In a 1996 paper, Chicago economist Willard Manning (now deceased) and Susan Marquis (who now leads RAND) used the HIE data to calculate what they supposed would be an optimal coinsurance rate of 50%, with no cap on cost exposure (and again no scaling to income).[34] On their view, the best way to strike the Zeckhauser bargain is to expose people to catastrophic health expenses.

Continuing the drumbeat, when President George W. Bush proposed to expand health savings accounts, he complained that patients "pay a flat rate for insurance, but they really don't know the true costs of medical services they receive. . . . When consumers don't have the incentive to get better prices, costs go up."[35] In 2003, President Bush signed the Medicare Modernization Act, which included for the first time a prescription drug benefit, though it had a convoluted cost-exposure scheme with a deductible, followed by a 25% copay for costs up to $2,400. Then, patients experienced an infamous "donut hole" period of spending without insurance coverage whatsoever, until they reach another annual limit.

Over these same years, evidence was beginning to mount that such policies of incomplete insurance, which left patients exposed to substantial costs, were failing to really protect them from risk and could be causing other problems as well. In a series of studies in 1981, 1991, 1999, and 2007, a research team led by Harvard law professor Elizabeth Warren, who would later become a U.S. senator and presidential candidate, documented the prevalence of medical problems among those in bankruptcy. The standard story is that consumer bankruptcies are caused by profligate spenders. With increasingly large samples and rigorous methods, ultimately relying on official court records, which were completed on the penalty of perjury—the authors estimated that over half of bankruptcies were caused by illness and injury. These case files and interviews told of a perfect storm of medical bills and lost work, combining with credit problems and other factors.[36] Even middle-class families who enjoyed health insurance were not safe from the risk of medical bankruptcy.

Following the Warren team's methods, in 2008, I put together a team of researchers to conduct a similar study of families going through foreclosure, and we found an almost identical proportion of foreclosures that were driven by medical problems.[37] Indeed, we found that families in foreclosure, even if they had health insurance, had paid an average of $5,100 in medical bills in the recent two years, and a sizable proportion had even taken out second mortgages to cover such costs. We titled our first paper, "Get Sick, Get Out," and followed up years later with a more rigorous study finding similar results.[38]

These striking findings about bankruptcies and foreclosures launched a running debate. Other scholars sought to challenge the definitions, methods, and implications of the burgeoning literature showing the association between financial distress and healthcare expenses.[39] We revisit these issues in Chapter 3, but the point here is historical.

This evidence was part of the groundswell of support for President Barack Obama's 2009 effort to reform the U.S. healthcare system. Even here, however, the president's proposal did not at all retreat from the fundamental U.S. commitment to cost exposure as a primary mechanism for financing healthcare. But he did propose scaling it back. The ACA eliminated cost sharing on a range of preventative services. It also tried to protect patients against catastrophic costs. "We will place a limit on how much you can be charged for out-of-pocket expenses, because in the United States of America, no one should go broke because they get sick."[40] In another speech, President Obama targeted insurance companies and promised that, under the ACA, "no longer would they be able to force you to pay unlimited amounts of money out of your own pocket."[41] Nonetheless, as we will explore further in Chapter 3, the actual limits were so high—$15,800 for a family in 2019—that they could still easily bankrupt middle-class families.

In 2017 and 2018, with the Trump election and a Republican sweep through Congress, we saw a renewed interest in cost exposure. In 2018, the Cato Institute published a book by Charles Silver and David Hyman, reiterating the standard story that "Medicaid, Medicare, and private health insurance all tempt beneficiaries to use medical services imprudently. That's a big part of the reason why America is awash in unnecessary treatments."[42] Indeed, the authors went so far as to claim that Medicaid does more harm than good; it should simply be replaced by a simple wealth transfer, so that the impoverished beneficiaries can spend more efficiently for themselves. This is a more radical version of the idea of "block granting" Medicaid to the states, which has currency among right-leaning politicians, including those in the Trump administration.[43]

The most recent empirical work on cost-exposure has also been disappointing. In 2017, one of the top economics journals published a study of one large employer, who dramatically expanded cost exposure for its health plan beneficiaries. The scholars observed a substantial reduction of spending of about 12%, but even in this highly educated and well paid population of employees, the cuts were indiscriminate across both potentially valuable care and potentially wasteful care. Even worse, traditional economics would predict that when exposed to the costs of their own care, patients would become better shoppers, and thus demand lower prices from providers. Ironically, the scholars observed just the opposite: "after the required switch to the HDHP [High Deductible Health Plan] consumers are actually increasing the expense they are paying for a given procedure rather than price shopping and moving to lower priced providers when they face a higher marginal price for care."[44]

A 2019 working paper for the National Bureau of Economic Research is similarly disappointing. Michael Chernew and colleagues studied patients

who had an online price transparency tool and faced cost exposures designed
to make them shop for cheaper imaging services (lower limb MRI scans).
Less than 1% of patients used the tool to search for the lowest cost provider;
instead they tended to go wherever their referring physician sent them.[45] We
will return to this theme at the end of the book, but for now we simply observe that traditional economic theory is unravelling, to the extent that it
conceives patients simplistically as consumers.

## MAYBE HEALTH INSURANCE IS NOT SO BAD AFTER ALL?

Looking back, we see a common ideological thread running through textbook economics and decades of federal policy. The drumbeat of theory and
politics has reiterated that wasteful spending on healthcare is driven by overinsured patients demanding more healthcare than they really need, since
they lack proper incentives to decline wasteful healthcare. Thus, we can reduce that problem by making health insurance less comprehensive (or even
repealing it altogether) so patients will be exposed to a greater risk of large
medical bills.

It is hard to argue with the textbook economic prediction that insurance
will cause people to consume more healthcare than they otherwise would.
That is both a well-documented empirical fact, as well as common sense:
people will consume more of anything when it is free to them, compared to
when it costs money out of pocket. It is true for cars, TVs, and ice cream,
and surely true of healthcare as well. When the price is zero, I'll have more.

### The Uninsurance Counterfactual

We should think more about how we interpret that behavioral effect, if we
are to evaluate its meaning for setting policy. We know how the textbook
economic theory interprets the effect. As Medicare was being expanded to
cover prescription drugs, Pauly recapitulated "the general theory that health
economists apply to insurance." He wrote that "'moral hazard' . . . is generally . . . inefficient, because some of the use of medical care that insurance
stimulates (compared with having no insurance, when a person pays the full
market price) must by definition be care that is *worth* less to the person than
its market price. [On standard economic assumptions] care that is worth less
than it costs is wasteful."[46] So, if uninsured people are not buying a $100,000

treatment, then the treatment is not *worth* $100,000. If insured people do buy it, that is waste, and insurance has made us worse off.

So, the standard theory is that uninsured people do not consume as much care because it is not worth its price. Yet there may be other reasons that an uninsured person might not purchase such a treatment. Perhaps a procedure is well worth $100,000, or perhaps even more, in its power to relieve pain, alleviate disability, prolong life, and allow a person to do whatever she may enjoy with the life she has. The patient might desperately want the treatment to secure those benefits, as anyone would. Nonetheless, the uninsured patient may decline to consume because she cannot presently afford to purchase it. In the real world, the patient may simply lack the liquid wealth (or credit) necessary to do so. Thus, when we observe her behavior in declining to consume, it may tell us more about which people have money than which healthcare interventions have value.

This may seem obvious to those not steeped in the professional field of economics. That field has, however, blinkered its own approach to such questions. American economists typically do not look at how much pain might be relieved by a treatment, or even how long it could extend life. Those questions require engagement with individual patients, listening to their experiences, and medical expertise to evaluate and measure those outcomes—what Pauly calls a "noneconomic medicalist approach."[47] Even more, those considerations beg huge normative questions. After all, relief of pain and extension of life are not the only things a person may value—some people may rationally prefer to leave a greater bequest for their child's education or enjoy one last vacation with their spouse. To prioritize such disparate goods would require a comprehensive, substantive theory of the good life and the good society. This sort of theory is the purview of philosophy and theology, not economics, which has in recent decades taken an emphatically empirical and mathematical approach instead.

Yet economics, perhaps more than other academic discipline, aspires to guide social policy. To do so, economists need a normative baseline against which insurance can be compared. As Pauly's summary makes clear, the counterfactual is the uninsured patient. She is acting in a situation most like the idealized free market, where she can make rational trades between her wealth and various consumption alternatives. Here, price paid reflects value perceived. We assume that the patient compares the potential benefits of a treatment against the price charged. When we observe that such a trade did (or did not) occur, we can infer that the value of the product to her was above (or below) the price demanded. As far as it goes, the analytic model is a powerful way to identify healthcare value and waste, because those consumption choices can be observed and measured, making valuation into a science.

Notably, however, this idealization is not completely neutral. The idealized individual patient faces healthcare decisions with her own wallet in hand. In this way, healthcare spending is conceived already as a question of individual choice, not collective bargain or social commitment. And the theory assumes a particular distribution of wealth and access to credit that happens to exist in the time and place and for the person who decided to decline or consume the particular healthcare, under the economist's watchful eye.

This individualism does not merely appear in the standard theory of moral hazard. It exists in the fundamental theory of insurance itself, as the protection against risk. As we saw briefly, on the now-standard view sketched by Arrow, insurance is primarily about individuals protecting themselves, by shifting money from their own good years to their own bad years. To make this work in practice, insurance is admittedly a contract with another party who agrees to pay the person back in the worst years and thereby "smooth out" the person's wealth. But the other party is just a facilitator—the real transaction is from the premium payor to her own future self, who suffers a bad year. We could call this the "intrapersonal" theory of health insurance.

### Insurance as Access Pact

In the mid-1990s, University of Minnesota economist John Nyman suggested an alternative theory of health insurance, which, as he put it, "stands conventional theory on its head."[48] Nyman explains in the preface to his 2003 book that his fundamental theory was first submitted to peer-reviewed economics journals in 1995, but was rejected for four years before eventually being published and later synthesized into a book.

The story goes back to the fundamental question of why we want insurance in the first place. Rather than the traditional economic focus on risk, Nyman focuses on access. The point of health insurance is not just to smooth out our wealth across low and high years of healthcare spending. Rather a primary purpose is to give us access to healthcare we otherwise could not afford. This effect becomes most apparent when we consider expensive treatments such as organ transplantation, a heart stent, or a cancer drug—the costs for which can easily be substantial portions of, or even multiples of, median U.S. income. For these sorts of care, insurance (whether public or private) might be the only feasible way to gain access.

It is critical to understand that healthcare costs are not distributed evenly across the U.S. population, or even in the familiar shape of a bell curve, which statisticians call a "normal distribution." Rather, healthcare spending is concentrated in a small portion of the population, which is unlucky to consume a huge and disproportionate slice of our healthcare budgets in any given year.

Specifically, in 2015, nearly a quarter (22.5%) of healthcare costs fell on only 1% of the population, where each individual incurred more than $112,395 in healthcare.[49] Slicing the data at another point, it is also true that half of all health expenditures fell on just 5% of the population, and that group spent $50,572 on average. The median split is also interesting: 97.2% of health spending was consumed by half of the population, while the other half incurred only 2.8% of aggregate health spending. This is nothing like a bell curve.

It is also instructive to see the causes of the high-dollar spending. Among those with very large healthcare expenses (the top 5% by spending), about half of those people (49%) had experienced a discrete event generating large costs.[50] Scholars who have studied these patterns explain that "some examples of this illness trajectory might include people who have a myocardial infarction, undergo coronary bypass graft surgery, and, after a period of rehabilitation, return to stable health; individuals who are diagnosed with early-stage cancer, complete surgical resection and other first-line therapies, and achieve complete remission; and those who are on frequent hemodialysis while waiting for a kidney transplant and then receive a transplant and return to stable health."[51]

A second large category of high spenders (40% of them) are those who suffer from chronic conditions and functional limitations, many of whom are older. These include commonly treated conditions like hypertension, followed by osteoarthritis / other nontraumatic joint disorders, and hyperlipidemia, but also mental disorders, heart disease, chronic obstructive pulmonary disease / asthma, and diabetes mellitus.[52]

This fact of spending concentration is essential for understanding the feasibility of various mechanisms for financing healthcare consumption. If everyone had relatively predictable and modest costs, then comprehensive insurance would not be necessary. But, in fact, healthcare costs are concentrated in such a way that it is very difficult for individual persons to bear a substantial portion of their own costs, especially if they are unfortunate enough to be very ill. That is the purpose of insurance—to pool those risks across the entire population and then spread the costs among us.

This theory depends on a different analytical baseline. Rather than the lodestar of the individual patient holding her own wallet—and the intrapersonal notion of insurance that it presumes—we can instead imagine a population of consumers who are binding themselves together to purchase in advance the right to later consume healthcare, as specified in a health insurance contract. On this view, the health insurance contract can create a right to consume all sorts of healthcare that these consumers seek collectively, regardless of whether they could afford to purchase that care individually. Risk is still important on this view, but it is not so much borne across time as it is across the many people bound together in an insurance pool. In a given year, for whom will the risk materialize?

To simplify, imagine not just one, but 10,000 people each with $50,000 of income, but who plan on spending the vast majority each year on housing, food, education, and everything else. Nonetheless, they all fear that they will someday need a $100,000 treatment for a rare disease that will strike only one of them. None of them could individually afford such a treatment, but they all want it. So, they each contribute $10 to a common pool, for the use of whoever happens to need the $100,000 treatment that year. This insurance premium is a measly $10 but imagine adding on 199 other such treatments that the people may want to access, and a full insurance contract emerges. We see individuals rationally agreeing to spend, say, $2,000 per year on such common pool agreements that cover all medically necessary healthcare.

Nyman shifted the frame from the lone individual holding her wallet to the group choosing to collectively purchase a right to consume healthcare. The theory is fundamentally redistributive, moving money from those who are luckily healthy to those who are unluckily sick with large medical expenses. Still this point should not be confused with a moral thesis, such as one expressed by bioethicist Gregg Bloche, who says that "medical coverage is more than a business proposition; it is an expression of our commitment to each other."[53] Or law professor Timothy Jost suggests that "the health care systems of virtually all developed nations are based on an underlying commitment to solidarity."[54] We are all at risk of illness, and all ought to contribute to the costs of such care to the extent that we are able. Although we will delve deeply into such overtly normative approaches in Chapter 4, for present purposes I am not so sure that we need such an expansive social notion to provide a counterpoint to the textbook economic notion of rational purchasing behavior.

Under Nyman's theory, the shift in frame can be a mere business proposition, not necessarily involving a moral or even political commitment by each person to another. In the hypothetical case, every single person earned the same $50,000 annually—without inequality, there was no need for compassion or solidarity. Instead, the fellow members of an insurance pool can be ruthlessly rational individuals. They are bound together by a legally enforced contract through the intermediary, an insurer. Thus, although my reading of Nyman's theory shifts away from individualism, insurance pools are no more leftist than, say, the modern corporation, which similarly uses voluntary contracts to pool assets to achieve a common goal.

Similarly, scholars and advocates have long conceived the decision to donate cadaveric organs for transplantation as if it were a paradigmatic case of altruism. (The concept is implied by the very word, "donate.") On this view, it is perhaps unsurprising that there are persistent shortages of organs. In contrast, consider the supply and demand for organs as a collective action problem, where we all have an interest in protecting ourselves from the risk of someday needing an organ, and where we can all contribute our own cadaveric organs. In 2007, I argued for a mechanism of linking decisions to give and get organs, where participation is a rational strategy for those seeking to protect their own health.[55] In 2008, indeed, Israel implemented such a system, giving priority access to cadaveric organs to those who had signed up to donate their own organs. As one would expect, this solution increased organ donor registrations.[56]

Accordingly, let's see how far we can get with a rational conception of health insurance as an access pact. Such an approach is likely to be more stable than one depending on contingent and shifting sentiments of solidarity or altruism.

Now, on the access view for insurance, we will still expect that insured people will consume a lot more healthcare than uninsured people. But that is not a wasteful side effect. It's the very purpose of buying health insurance in the first place! We buy health insurance for fear that, without it, we may not get the healthcare we need. In this sense, a health insurance premium is like a lease on an apartment, or an advance purchase ticket to a movie, a membership to a gym, or a stock certificate—these create rights to receive benefits, which we otherwise would not receive. And, of course, people with leases on apartments are more likely to use apartments than people without such leases. Of course, those who have bought tickets to the movie will be more likely to see the movie. Nobody would suppose that lease agreements need to be reformed so that on top of their monthly rent, renters must also pay out-of-pocket for every night they sleep at home. And likewise, on the access theory, health insurance need not be made incomplete, with deductibles, copays, and coinsurance to deter people from consuming the healthcare that is covered by their insurance.

In Chapter 3, we will review the phenomenon of "underinsurance," where insured individuals have so much cost exposure that they are in fact deterred from using their insurance benefits. Imagine if a quarter of the people who had signed leases and paid monthly rent payments were nonetheless made to sleep on the street, because they could not afford the additional nightly payments that their landlords required to actually sleep in their apartments. Or imagine that a quarter of the people who bought tickets to the movie were locked out of the theater, because they were unable or unwilling to pay the additional "user fee" charged at the door. Thank goodness the beds and seats were not "wasted" on such people! If we understand that the original premium payments were made specifically for the purpose of allowing additional healthcare that would not otherwise be consumed, then such user fees at the point of service would seem like a counterproductive policy.

## Assessing the Alternative Theories

So, who has the better theory for understanding health insurance? Is it the standard textbook economic approach, focusing on intrapersonal risk? Or is it Nyman's alternative focusing on redistributing funds among persons to ensure access to care that individuals could not afford alone? This choice has big implications for whether and how to expose patients to costs.

The answer to this question depends on both the price of the healthcare and the individual's ability to bear it. For relatively inexpensive healthcare and relatively wealthy people, insurance is largely unnecessary to achieve access, making the traditional economic theory apt. For relatively expensive healthcare and relatively poor people, insurance is essential to achieve access, making Nyman's theory quite compelling. The answer is also dynamic. In 1963, when it was pioneered, the traditional economic theory of risk may have been sensible. The explosion in expensive medical technologies had not yet happened. Nor had wages stagnated for thirty years.

Now, from a policy perspective, not only are healthcare costs very high but they are also very concentrated. As we have seen, the vast majority of health spending is incurred by the few people who have very substantial medical expenses. If we care about health spending overall, we should focus on the $50,000 and more courses of care that are in the aggregate driving health spending overall. And that is precisely the sorts of care that motivate Nyman's theory.

To some degree these alternative theories are testable, because they make distinct predictions. The traditional theory predicts that exposure to cost should disproportionately reduce consumption of lower-value healthcare, which does not deliver much health per dollar charged. As people become exposed to more of the costs of their own care, they should continue buying valuable care but start to decline the low-value, high-price care that was only being purchased because it was subsidized. The access theory, in contrast, predicts that cost exposure will disproportionately reduce consumption among poorer people who otherwise lack access, and it will do so, regardless of the real value of the care. A large body of research is lending credence to the access theory.

The evidence is now clear: cost exposure causes individuals to not get care that we know is highly valuable. This was one of the most interesting findings of the RAND HIE, which actually tracked health status of each participant rather closely. For those who were relatively healthy and wealthy, cost exposure made little difference to their health. As the research team's leader, Joseph Newhouse, explained, "For high-risk individuals, however, particularly if they were low income, there were important benefits to health from free care."[57] That is to say, exposure to costs harmed health for these populations, causing them to not consume healthcare that would have been beneficial.

In 2013, a team of MIT and Stanford professors went back to re-analyze the RAND data.[58] One key concern was that some of the people recruited into the study actually refused to participate, and others exited the study before it was complete, both of which could bias the results. Indeed, when offered plans with the greatest levels of cost exposure, more people refused to join or refused to stay in the experiment, and the differences were statistically significant. The researchers confirmed that the exits were by choice, rather than involuntarily due to death, joining the military, or becoming eligible for Medicare. Overall, 88% of the free-care plan participants completed the study compared to 63% in the highest cost-sharing arm.[59]

This effect essentially undermined the landmark feature of the experiment: randomization, making it more like the sort of routine observational study that economists do all the time. In the original book on the project, the authors acknowledged this potential limitation, but claimed that "the additional refusal and attrition appear to have been random with respect to the characteristics of the participants, and therefore free of bias."[60] By this, the authors mean that their post hoc analyses were unable to predict who, among those randomized to a condition, were most likely to refuse or drop out. Still, the differential participation across experimental conditions suggests adverse selection, whereby patients who predicted the greatest healthcare need would rationally act on that information to avoid high cost exposure. If so, then the experimental estimates of the effects of cost exposure would yield unrealistically low estimates of adverse outcomes. Other scholars, such as John Nyman, have argued that the HIE was "biased by attrition and that the attrition accounts for the lack of a health effect from the reduction in health care use, especially hospitalizations, among the participants assigned to the cost-sharing arm."[61]

More recent research has shown that cost exposure can backfire. A 2004 *Journal of the American Medical Association* (*JAMA*) paper reported on the effect of doubling copayments on prescription drugs. Although healthcare consumption decreased, "copayment increases led to increased use of emergency department visits and hospital days for the sentinel conditions of diabetes, asthma, and gastric acid disorder: predicted annual emergency department visits increased by 17% and hospital days by 10%."[62] One might suppose that healthcare that keeps you out of the emergency room is probably pretty valuable healthcare.

In the Introduction, I also mentioned a study on heart attacks (acute myo-cardial infarctions). After a severe heart attack, patients need follow-up care and medication; there can be little doubt about their value. A 2007 survey of patients with this condition found that one in seven experienced finan-cial barriers to getting that care, and over two-thirds of them had health insurance.[63]

In a similar vein, a 2010 cross-sectional study followed nearly 150,000 type-2 diabetic patients, examining both their cost-sharing exposure and their adherence to insulin and oral antidiabetic medicines.[64] In this population, the medicines are essential; nobody would suppose they are low value. The authors examined adherence and complications, including neu-ropathy (permanent damage to nerves, often causing numbness and pain), as well as medical service utilization and workplace productivity. Even a relatively small amount—a $10 increase in patient cost exposure—was associated with a 5%–6% reduction in adherence, which then substan-tially worsened health outcomes and led to emergency room visits.

Many American families seem to be living on very thin margins. A 2017 *JAMA Internal Medicine* article reported similarly that, among low-income families, imposition of high deductibles was associated with a 22% increase in emergency department acute complication visits.[65]

A 2013 study of high-deductible health plans focused on emergency room visits, and it was able to distinguish between appropriate utilization for high-severity incidents (such as kidney stones, cardiac arrhythmias, and open head wounds) versus inappropriate utilization for low-severity incidents (such as sore throats and back pain), which cost exposure should hopefully deter. The research team found that when patients are moved to high-deductible health plans, richer patients reduced their consumption of low-severity (low-value) emergency care, as the risk theory would predict. However, for high-severity (high-value) emergency care, poorer patients, but not richer patients, dramatically reduced the care they consumed.[66] Cost exposure sorted out poor patients from getting good care, just as the access theory would predict.

Similarly, in a 2015 *Health Affairs* article, Kenneth Thorpe found that cost sharing for prescription drugs may be counterproductive for patients with one or multiple chronic conditions.[67] While higher copayments and coin-surance rates reliably reduce spending on the drugs themselves, for patients with multiple chronic conditions, increased cost exposure reduces adherence and leads to more spending when these patients eventually sought care for the complications thereof.

All these studies (and others we discuss in other chapters), reaching back to the HIE and forward to the present day, tell a coherent story. Harvard economist Kathy Swartz concludes her own review of this literature: "The better studies reinforce the HIE findings that low-income people in poor health are more likely to suffer adverse health outcomes, such as increased rates of emergency department (ED) use, hospitalizations, admission to nursing homes, and death, when increased cost-sharing causes them to reduce their use of health care."[68] Comprehensive insurance solves an access problem, and the consumption that it stimulates improves health.

Notwithstanding the clear theory and compelling evidence, Nyman's work has failed to change the paradigm of health economics. Indeed, young economists are still trained on health economics textbooks, which continue to equate moral hazard with welfare loss and "emphasize" that "only risk-averse individuals demand insurance," ignoring the possibility that a risk-neutral person might rationally buy a health plan that creates access to care that he otherwise couldn't afford.[69] In a recent review article in a minor economics journal, two scholars outside the mainstream of academic economics reviewed this history and regrettably concluded that Nyman's "major challenge" to economic thinking about moral hazard has been largely ignored.[70]

I am reminded of Thomas Kuhn's pioneering work describing how scientific fields are not merely objective instruments calibrated to the truth; they are really contingent sociological cultures of prestige, hierarchies and incentives, populated and organized by humans.[71] The idea of the lone consumer holding her own wallet is powerful in its simplicity. Scientific fields reluctantly deal with anomalies, always trying to save and reinforce core doctrines, and only rarely change fundamental paradigms.

One reason that health economics may have largely disregarded Nyman's theory is because the theory is disabling. With Nyman's theory, it is much more difficult for economists to speak to policy-relevant questions, by merely marshalling and analyzing data about consumption behavior. As we have seen, the mere fact that insurance increases consumption reveals nothing about whether that is a good or a bad thing. Nyman challenges the normative baseline of the uninsured person spending her own wealth but offers no other economic lodestar. Instead, to make smart policy we need experts who can identify good and bad healthcare on its own merits—indeed, that's why we rely on the Food and Drug Administration (FDA) to screen medical technologies and rely on physicians to recommend specific treatments for patients.[72]

## USING INDEMNITIES TO IDENTIFY REAL WASTE

It is important to concede that the price effect of classic economic theory remains a problem. We cannot rely on fully insured persons to make good cost-benefit trade-offs, since they are not exposed to costs. Even under the access theory, *some* of the marginal additional spending caused by health insurance coverage may be wasteful and should be targeted with cost exposure or other interventions. But since we cannot infer that *all* the extra spending is waste, we need a more nuanced identification strategy. When it comes to waste versus access, Nyman himself says, "The challenge for policy is to distinguish one from the other."[73]

To identify waste, we need an analytic lodestar for comparison, just as textbook economics has for decades used the uninsured person as its counterfactual. As that new lodestar, I propose a fully insured person, whose insurance benefit is paid in cash (as an "indemnity"), rather than paid in-kind to providers, as in extant health insurance plans.

### Indemnity Insurance

The current arrangement of health insurance is actually rather odd, when you think about it. Let's suppose someone has already met the annual cost-exposure maximum and goes to an oncologist, who recommends an expensive treatment for cancer. The patient's health insurance company pays for the treatment. But the mechanism of the insurer's payment is important. Although the patient is the beneficiary of the insurance contract, the payment bypasses her and instead goes directly to the oncologist who will dispense the drug. While this routing of the funds works perfectly fine to guarantee access, this form of insurance makes the benefit nonfungible—the patient cannot use the money for anything else such as housing, education for herself or a child, acupuncture, or a vacation, any of which she may rationally prefer instead of the expensive drug. Even among alternative healthcare treatments—say a generic drug that the FDA approved for the specific condition versus a patented drug that your oncologist proposed to use off-label—this form of insurance provides no incentive for the patient to consider the relative costs and choose the best bargain.

In this way, our health insurance money is locked up in this particular form of consumption, which may not maximize welfare. The patient deciding whether to consume thus only need ask herself whether the expensive healthcare is likely to be better than nothing, since nothing is all she can get instead. For this same reason, healthcare providers need not compete on price, since the decision maker is immune to the price.

It may seem that I am only repeating the fundamental economic story about how insurance causes moral hazard. But note that the problem is caused not by insurance, but by one peculiar and unnecessary feature of insurance—the indirect payment to the provider rather than to the beneficiary-patient. As Charles Silver and David Hyman have argued in a recent book, insurance "will only buy something . . . if the money goes into the pockets of health care providers," even if that is not the best-value use of the money.[74] It need not be this way. Instead of paying the provider, suppose that insurers simply paid patients cash when the patient became ill and eligible to consume an expensive treatment. The patient could, if she chose, use the money to buy the treatment recommended by her oncologist, or not. The patient would be allowed to spend it on anything she may desire, including other treatments or other things she may value more. This "indemnity" mechanism maintains an opportunity cost for patients—all the alternative things they could do with the money instead of consuming healthcare. An indemnity would recreate a market discipline.

This approach is sometimes called "contingent claims insurance." Over the years, a few scholars—including Mark Pauly—have proposed such an indemnity system, where health insurers would pay a cash benefit to patients rather than paying providers.[75] Indeed, in other insurance markets, insurers sometimes pay cash benefits. Suppose you get a small dent in your car, bigger than your deductible but perhaps not big enough to merit a repair. The insurance company will send an appraiser out to estimate the cost of covered repairs. Under some insurance policies, car owners decide whether, when, and how to repair their car.[76] For homeowners in California, a state law provides for a "replacement cost" policy so that the homeowner who suffers a covered loss, like a forest fire, can purchase a new home, rather than rebuild their old one.[77] This sort of provision makes a lot of sense, to potentially allow people to move away from areas particularly prone to risks, such as forest fires.

Scholars have nonetheless supposed that for healthcare, an indemnity might be infeasible, because it would be difficult for an insurer to observe the severity of each particular patient's illness so as to tailor the amount of the indemnity accordingly. In fact, in the 1980s, Medicare changed its hospital reimbursement policy to something like an indemnity payment, although the payment still goes to the hospital rather than the patient. Depending on which diagnosis-related group (DRG) the patient falls into, the hospital receives a specified payment that represents the average cost of treating the condition. Of course, some patients will turn out to have more severe and costly versions of the disease compared to other patients. Thus, some will be overcompensated and others undercompensated. Since hospitals treat thousands of patients, the differences wash out; the DRG payment does not have to be accurate for any particular patient.

For an indemnity to work for individual patients, it would have to be tailored more narrowly. Under most insurance policies (and state and federal laws), insurers must cover all "medically necessary" care. In the current system of in-kind benefits, insurers already depend on physicians, in the first instance, and on other claims reviewers, secondarily, to determine what sorts of care a patient needs. These decisions are subject to certain exclusions defined by the policy and subject to various appeals processes, initially within the company and then through independent reviewers required under most state laws. Those same mechanisms to determine the amount of coverage would exist under an indemnity system. The only difference would be that the payment would go to the patient rather than the provider, and the payment would be predicated on eligibility for the treatment rather than eligibility-plus-consumption of the treatment.

Another practical challenge for an indemnity is that we would have to be willing to hold patients to their choices. Suppose the patient receives an $80,000 check and declines the expensive cancer drug to instead spend the money on something else. If the patient comes back a month later now wanting the cancer drug, the insurer has to be willing and able to say no. That is an implication of consumer-driven healthcare.

We do see some indemnities in other countries. For example, a German disability insurance program uses an optional indemnity mechanism for home healthcare. Patients choose between an in-kind benefit of healthcare workers visiting their homes, or a smaller cash payment instead, which the patient can use to hire his own help or perhaps rely on family or informal support relationships instead, pocketing the difference. Data from the 1990s show that "more than 75% of home care beneficiaries chose cash rather than services."[78]

In my view, there is some potential to innovate U.S. health insurance along these lines. For too long, we have been locked in a zero-sum game, either trying to increase insurance coverage, to capture its access function, or trying to reduce insurance coverage to create more cost exposure, to reduce waste. In Chapter 5, I will propose a partial indemnity reform, which I call the "split benefit," as a way to make the insurance benefit more fungible, achieving the access benefits without inducing waste. For now, however, there is more to say about economic theory, which will drive our approach to this and other reforms.

## Testing the Access Function

Regardless of the real-world feasibility, indemnity insurance can serve as an analytical lodestar to identify waste under the access theory. Imagine yourself someday receiving a colon cancer diagnosis and facing a choice between a standard chemotherapy regimen versus a cocktail with a newly patented drug, which costs an additional $80,000. If uninsured, most Americans would likely have to decline the novel treatment, regardless of its value. Under a typical insurance policy, a patient will spend a few thousand dollars out of pocket and meet their cap on cost exposure, regardless of whether they choose the basic treatment or the novel treatment. The oncologist will be paid one rate or the other, but the patient will never see the money. So, we might suppose that nearly all insured patients would opt for the expensive treatment.

The difference in consumption between those who do and do not have insurance—likely humongous—is the effect of insurance. However, it is unclear how much of that difference is due to insurance's access function or due to its moral hazard side-effect. As I have argued, standard economic theory and research has used the wrong counterfactual, or the wrong benchmark, to assess moral hazard.

But imagine a third condition where the patient has a hypothetical insurance policy that pays an indemnity. Upon notification that his physician

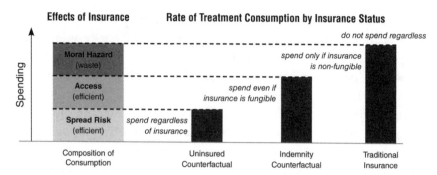

*Figure 1.1* Theoretical Model for Decomposing Effects of Traditional Insurance from Two Counterfactual Conditions (Hypothesized Values)

recommends the premium novel care, the patient receives a check for $80,000. Now, what proportion of those individuals—who can now afford the expensive care but also has an incentive to weigh its value against alternatives—would accept the care nonetheless? The difference in consumption between this indemnity group and the traditional-insurance group is the true waste caused by our status quo insurance. It may turn out to be quite small, if patients highly value the healthcare or tend to defer to their physicians' recommendations whenever they can afford to do so. This new model for understanding insurance is shown in Figure 1.1.

Thus, to be clear, the difference in consumption between uninsured people and those insured with indemnity is the access function of insurance. The difference in consumption between people insured with indemnity versus insured with traditional, in-kind health insurance is the wasteful function of insurance (aka true moral hazard).

Although indemnities exist in other domains, like car and home insurance, they do not have the same access function as in the health insurance domain. In those other domains, the beneficiary has already somehow purchased the asset that she wishes to protect. Thus behavior in those domains does not shed much light on moral hazard in health insurance.

Nyman's research team published a 2018 paper, in which they observed self-reported spending patterns of uninsured persons, and used exogenous increases in assets (e.g., an increase in stock prices) to simulate what an indemnity might do compared to those who did not enjoy such an increase in assets. The findings varied wildly, depending on the particular disease studied; for diseases like diabetes or cancer, over half of the spending was found to be "efficient," meaning that it would be purchased even under an indemnity payment.[79] This simulation approach required lots of assumptions to make an analogy between uninsured people receiving assets from other sources to insured people receiving hypothetical indemnities, and then compare them to data of actual people with traditional insurance. One particular challenge is that uninsured people are less likely to have a regular relationship with the healthcare system, which would allow them to get diagnoses and screenings, which then lead to expensive courses of healthcare. Merely having a few thousand dollars does not change those fundamental behavioral pathways, which create the opportunities for large dollar healthcare spending.

Still, this research at least asks the right questions. Someday perhaps we will have a RAND HIE sequel, which tests such a full indemnity health insurance policy to generate estimates for each effect. Even without randomization, it would be useful to simply observe such a healthcare indemnity program in the field.

In the meantime, my research team has simulated the effect of indemnity insurance, using vignettes—short stories asking respondents to imagine themselves as patients in the cancer scenario like the one described above, which a physician coauthor drafted to be realistic.[80] Vignette research has become a staple of social science methodology, and has been validated, meaning that vignettes accurately predict real-world behavior.[81] In particular, this research method allows us to test an insurance scenario that does not exist in the real world, and it allows perfect head-to-head comparisons, because all else can be held constant in the randomized experiment.

In this new work, we recruited 600 people from an online population, blinded them to the purpose of the study, and randomly assigned each person to one of the three insurance scenarios just described. We included one more manipulation: half of the respondents learned that the expensive drug was FDA-approved for colon cancer, because it was proven safe and effective. The other half were told that it was not FDA-approved for colon cancer, but that their oncologist proposed that it be used off-label, suggesting that it may be promising even though it had not yet been proven effective. For analytical purposes, we could consider the former "high-value" care (likely to be effective given the scientific basis and FDA review) and the latter "low-value" care (lacking such indicia of quality). The drug was offered at the same price in either condition. Everyone was asked whether they would consume the expensive drug on top of the regular chemotherapy regimen.

Recall from Figure 1.1 that the difference between the first two bars is the access function of insurance, as the patient receives sufficient wealth to cover the treatment under the indemnity. But the difference between the second and third bars is the waste of moral hazard, as the benefit is fungible in the second but not the third condition, which represents the standard sort of health insurance now existing. As expected, we observe a huge difference in consumption between uninsurance and traditional insurance—for this expensive cancer treatment, insurance increases the rate of consumption by a factor of ten. In this scenario, involving a treatment that is much more expensive than most people could afford out of pocket, the access function of insurance was on clear display.

Perhaps surprisingly, however, there was little or no difference between traditional insurance and the indemnity payment. Even with 600 respondents, the difference is not statistically significant at traditional levels. (We confirmed that respondents understood the cash-payment mechanism and excluded those who did not. The results were robust.) Thus, from these data, we could not conclude that there is any moral hazard waste whatsoever.

In particular, economic theory might expect to see more such waste in the low-value conditions—with traditional in-kind insurance patients saying "what the heck, might as well try it since it's free to me." In this condition, people with cash indemnity should be much more sensitive to the low value of the care, and the gap should grow compared to traditional insurance. To the contrary, for the people who learn that the treatment is unproven, we see a substantial reduction in their intent to consume in both the cash indemnity and traditional insurance systems. The hypothesized gap does not appear. While consumption of the low-value treatment remains substantial, it seems to largely reflect the considered judgments of those patients that the treatment is worthwhile at the price demanded.

This research suggests that the waste from moral hazard appears remarkably small, if it exists at all. It thus helps us decide between the traditional textbook economic theory versus the access theory of health insurance. Major questions of policy should not be driven by a single such experiment, however. My research team worried that this finding may be simply a fluke, perhaps limited to the particular cancer scenario we tested. So my physician coauthor, Keith Joiner, drafted seven other realistic vignettes in a range of cases, from cancer to arthritis, and from relatively superficial concerns like psoriasis to deadly problems like heart failure. We did focus on expensive situations, where the access function of insurance could be most important (conceding that it is irrelevant for a middle-class person filling a $4 prescription at Wal-Mart). We recruited 2,400 more respondents from another online population, and this time ensured that they were demographically representative in terms of age, gender, and income for the U.S. population. As law professor and economist Kathy Zeiler explains, "Replicating reported results and testing whether principles hold up under a variety of conditions helps to shore up confidence that the principles are generally reliable."[82]

Strikingly, our new data replicated our finding for the cancer scenario and found similar results for every other clinical situation. In almost every case, we found health insurance providing a huge access effect (when compared to uninsurance), but we were unable to detect a significant moral hazard effect (when compared to indemnity insurance). Our much larger sample allowed for very precise estimates that, when controlling for everything else, the effect of moral hazard was nil, or very close thereto.

We also asked people to explain their decisions. One frequent theme was around the special status of health. For example, in a scenario about an expensive drug for macular degeneration (an eye disease), one respondent said, he would try it "because you only have one chance to save your vision." In the cancer scenario, another said, "I want to survive at all costs. [Saving] 80k isn't worth my life."

Another frequent theme: respondents often decided to try the expensive treatment because "it was recommended by the doctor." And that was true, regardless of whether the details of the scenario portrayed the treatment as being highly effective or completely unproven, for the same price. So, our data did show insured people willingly consuming low-value healthcare. Our data confirm what we know from observational research: there is lots and lots of waste in the healthcare system. But our data suggest that health insurance is not the primary cause. Instead, it is driven by the physicians who recommend such low-value healthcare in the first place. (In Chapter 6, I will argue that we should target those drivers of wasteful spending, rather than focus on patients.)

Our studies are largely illustrative. It is possible that real patients would respond differently than our respondents did when asked to imagine the situation, perhaps following even more stringently their physicians' advice or perhaps feeling more strongly the pull of alternative opportunities for spending. Nonetheless, this research suggests that, when properly understood, the wasteful consumption caused by health insurance might be minimal.

### The Lived Experience

If economic theory and empirical evidence are going to affect our ultimate judgments about healthcare policy, they must be weighed against and synthesized with everything else we know about the world.

Narrative can help. At age thirty, Kate Weissman was suffering from cervical cancer. She would fight through fifty-five rounds of radiation, seventeen rounds of chemotherapy, and ultimately surgery to remove cancerous lymph nodes, but her oncologist also recommended proton beam therapy, a very expensive intervention.[83] She was getting world-class care from Harvard physicians at Massachusetts General Hospital. Her health insurance company, United Healthcare, is the largest insurer in the United States. Because of the high cost of proton beam therapy—$95,000—the insurer imposed a pre-authorization review. Notwithstanding the recommendations of Kate's physicians, United ruled that there was no good evidence that proton beam therapy was appropriate for cervical cancer. Kate appealed the decision, but United stood firm.

She and her husband, Matt Eonta, were devastated. The hospital would still provide the procedure if they could come up with the $95,000, but they could not afford it out-of-pocket. As journalist Wayne Dash puts it, "Through tears, the couple called Weissman's parents and asked for help. Lauren and Cindy Weissman jumped at the chance, raiding their retirement savings and wiring the money to the hospital so she could begin proton treatment immediately."

It's tempting to focus on the insurance company's denial as the story, considering and pining for the counterfactual where they had paid and Kate surely would have consumed the healthcare. But in that scenario, health economists might well have assumed that her consumption was a case of moral hazard waste, since after all she did not personally have to bear the costs of the proton beam therapy under that scenario. And, to buttress that story we could look at the other counterfactual—so many uninsured patients, who do not consume proton beam therapies. Insurance would seem to cause the consumption, and that seems wasteful.

But, for our purposes, the interesting point is that when Kate's parents opened their wallets for her healthcare, it was as if they were an insurer providing an indemnity. And Kate consumed the expensive healthcare, just like the people in our vignette experiments said they would if they received an indemnity. Of course, Kate's parents or our respondents could have held on to the money, saving it for a lake house or a bequest, or something else, but it is hard to imagine them doing so. For many of us healthcare is special, and saving our lives is a precondition to everything else we may enjoy.

"Sitting on a couch in their daughter's home, Lauren and Cindy Weissman express relief she's cancer free. They're proud they were able to help when she needed it most, . . . 'There was never any question, because her health was the most important thing,' her father says." Thankfully, Kate got the care and has since made a full recovery. As the exceptional case who found a way to afford expensive care, even when uninsured, she is our third counterfactual. Kate illustrates the way that insurance can create access to the valuable care that people would purchase themselves, if only they could.


We know that health insurance creates more healthcare spending. But this chapter has shown that we cannot equate the additional spending with waste. Insurance is designed to give us access to care that would be otherwise unavailable.

# CHAPTER 2

# HOW WE EXPERIENCE EXPOSURE

How do patients make healthcare consumption decisions? This chapter is about the phenomenology—the experience and meaning—of healthcare under cost exposure. We consider the competence of patients to make these decisions about whether healthcare is worth its exposed price, and how the particular situation of illness and injury, with its stress, fear, exhaustion, and distraction impinges that competence. What does it mean for cost exposure to frame those healthcare choices as being about money, and how does that affect the treatment relationship? We see that, even if insurance did stimulate substantial wasteful spending, consumers might well have reasons to prefer a policy that does not expose them to marginal costs. Rather than "do it yourself," they may instead rationally prefer to outsource the rationing function to trusted institutions.

---

"Rationing" can seem like a dirty word.[1] Nonetheless, in healthcare, there are some fixed items, like transplantable organs or hospital beds in an epidemic, which must be literally rationed, as there are just not enough to go around. Ultimately, someone must say who gets them and who doesn't. But, less overtly, rationing must also happen in any system where money is limited. So I don't think that the term "rationing" should be pejorative. We do need to decide *how* best to allocate those scarce resources, and *who* should have that job.

Cost exposure is one way to perform health-system rationing—it pushes to the consumer the task of determining whether a given healthcare intervention is worth its price. Alternatively, insurers and health-system policy-makers could assign the task of determining what treatments are worthwhile to some other person or institution, such as a government regulator, the patient's physician, or her insurer. Any of those decision makers could decide that a patient should not receive a given treatment, given its cost and the scarcity of healthcare resources. Here, I just want to highlight this particular policy mechanism—to assign the patient the rationing task.

## THE PATIENT'S PERSPECTIVE

If cost exposure is to empower the patient with the task of rationing, let's examine the patient's capacity to do so. How does she grapple with healthcare decisions, and how does adding a new factor (cost) impinge those choices?

### Complexity and Expertise

Healthcare decisions are particularly fraught for patients since they are often highly technical and complex. Patients must choose between different treatment options with very different trade-offs of risk, benefit, and cost—each of which may be only estimated probabilistically. Should I treat my cancer with chemotherapy, proton beams, radiation, or surgery—or some combination thereof? And if chemotherapy, should it be the standard cocktail or the new patented one available off-label; if surgery, with a robot or by hand, and by which surgeon? This selection task requires accurate predictions of both the physiology of how the body will respond to an intervention (and comparing it to the counterfactual of how the body would fare without the particular intervention) and accurate predictions about the patient's subjective experience (pain, anxiety) with the intervention (and comparing it to the subjective experience without the intervention). A patient must ask which healthcare option will deliver the most health and happiness, and are those marginal benefits worth the cost? The difficulty of these questions is precisely why patients consult doctors in the first place—they have the expertise that we laypersons lack.

We can imagine patients going onto PubMed, a free search engine for medical literature, to try to research the various potential treatments, just like they might go on the Web to research a new car purchase. Unfortunately, much of the biomedical literature is behind paywalls, but even if they found an article, could they make sense of it individually much less synthesize the finding with the broader background knowledge that we expect a physician to master? A mountain of evidence has shown that the American population suffers from low levels of numeracy, health literacy, and financial literacy. Pulling together this literature, law professor Alison Hoffman has explained that many Americans are unable to solve very basic math problems, for example determining whether they have enough gas to get to the next gas station, when given all the relevant inputs (distance to the station, gallons in the tank, and the fuel efficiency of their car).[2] Even basic health-care questions, such as when to take a drug in relation to eating given the explicit instructions on the label, stymie many Americans. Asking a patient to second guess their oncologist's treatment recommendations due to cost concerns is a decision orders of magnitude more difficult.

Consider another such context, where we rely on trained experts to help us make life-or-death decisions under such conditions of uncertainty. Imagine sitting as a passenger on a transatlantic flight, and the flight attendant summons you to the cockpit. The pilot explains that there is a small aberration in the performance of the right engine. Should we divert back to Boston, or land in Greenland, or proceed on to London? And should we dump fuel to minimize the chance of an explosion, or keep fuel to preserve our options and range? It's only fair to ask you the passenger, of course, since you will bear the risk of harm for a bad choice. Feeling waves of fear wash over you, you rack your brain to imagine the different possible scenarios and assign probabilities to each.

All of this may seem a strange question to ask, since the pilot is supposed to be the expert, who can weigh the risks and benefits of each option, understanding the likelihood of the risk materializing and the severity of the risk if it does. But this pilot's hypothetical question to a passenger is not unlike the question a physician poses to a patient. (Of course it is an imperfect analogy—in a commercial airplane, there are other passengers, and even the pilot's life is at risk as well. The point here is about the difficulty of asking the layperson—whether passenger or patient—to make a difficult cost-benefit tradeoff, when the expert (physician or pilot) is sitting right there.)

How does a layperson cope with this challenging question? Feeling overwhelmed and incompetent, the passenger might adopt some heuristic to achieve the obvious goal of safety. How about just doing whatever the pilot recommends? One can imagine the passenger saying to the pilot, "Yes, it's *my* body that is at risk, but it is best protected by *your* expertise."

## Stress and Exhaustion

Not unlike the ailing plane, major medical problems are very stressful experiences, even if they are not always so emergent. And there is sometimes no good choice, just an assortment of equally dissatisfactory choices. A commonly used stress assessment tool, the Social Readjustment Rating Scale (SRRS), has been used in large population surveys asking people to rank life events. Perhaps unsurprisingly "major injury / illness to self" ranks third, after "death of spouse / mate" and "death of close family member."[3] "Major injury / illness to close family member" ranks fifth.

This experience of being called upon to make a decision in a domain where we are incompetent is particularly stressful. As an industrial and organizational psychology handbook explains, "There is a potential for stress when an environmental situation is perceived as presenting a demand which threatens to exceed the person's capabilities and resources for meeting it, under conditions where he expects a substantial differential in the rewards and costs from meeting the demand versus not meeting it."[4] Life versus death would be such a "substantial differential."

Returning to our airplane analogy, suppose that the pilot mentions that landing in Greenland would be one option, and that sounds pretty good to you. The logistics involved with landing in Greenland—refueling the plane, providing alternative travel arrangements for passengers—will cost the airline $250,000, and you will personally be charged $10,000, under a new federal mandate. But the pilot pauses for a moment, as he scrutinizes the shocked look on your face. He mentions that Bermuda is just a bit further away but has a longer runway. Since you are the one paying, the pilot says that you should also know that Bermuda will only cost you $7,500. Now, what should we do?

In addition to thinking about the safest approach for landing the plane, you also have to think about whether you can bear that cost, and what it may do to your longer-term financial future. How likely are you to keep your job? From whom could you borrow money? How might that affect your relationship with them? When might you pay them back? Should you move into a less expensive home? Sell your car? If you take the cost question seriously, it would be difficult to continue focusing on the merits of where and how to best land the plane.

Asking someone to think about money may actually distract them from assessing the quality and value of the healthcare options facing them. If fifty years of behavioral science has proven anything, it has shown that humans have limited cognitive bandwidth.[5] Ironically, this is another form of scarcity, not unlike the financial scarcity that requires someone to do healthcare rationing in the first place. For cognitive science, the implication is that, in making a given decision, there are only so many attributes that we can weigh at once.[6] As an alternative to centralized rationing, cost exposure can create more treatment alternatives (like adding Bermuda to the list of landing spots). This particular rationing mechanism necessarily adds one more attribute for the patient to consider: cost.

As we have said, somebody must weigh all the options, and somebody must consider cost. But as a policy mechanism for rationing, cost exposure puts that cognitive work on the patient herself (and perhaps her family). Yet, those people are facing severe stress at that very moment.

Notably, on the standard list of major life stressors (the SRRS), "experiencing financial problems / difficulties" is also very significant, ranking fourteenth on the scale of fifty-one stressful events.[7] And these financial problems can also be exacerbated by losing one's job (thirteenth on the list), which is also a risk of getting severely ill or injured (as Chapter 3 shows, it's hard to work when you are flat on your back in a hospital bed).

Medical bills can be precisely such a stressor. In one study of cancer patients, 42% reported that their medical bills represented a "significant" (33%) or "catastrophic" (9%) burden.[8] In another study of 104 cancer patients, four-fifths reported financial stress related to their treatment, and these concerns were reflected in standard measures of depression, anxiety, and quality of life.[9]

From a physiological point of view, the human stress response is complex and not yet fully understood, but we are increasingly understanding that stress influences health. After intensive healthcare episodes, additional stress has been shown to worsen health outcomes in particular.[10] For employers considering whether and how to use cost exposure as part of their health benefit plans, this stress response should be particularly interesting. Research suggests that among employees stress is associated with decreased productivity and quality, additional accidents and injuries, and more absenteeism and turnover.[11]

Stress can change the way decisions are made. Even at the neurological level, stress has a role in the way memories are encoded and neurons are replaced.[12] Stress also changes how people think about the risks and benefits. Scholars posit that stress causes potential *benefits* of a decision to seem more salient than they otherwise may be. For example, when people are stressed, fatty and sweet "comfort" foods may seem all the more attractive, while the longer term health consequences may seem less salient.[13] This may seem like an odd response to stress, but the effect has been observed in lab studies with rats, whose dopamine receptors fire more frequently when stressed, and in brain-scan studies with humans. Scholars have also found behavioral correlates—"stress enhances learning about positive outcomes while diminishing learning about negative outcomes."[14]

Imagine sitting in the oncologist's office and hearing about a treatment that will cost $10,000 out-of-pocket. The focal question is then, *what will this expenditure do for me?* It seems easier to understand and remember the potential benefits of the treatment, while the risks and side effects blur and fade away. If we are going to spend that much, we *need* it to be a worthwhile expenditure. Similarly, patients often wrongly suppose that participating in risky scientific research studies will be more beneficial than there is any basis for believing—a bedeviling phenomenon known among bioethicists as the "therapeutic misconception."[15] As Katrina Starcke and Matthias Brand conclude in their review of the literature on the effects of stress on decisions under uncertainty, "Stress deteriorates overall decision-making performance."[16] Nonetheless, the research in this field is still nascent and conflicting.[17]

When confronted by these stressful and complex healthcare decisions, patients and their surrogates are often utterly exhausted as well. Even at home, it's hard to get sleep when your back hurts or you are having trouble breathing. If you are in the hospital—with its beeping monitors, shared rooms, and pokes and prods—it is much worse. In one study of patients in an intensive care unit, patients were only getting 50%–60% of the sleep they normally got at night.[18] In a recent study of hospitalized older patients receiving usual care, 46% were suffering from sleep deprivation.[19]

Harvard professor William Kilgore has summarized the literature, explaining that sleep deprivation is "associated with a reduced tendency to think positively, decreased willingness to take effective behavioural action to solve problems, and a greater reliance on unproductive coping strategies such as superstitious and magical thinking processes."[20] Sleep deprivation also reduces "impulse control, and the ability to delay gratification."[21] Finally, "A large and growing literature suggests that sleep is critical to learning and memory, and when sleep is hindered, memory processing is correspondingly degraded." In particular, "sleep is important following learning to facilitate the consolidation (i.e. stabilization) and integration (i.e. assimilation) of newly learned information into existing memory structures." These are the people that cost exposure depends upon to make wise healthcare decisions.

As a social policy mechanism for healthcare rationing, patient cost exposure depends on these people to make good cost-benefit tradeoffs. It does not help that these are the very same people that are sleep deprived, stressed, distracted, and not especially competent at understanding the medical technicalities involved. Even worse, they are afraid.

### Fear

While stress can arise from decisional complexity itself, adding financial considerations can increase fear in particular, because large healthcare costs are associated with financial ruin, including bankruptcy as we will see in Chapter 3. There, we will explore how cost exposure actually makes our healthcare more dangerous, as it increases risks of subsequent financial problems, reduces our access to subsequent care, and undermines our housing security through eviction or foreclosure. We will explore the objective basis for those risks later, but here the mere fear of them may change the experience of healthcare. A patient may decline to consume worthwhile care for fear that the expenditure of funds will create even worse problems for her. In a sense, that's the point of cost-exposure—to give patients some "skin in the game." It's not just, "think about how much this costs," it instead primes the patient to "think about how much this will cost *you*."

That sense of fear may itself degrade decisional quality. Psychologists have demonstrated that negative mood states, like fear, cause people to think about things that are irrelevant to the decision task they face, an understandable coping mechanism that nonetheless diverts scarce cognitive resources.[22] While the physician drones on about huge costs and the innumerable risks of the surgery, a patient could be thinking *I wonder if this is related to my dad's illness years ago? Dad loved baseball. Gosh, that is nice to think about. But why didn't I go to more games with him? I wonder who will win the World Series this year, by the way? Oh, wait, what was that doctor saying?*

As scholars surveying this literature conclude, "By increasing decision complexity or difficulty, negative task-related emotion will encourage less extensive . . . processing."[23] They offer the example that "a decision maker feeling distress at the prospect of choosing between two job offers may conclude that thinking through various decision criteria and potential outcomes is too taxing, and he or she may therefore develop a simple decision rule (e.g., taking the higher paying job)."[24] Analogously, we can imagine fearful healthcare consumers adopting decision heuristics, such as *do-whatever-my-doctor-recommends*.

More generally, decision making under fear can create a feedback loop, as Loewenstein and colleagues explain: "Fear increases arousal and arousal increases the intensity of new fear responses."[25] Although this dimension has not been studied in healthcare directly, it is possible that cancer patients fearing financial devastation might actually then fear the cancer even more, thereby preferring more intensive interventions. By exposing individuals to cost, and thereby making choices more complex and fearful, it may undermine the quality of their decisions.

More specifically, recent research suggests that the very consideration of financial constraints can undermine decision quality. In one experiment published in *Science,* Oxford University behavioral economist Anandi Mani and her research team recruited shoppers at a New Jersey mall to make a series of hypothetical decisions implicating their finances.[26] One scenario, for example, stated, "Your car is having some trouble and requires $X to be fixed. You can pay in full, take a loan, or take a chance and forego the service at the moment. . . . How would you go about making this decision?"[27] Some participants were assigned to a "hard" condition, where it would take $1,500 to fix the car and others were assigned to an "easy" condition requiring only $150 to fix the car. Subjects then completed two tests of cognitive function and reported their demographics, including wealth. The central finding was that, although "poor" and "rich" subjects performed equally well on the cognitive tests following easy financial decisions, the poor subjects performed worse after hard decisions that evoked onerous financial situations. The effect size was substantial, on the same scale as losing a full night of sleep, or suffering from chronic alcoholism, or a thirteen-point decrease in IQ.[28] As the authors interpreted their findings, "Preoccupation with pressing budgetary concerns leaves fewer cognitive resources available to guide choice and action."[29]

Three additional experiments replicated the finding and ruled out alternative explanations. Most striking were field data from a random sample of 464 sugarcane farmers in India, surveyed before and after harvest season. Before harvest season, the researchers documented that the respondents faced severe budgetary constraints (e.g., more often pawning off personal property to generate needed funds). On two different measures of cognitive function, the farmers performed substantially and significantly worse when they were poorer. The authors worried that the results could be due to differences in nutrition or stress. They found no differences as to food intake, but did observe significantly elevated biomarkers for stress in the preharvest time frame. Nonetheless, regressions controlled for the stress effects, allowing the researchers to conclude that attention was itself the likely causal mechanism. The authors warn that "policy-makers should beware of imposing cognitive taxes on the poor just as they avoid monetary taxes on the poor."[30] This striking work has led to methodological debates about the validity of the research.[31]

This body of research suggests that the imposition of cost exposure may actually reduce the patient's ability to think carefully about the other attributes of her healthcare choices, whether by increasing complexity, stress, or fear, or by diverting attention. Concededly, much of the literature that I have reviewed does not pertain directly to healthcare—I have drawn on a broad body of behavioral science. But health policy must begin with the recognition that these healthcare consumers are in fact humans.

These findings also provide a groundwork for understanding topline effects that we do see in the healthcare domain. Recall that the RAND Health Insurance Experiment found that increased cost exposure may have had deleterious effects for poorer and chronically ill patients, even though the experimental design included special protections for lower-income individuals. And the imposition of cost sharing caused reductions of both high-value and low-value care. This newer body of research fills in the rest of the story, providing a plausible mechanism for these deleterious effects of cost exposure.

## PUTTING A PRICE ON HEALTH AND THE
## TREATMENT RELATIONSHIP

Bruce Vladeck, who led the Medicare and Medicaid programs in the 1990s, argued that "consumers . . . don't wish to be forced to make rational trade-offs when they are confronted with medical care consumption decisions. [M]edical care is about living and dying, something considered by many to be of a rather different character from the purchase of tomatoes."[32] Cost exposure threatens to change the way we think about ourselves and our own bodies, and it may undermine trust in our treaters and erode the treatment relationship. In this section, we explore the meaning and experience of putting a price on such things.

### Commodification

Vladeck suggests an incommensurability between money and health that, when forced upon sick people or their loved ones, may feel bewildering. Sunstein defines "incommensurability" as arising when "the relevant goods cannot be aligned along a single metric without doing violence to our considered judgments about how these goods are best characterized."[33] Here the relevant goods are health and healthcare. The "single metric" is dollars and cents. Are dollars and cents the best way to characterize health and sickness, life and death?

The concern with incommensurability may be the same as the concern about "commodification," which professor Margaret Radin has compellingly developed to explain why we resist having our humanity reduced to a mere thing that can be traded for another. "We feel discomfort or even insult, and we fear degradation or even loss of the value involved, when bodily integrity is conceived of as a fungible object. [It] is threatening to personhood, because it detaches from the person that which is integral to the person."[34] These concerns have been implicated by the examples of selling organs for transplantation or leasing a womb for a surrogate mother. Although extreme cases, they illustrate the fundamental point.

Similarly, the point of cost exposure is to put a price on the goods and services that are healthcare. The patient sees these particular widgets or procedures as the means to achieving a healthy and thriving version of herself.[35] For someone needing an organ transplant, cost exposure puts a price on that sought-after organ, even if the actual charges are enumerated for the surgeons' time, the hospital bed, and the drugs to ensure that the body does not reject the transplant. A patient who seeks a body free of cancer or a hip free of arthritis pain faces the cost of treatment as the cost of securing that healthy body she seeks. Cost exposure creates a quid pro quo—a this for that—exchange.

Libertarian professor Richard Epstein has pressed a line-drawing problem here.[36] After all, Vladek's purchase of tomatoes implicates health concerns and our bodies too, but we do not suppose that it is problematic to price produce. And we project our sense of self into all sorts of things and personal projects, such as our professional educations or even the cars we drive. Yet I am not eager to eliminate the price mechanism in all those domains. Even in a broadly capitalist society, such as the contemporary United States, there are nonetheless some things that we hold as too sacred for a quid pro quo exchange.[37]

Politics is such a domain. Although U.S. law tolerates virtually unlimited spending for political advertising, we have not yet come to allow candidates, or their advocates, to actually pay voters for their votes. Likewise, politicians must routinely solicit campaign donations from their benefactors, but they are not allowed to earn any payment for official actions, such as vetoing a bill. Of course, it's not always easy to determine whether any given transaction was made with such a corrupt intent. Yet, in some of my other research, I have found that Americans are quite willing to infer quid pro quo arrangements from banal political transactions.[38]

Even in healthcare, we allow physicians to accept money from the drug and device industry on the side as a supplement to their salaries. Still, we have an elaborate system of laws and regulations to make sure that those payments are not quid pro quo kickbacks for each prescription they write.

Harvard bioethicist Glenn Cohen offers another stark example of something beyond the pale: the buying and selling of children for money. Sure, there are people with money that might like to simply purchase a child reflecting their preferred characteristics. There are all sorts of problems that come to mind when considering a proposal for a free market in children, but one of the most salient is that "exchanging children for money corrupts the value of children because money and children belong in different spheres of valuation."[39] To say that the child's blue eyes or skillful cartwheels are worth $75 or even $7,500 is to make a category mistake.[40] The illegality of markets in children reflects these settled insights.

These sorts of proscriptive laws help a society avoid a fundamental category error. Raising children is supposed to be about love. Even if the person who would seek to purchase a child really would love him or her, the monetary transaction would corrupt the meaning of the relationship. Similarly for political decisions or physician prescribing—bribes and kickbacks are not tolerated because they corrupt. We keep these things beyond the domain of the *quid pro quo*.

Yet cost exposure creates exactly this sort of *quid pro quo* for our own bodies. This problem is even more obvious when the person deciding is a surrogate, such as a parent, who must make a decision on a child's behalf. How much is the life of your loved one worth to you? In this way, we may end up putting a price on our child's life after all. You cannot sell your child, but with the right healthcare, you can purchase her life.

### Trusting the Treaters

There is a unique dependence between a patient and her physician. David Mechanic and Mark Schlesinger have argued that "the success of medical care depends most importantly on patients' trust that their physicians are competent, take appropriate responsibility and control, and give their patients' welfare the highest priority."[41] This dependency is partly epistemic—because the layperson patient is often unable to independently assess the advice she receives.

In the 1980s and 1990s healthcare reform was focused on "managed care," which gave physicians oversight and incentives to control costs. Scholars and courts worried, and some evidence suggested, that financial oversight of physicians could undermine patients' trust and erode the doctor-patient relationship. In a 1997 survey, only 30% of Americans in such managed-care plans agreed that they trusted their health plans to do the right thing for their care "just about always."[42] More recent initiatives, such as the "accountable care" movement, have rekindled such concerns that physicians will act on their incentives to deliver less care or cheaper care.

Interestingly, patient cost-exposure mechanisms, such as copays and deductibles, impose incentives for thrift on the patient rather than the provider, and thus ostensibly should avoid the risks of managed care. Still, cost exposures may reshape the treatment relationship in a different way, as it changes the relationship between the patient and the physician.

Cultural practices of healing and treatment have ancient roots, often intertwined with supernatural notions. The physician is the one who brings those powers to bear on the patient, who knows not how they work. Notwithstanding the move toward materialism and scientific explanations, and then progressive changes in the particular technologies employed, the doctor-patient relationship continues to turn on trust, care, deference, and expertise.

Bioethicists David Schenck and Larry Churchill have studied how the most effective physicians interact with their patients. Even in this era of science and technology, they describe a "ritual" process of forming a treatment relationship, the "rite of passage" as a patient moves into that relationship, and the relationship itself as an "ancient and archetypal journey" where the physician serves as the "guide" and "companion."[43] In this vein, health policy expert Mark Hall has described a "power of healing" as "the dimension of doctoring that enables physicians to confer relief through spiritual or emotional means akin to those used by parents or priests."[44]

Let me highlight two particular instances where the commercialization frame, encouraged by cost exposure, can affect the healing relationship. The first is the selection of a provider. The second is the interaction with the chosen provider.

One key purpose of cost exposure is to drive patients toward lower-cost providers or lower-cost treatments. To the extent that cost exposure succeeds in driving patients toward lower-cost options, then those chosen providers and treatments will be perceived as "lower in cost." This is not merely a tautology: other institutional arrangements (e.g., central rationing) could drive patients to lower-cost options without the patient necessarily conceptualizing them as such. Patient cost exposure uniquely harnesses and exploits the patient's own mind for this purpose.

A vast literature shows that consumers perceive higher-priced products and services to be of higher quality and lower-priced products and services as lower in quality.[45] In a series of health-related studies, Baba Shiv, Ziv Carmon, and Dan Ariely manipulated the prices of products and then observed outcomes. For example, in one preliminary study, they gave members of a fitness center a performance-enhancing drink prior to their workout, but told half of the participants that it had been purchased at a deep discount. This design likely muted the effect, since the lower cost was described as a special discount off of a disclosed higher price, which could still signal higher quality. Nonetheless, "the results show that participants in the reduced-price condition rated their workout intensity as lower than did those in the regular-price condition, and participants in the reduced-price condition indicated that they were more fatigued than did those in the regular-price condition."[46] In another experiment, the authors found that respondents were able to solve fewer puzzles after having consumed a discounted-price drink, compared to those randomly assigned to an otherwise identical full-price drink.

The authors analogize this dynamic to the placebo effect, in which expectations modulate the body's response, and higher prices generate higher expectations. In a related phenomenon, Thomas Kramer and colleagues have demonstrated a "no pain, no gain" heuristic for evaluating pharmaceutical products. People judge a bad-tasting cough syrup to be more effective than a good-tasting one.[47] In a research letter published in the *Journal of the American Medical Association* (*JAMA*), Rebecca Waber and colleagues tested whether respondents who thought they were taking a painkiller drug experienced better pain relief, when they believed it was a higher-priced drug. Although all patients received a placebo, the response was almost 25% greater among those in the higher-priced condition.[48] This effect may explain why, although most Americans think that more people should use generic (lower-priced) drugs, only 37.6% of them prefer to take generics themselves.[49] In recent years, however, confidence in generic drugs appears to be increasing.[50]

Of course, these effects will not arise where the costs are not transparent or the patient is not in a position to weigh them. Indeed, in one recent study of people who had received care in the last year, only 5% reported that they had compared costs across providers for their most recent visit.[51] Of course, the cost-exposure agenda seeks to make that behavior much more common.

I want to be quite explicit in saying that the research base is merely suggestive here.[52] We do not have strong evidence that cost exposure is reducing perceived efficacy of healthcare. But I think the evidence does suggest a risk that when a patient perceives that she is receiving less expensive healthcare, that perception may in fact generate lower expectations of healing and worse treatment outcomes. If healthcare consumers shop around and find a range of prices for, say, surgeons offering knee arthroscopy procedures, they might be even more likely to suppose that the lower-cost providers somehow provide lower-quality surgery. We should be especially concerned in contexts where the price is salient, where patients are exposed to marginal differences in price, and where providers compete along this dimension.

There is a second way in which cost exposure can shape the treatment relationship. Once a patient selects a physician or other healthcare provider, cost exposure frames the relationship as between a consumer and a seller in a market, which is premised on the idea of "rational contractors" negotiating a quid pro quo exchange, as philosopher James Childress and physician Mark Siegler have noted.[53] Indeed, the point of cost exposure is to make consumers ask whether this healthcare is the best possible expenditure to promote their own welfare. We want the consumer to be wary of waste. We want her to veto recommendations that will fail to deliver value commensurate to the prices charged.

Scholars Analee and Thomas Beisecker have described this perspective of the arm's-length consumer as a profound reorientation. Unlike "the client [who] comes to the professional for advice and accepts the professional's opinion; the consumer, in contrast, listens to the thoughts of the provider, or of several providers, but ultimately makes his or her own decisions."[54] As sociologist Leo Reeder puts it, "When the individual is viewed as a consumer, he is a purchaser of services and tends to be guided by caveat emptor. Thus, the switching of labels tends to change the fabric of the social relationship."[55]

In one sense, we should applaud the reorientation of healthcare from a physician-knows-best paternalism to focus on the patient's own intelligent choices and preferences. It is perfectly consistent with the trend toward patient autonomy, enunciated by Justice Benjamin Cardozo over a century ago, writing in a landmark case now cited thousands of times, that "every human being of adult years and sound mind has a right to determine what shall be done with his own body."[56] But informed consent is in some tension with the reality of epistemic dependence and vulnerability. In the landmark 1972 case of *Canterbury v. Spence*, the District of Columbia Court of Appeals held that "the average patient has little or no understanding of the medical arts, and ordinarily has only his physician to whom he can look for enlightenment with which to reach an intelligent decision."[57] A good clinical encounter synthesizes all the scientific information with contextual factors and patient preferences in a realm of gray uncertainty, to make a shared decision about how to proceed. Although there is some heterogeneity between patients, surveys suggest that many in fact prefer a model of "shared decision making," where "the average respondent would request information in case of illness, but would leave the responsibility for the medical decisions to his or her physician. In other words, most respondents did not want an active role, but neither did they want to be entirely passive in the doctor-patient relationship."[58]

Can this process of shared decision making be squared with the market-oriented point of view, which cost exposure encourages? At one extreme it can become overtly adversarial, where the Beiseckers argue that "consumer-oriented patients are motivated to approach any doctor-patient relationship warily."[59] They should clutch their wallets in hand and think and second-guess each suggestion offered by the physician as potentially just another attempt to extract hard-earned money. Just as when a car salesman offers undercoating, or custom floor mats, or an extended warranty, rational "consumers distrust sellers' motives, and they expect this distrust to be reciprocated."[60]

Legal scholar Matt Lawrence explains how physicians may reflect this wariness. Rather than being the patient's agent or ally, patient cost exposure creates a zero-sum game of collections. "When it comes to medical billing physicians are more like adversaries than allies."[61] Even if the larger exchange is welfare enhancing, once the healthcare is provided, the extraction of money from the patient—perhaps referring her to collections or even suing her—is contrary to her interests. In extreme cases, hospitals have even foreclosed on their patients' homes to extract the funds that the law said they owed.

If cost exposure does create this sort of untrusting adversarialism, what are the implications? Several studies have empirically shown correlations between trust in physicians and health outcomes, although the mechanisms are not well understood. A 2001 systematic review published in *The Lancet* found twenty-five randomized controlled trials focusing on how the doctor-patient relationship affected health outcomes. They found inconsistent results in various details, but "one relatively consistent finding is that physicians who adopt a warm, friendly, and reassuring manner are more effective than those who keep consultations formal and do not offer reassurance."[62] One study of colon and breast cancer patients found that trust in their physicians was associated with earlier detection of their cancers, which is itself a primary factor for successful treatment.[63] Some of this is likely driven by physician characteristics. For example, in a correlational study, Mohammadreza Hojat and colleagues found that physicians who scored higher on an empathy scale had patients who were better able to manage their diabetes, as assessed by blood tests.[64] The authors speculate that the greater empathy enhances the physician-patient relationship, "which in turn promotes sharing without concealment, leading to better alignment between patients' needs and treatment plans and thus more accurate diagnosis and greater adherence."[65] Physician trust is especially important when patients are considering whether to comply with treatment recommendations when cost is itself a factor.[66]

This literature suggests that a successful healthcare treatment relationship may be different than other sorts of quid pro quo relationships that we see in the modern economy, such as the hiring of an automobile mechanic. British scholar Fred Hirsch has described a "commercialization effect," in which the way a product is exchanged can actually change the product.[67] Hirsch speculates that basing healthcare on a quid pro quo exchange encourages patients to view their physicians warily, which then increases the chance of the patient suing the physician when a bad outcome occurs.[68] That liability risk then causes physicians to practice more "defensive medicine," driving up healthcare spending with unnecessary procedures. As far as I can tell, this mechanism has not been studied directly, but it is a plausible story.

At the macro level of health systems, we see such an effect. Physician Ellery Chih-Han Huang and colleagues used a survey of over 45,000 respondents in twenty-nine countries to compare answers on the question of whether "all things considered, doctors in [your country] can be trusted." Separately, the authors rated each country's healthcare system on the degree to which it was commodified, considering how much of the expenditure came from private funds and the percentage of hospital beds that were private, versus the breadth of the public healthcare system. Unsurprisingly, the United States scored as the most commodified healthcare system, and it also had the third-lowest score for trust in physicians. Countries like the United Kingdom, Norway, and the Netherlands—where healthcare is not conceived as a commodity to be bought and sold—had substantially greater degrees of physician trust.[69]

At a more granular level within the United States, another study used a household survey to obtain standard measures of physician trust, such as whether your "physician puts patients' needs above all other concerns" and more particular concerns such as the "physician performs unnecessary tests."[70] In this study, sociologist Peter Cunningham focused on people who had "high out-of-pocket medical costs relative to their income and / or problems paying their medical bills," and he found that they were more likely to distrust their physicians on every question studied.[71] Although this sort of observational study cannot show that the cost exposure *caused* these reactions, Cunningham used statistical controls for demographics, including income and insurance status, to try to isolate the cost-sharing exposure as the likely cause of the difference in trust. He concludes that "patients with high medical cost burdens are more likely to view their medical encounters in terms of financial transactions and medical providers as economic actors. Such response patterns may reflect a consistent belief that the physician is more interested in financial gain from the patient than ensuring they are receiving appropriate and necessary services."[72]

Contrast this perspective with the themes developed by Larry Churchill and colleagues in their model of "relationship-centered healthcare," based on their observations of the most effective physicians. They counsel physicians to "invest in trust" as an essential ingredient in the relationship, because patients identify "caring, empathy, and compassion" as the most important clinician traits.[73] By framing the physician as an arm's-length seller instead, cost exposure is a potential barrier to this sort of treatment relationship.

## CHOOSING WHETHER TO CHOOSE

Looking back on this chapter, we see a range of ways in which the cost-exposure strategy of putting prices on healthcare consumers has unintended consequences. That strategy is cognitively burdensome and creates dissonance with our experience and valuation of health and healthcare. It drives a wedge between us and our physicians, at a time when we need to trust them profoundly.

Nonetheless, one of the advantages of cost exposure is its preservation of patients' choices, compared to alternative rationing mechanisms. In recent years, health policy has been preoccupied by "consumer-directed health care," and the idea of "choice architecture," by which a policymaker uses a "nudge" that "alters people's behavior in a predictable way without forbidding any options."[74] Nudges, like cost exposure mechanisms, preserve choices. In contrast, centralized rationing is used much more heavily abroad to simply eliminate options. George Loewenstein points to Britain's National Institute for Health and Clinical Excellence (NICE), "which makes national decisions regarding the cost effectiveness of treatments and ensuing coverage" as an example of a "good shove that advances individual and social welfare considerably more."[75]

To be sure, even in the U.S. healthcare system, there are some inchoate forms of such shoves. Federal law prevents the sale of drugs and devices that lack proof of safety and efficacy, and state laws put the licensed physician in the role of gatekeeper between patients and many treatments and then holds those doctors liable if they exercise that role negligently. Similarly, insurers sometimes simply refuse to pay for high-cost, low-value treatments by saying that they are "experimental" or not "medically necessary"—the criteria in most insurance contracts. Medicare generally excludes drugs that are not approved by the Food and Drug Administration (FDA) and also excludes alternative treatments such as acupuncture. Insurers also impose pre-utilization reviews and "fail first" policies that require patients to try inexpensive treatments before seeking reimbursement for more expensive treatments.

In these ways, government regulators, physicians, or insurers simply take items off the patient's treatment menu. In fact, however, in the United States, these mechanisms currently function poorly compared to ideal rationers, who would bar treatments that lack value commensurate with their costs. For their part, many physicians remain in fee-for-service and self-referral relationships, where they "get paid more for doing more," as the president of the American Board of Internal Medicine has said.[76] The FDA's statute does not even allow it to consider costs; its approval of a new therapy includes no suggestion that it is actually worth its price, or even better than the alternatives already on the market. Responding to political pressures by groups of demanding patients, state and federal governments have imposed over two thousand mandates on insurance providers, requiring that, regardless of their cost, insurers must cover particular treatments that they might otherwise exclude in their contractual bargains with their insureds.[77] Insurers enjoy subsidies from employers and the government, directly and through the tax code. Accordingly, many "insurers have largely abandoned direct attempts to limit coverage for most medical procedures and instead have adopted a pass-through attitude toward medical spending."[78]

Thus, the U.S. status quo is an odd mixture of shoves and nudges, where the shoves are not attuned to the value of care and in a broad middle range of healthcare options, patients are nonetheless charged with making rationing decisions themselves. Cost exposure can be evaluated on this dimension of preserving options.

## The Paradox of Choice

Compared to the alternative strategy of having some sort of central rationer, we normally suppose that choice is good. Former Speaker of the U.S. House of Representatives Newt Gingrich has expressed this standard view: "If you were to walk into a Wal-Mart and say to people, 'Don't you feel really depressed by having 258,000 options; shouldn't it be their obligation to reduce the choice you must endure?' They would think you were nuts."[79] In contrast, President Clinton's Medicare administrator, Bruce Vladeck, has suggested that there may be a dark side to choice: "Consumers of medical care . . . are scared. They are scared of dying, or disfigurement, or permanent disability; and these are serious matters. . . . As a society, we may be prepared to pay a substantial economic premium to insulate people from having to make such decisions."[80]

In a well-known book, psychologist Barry Schwartz has described this as the "paradox of choice."[81] He reviews a range of social science research that has now become nearly famous. In one such study, Sheena Iyengar and co-authors examined enrollment rates in 401K retirement plans, comparing enrollment in companies that offered choices between as few as two funds to as many as fifty-nine.[82] Participation was highest when only two options were offered (75%), but lowest when fifty-nine funds were available (60%). Having more choices seemed to paralyze some employees; they "chose not to choose" by simply not creating a retirement plan at all.

A *JAMA* study of physicians shows a similar dynamic. In an experiment based on hypothetical situations, physicians were asked to consider an elderly patient with osteoarthritis and decide whether to prescribe a new medication until a future orthopedic consult. Half of the physicians were given two drugs to choose from, while the other half were given only one choice. Those with two choices were more likely to recommend none at all! As the authors concluded, "Apparently, the uncertainty in deciding between two similar medications led some physicians to avoid this decision altogether and recommend not starting any new medication."[83] Sorry, patients, you'll just have to suffer with untreated pain for a month or so, because your physician hit a mental speedbump!

These remarkable findings—that people avoid choices and do worse when they have more choices—have ignited a debate among social scientists.[84] In situations where a person already has very strong preferences, has clear expertise, or is faced with one option that is so obviously better than others, then choice is unproblematic. In healthcare, the opposite is often true—patients are unsure as to their preferences, they lack expertise, and all the options might seem equivalently unclear. A broad menu of treatment options, with cost exposures for each, can make the choice harder. Patients may actually do better in health insurance systems that use physicians and formularies to reduce the number of salient treatment options and then highlight only the best ones.

Concededly, unlike a retirement-plan buyer, a patient with a particular illness typically does not have dozens of treatments to choose from. More often, it is one or two: surgery or chemotherapy, or perhaps hospice care instead of either treatment. But there are various permutations, including which hospital to use and which surgeon within the hospital.

A related phenomenon is seen in the literature on defaults, even where there is only a binary choice—to do or not do. For example, one can either donate their organs upon death, or not. It turns out that people are much more likely to allow their organs to be donated upon death, if that outcome is the default and does not require an active choice.[85] If patients instead must "opt in" to being organ donors, contributions plummet. Reducing the choice from two options to only one default seems to help.

Similarly, in the United States, some states require vaccinations as a condition of kids attending school, but vaccination is not typically structured as the default outcome—the parent is still asked to consent to the vaccination (or not), just like other healthcare. Ilana Ritov and Jonathan Barron have shown why some parents are reluctant to vaccinate their children if the vaccine itself carries a small risk of death, even if that risk is vastly outweighed by the benefits of the vaccine to the child.[86] To choose is, in some sense, to take a responsibility for the outcome. To choose is to take on a moral burden.

In these sorts of situations, people seem to not want to implicate their own decisions in the poor outcomes that may befall them. People seem to avoid choosing.

## Regret Aversion

Some research shows that the mere act of choosing produces a sense of immediate regret, and people start to instantly think of the nonchosen alternative as more attractive (like the grass is always greener on the other side of the fence).[87] Suppose you give someone a lottery ticket but you then offer to trade it for another lottery ticket that has the exact same chance of winning. In such an experiment, Maya Bar-Hillel and Efrat Neter found that people were unwilling to make the trade, even when offered a small incentive to do so.[88] By failing to maximize their own utility, people seem to be violating the most basic economic assumptions about human behavior. Why?

People seem to try to avoid experiencing regret. Making an active choice to swap lottery tickets creates a risk that you will feel responsible for the ultimate bad outcome of receiving a losing ticket. But if a ticket just falls out of the sky, and you happen to win there is only an upside. There's no risk of feeling bad about your choice, because there was no choice.

Behavioral scientist Terry Connolly and colleagues have delineated several distinct types of regret, based on the target of what is regretted.[89] Most obviously, decision makers can suffer *outcome regret,* when they prefer that the world may have turned out a different way ("if only my child had survived"). We might call this simple *disappointment.* In contrast, *option regret* focuses on the particular choice that a person made ("if only I had selected the chemotherapy treatment"). Finally, *process regret* targets the way in which the decision was made, including the factors considered, information gathered, and time consumed ("if only I had gotten a second opinion").

Marcus Aurelius and the Stoic philosophers famously argued that we should only worry about, and regret, that which we can control. We should be indifferent to the outcomes, because they are driven by other things, of which we are not responsible. As psychologist and author Janet Landman argues, we should probably think of bad outcomes in terms of disappointment, rather than regret: "The child is disappointed when the Tooth Fairy forgets his third lost tooth. The child's parents regret the lapse."[90] In contrast, however, Connolly and colleagues explain that process regret is "centrally concerned with mechanisms of self-criticism and justification."[91] More particularly, when a poor decision outcome occurs, "individuals tend to ask themselves whether the decision, or the process that led up to it, was justified[—if] it was partially or entirely unjustified, we feel regret, the intensity of which is increased by the seriousness of the outcome."[92]

Behavioral scientist Richard Thaler describes these sorts of dynamics in healthcare decision making: "Consider a couple which must decide whether to spend $X for a diagnostic test for their child. . . . There will surely be regret if the decision is made not to get the test and the child later is found to have the disease. . . . Yet once the test is ordered and the likely negative result is obtained, the couple may regret the expenditure, especially if it is large relative to their income. Obviously, these costs are avoided if all health care is prepaid," with no cost sharing.[93] Alternatively, these decisional costs can be avoided if a central rationer has eliminated the unreliable test as an option at all. Similarly, Thaler explains, if there are two different surgical procedures from which to choose, "clearly in this situation a rational consumer would want the physician to make the choice and furthermore, he would not want to know that a choice existed!"

Indeed, in a recent survey about one-third of physicians reported that they sometimes did not disclose treatment options to patients, when the physicians believed that the options would not be covered by insurance.[94] In this sense, the centralized rationing by the insurer (excluding some options from coverage) could help consumers narrow their range of healthcare choices, and thus avoid some regret on the margins.

We know that regret is quite common in healthcare settings, with, for example, nearly a quarter of prostate cancer survivors regretting their treatment choice.[95] Such regret can be painful and long-lasting.[96] Of course, suffering bad outcomes is inevitable; the question is whether we want to suffer with knowledge that we made a *choice* that caused that outcome.

Connolly and colleagues have called for much more research to understand regret in healthcare contexts in particular.[97] Because of the gap in the literature, we often must make inferences from other contexts. Marketing expert Itamar Simonson has studied the preference between brand names and generic products, and he found that when his research team asked consumers to consider the potential regret that they may feel as a result of their choice *prior* to making the choice, consumers tended to prefer the brand-name product more often.[98] People seem to want to avoid responsibility for choosing the less expensive product, and instead repose their trust in the brand as the more familiar and normalized option. If generics and brand-name drugs really are chemically equivalent, insurance designers might do better to just exclude coverage for the brand-name drug altogether, rather than preserving the option with a cost exposure differential (sometimes called, "pharmaceutical tiering").

Many healthcare decisions are even more emotionally laden. Scholars studying breast cancer patients, for example, note the prior literature showing that patients "are more likely to make hasty medical decisions when they are overwhelmed and numbed by the distress elicited by the diagnosis of advanced cancer. This implies that sub-groups of advanced cancer patients may be vulnerable to making emotionally charged decisions, which can result in irreversible regret."[99] The cost-exposure strategy for rationing puts the choices on such people and nudges them to think about money while making those choices. Contrary to the long-standing norm of informed consent, researchers have found that many patients prefer not to be involved in their own healthcare decisions, and "fear of regret for decisions that turn out badly" is one such reason.[100]

I will repeat once again that, in healthcare, there will always be bad outcomes, with or without cost exposure. Plausibly, though, a cost-exposure scheme heightens the risk of patients suffering process regret when there are inevitable bad outcomes. Process regret can be shielded, if the decision is outsourced to someone else, as in the Britain NICE committee. If the system declines to make a treatment available, a patient might regret any ensuing bad *outcome,* but he or she will not feel the pang of self-blame. Thus, process regret can be averted. If the other rationer also prevents the patient from becoming aware of other options, the patient may also thereby avoid option regret.[101] Cost exposure thus arguably increases these psychic costs by preserving choices for patients.

It seems fanciful to suppose that healthcare decision making could (or should) ever be truly outsourced from the patient. We have come too far in the last century along the agenda of patient empowerment to suppose that patients should defer blindly to their physicians' discretion. The law does require, and will continue to require, that healthcare providers secure informed consent from the patient, which will include disclosing the risks and benefits of the recommended treatment and reasonable alternatives (as circumscribed by regulators and payors). In this sense, with or without cost exposure, the final choice about whether to consume care will formally remain on the patient, even if the salience of that choice and the range of alternatives to choose from can vary wildly in practice. But if the healthcare system declines to make a treatment available, a patient might experience disappointment over any bad outcome, but he or she will not feel the pang of self-blaming regret.

## When Prices Are Themselves Costly

Thaler has observed that vacationers sometimes prefer a venue that includes lodging along with food, and perhaps drink and entertainment, in a single cost.[102] Club Med launched this model in the United States in the 1950s, and it now has five dozen such all-inclusive resorts around the world. Cruise ships similarly often include food in the trip price, and twenty-three million people partake in this packaged form of vacation annually.[103]

On the standard economic theory sketched in Chapter 1, these sorts of inclusive packages are clearly wasteful. If, like the RAND HIE, you randomly assigned people to either inclusive vacations or pay-as-you-go vacations, we would surely find more empanadas eaten (or left half-eaten on the table) when they are included in the cost of the trip. By the measure of classic economics, we could call these marginal food and drinks "waste." Since those paying out-of-pocket do not eat so many empanadas, then the extra ones are apparently not worth their real costs. Such an economic arrangement— that facilitates the spending of money on things not worth their costs— erodes social welfare.

The arrangement seems particularly silly in a domain where individuals can afford the empanadas either way (unlike heart transplant surgeries). The package deal is not expanding access to empanadas; it is simply causing them to be wasted. It is interesting that policymakers have not targeted the massive cause of social welfare loss, by instead requiring that vacationers pay out-of-pocket.

Nonetheless, we can also shift focus to see the meta-choice being made by consumers, when they select which sort of vacation they prefer as a whole. The fact that some people seem to prefer to purchase their vacation food as part of inclusive packages reveals their preferences. They do not like to be nickel-and-dimed. Similarly, we see people preferring airlines that include soft drinks and peanuts over other barebones providers, where every little thing is an upcharge. (One European airline even proposed a charge for using the bathroom![104]) Some successful airlines, like Southwest, have even resisted the temptation to charge for checked baggage, apparently recognizing that at least some consumers view the upcharges as frustrating.

On this putative measure, the prevalence of these inclusive packages suggests that at least for their consumers, they provide greater value than comparable vacations that expose marginal costs at the point of consumption. There is apparently some disutility (negative experience) in having to think about the marginal cost of each empanada, or some disutility in even seeing the aggregate cost of all those empanadas tacked onto the bill at the end of the vacation. Of course, vacationers must be willing to pay the overall price, which assuredly includes the cost of the "wasted" food. But this is not waste in the sense that it hurts overall welfare. Instead, the overall vacation transaction may *enhance* welfare by hiding the price at the point of consumption and thereby making the trip more enjoyable. This example reveals how cost exposure changes the experience of consumption.

The practice of gift giving reflects a similar insight. Americans spend $800 billion annually during the Christmas season.[105] This is a terribly inefficient practice—people spend time and money to go find a particular gift, like a blue sweater in size medium, which is unlikely to be how the recipient would spend the money herself. Even though the recipient can exchange or resell the gift to achieve a higher valuation, those processes can be costly in terms of time and, sometimes, money. In contrast, a simple cash transfer would be the simplest way to ensure that the recipient spends the money in a way she values most.

So why do we use such a convoluted and inefficient procedure to transfer value to the people we love? How is it that a tangible gift—like a blue sweater in size medium—may in fact provide greater value, even though it is less fungible, than cash?

Gift cards are similarly perplexing, though slightly less so. The cards represent purchasing power, but they have limited fungibility to a particular merchant, which seemingly makes the gift less valuable than cash itself.[106] Why would givers undermine the value of their gift by locking it down as such? Should Congress outlaw gift cards and all tangible gifts other than cold hard cash?

Of course not. One reason why givers limit fungibility of their gifts is to prevent the recipient from having to wrestle with broader opportunity costs. The medium blue sweater is supposed to be meaningful and different than mere cash, which may be forgettably spent on gasoline, toilet paper, or to-matoes. Similarly, a gift card, focused on a particular luxury retailer, has such an effect. In contrast, a gift of cash would transfer value, but it imposes on the recipient a burden of deciding how to spend it, making trade-offs against all her alternative spending priorities. Thus, nonfungible gifts may actually deliver greater value by avoiding all the various problems sketched earlier in this chapter—they reduce the number of choices, avoid the price criterion, and avoid commodification.

With the commodification issue in particular, we were left with a dif-ficult line-drawing problem above, but we need not resolve whether the commodification concern is dispositive in the normative, philosophical sense. We need only observe that some patients may subjectively experience cost exposure negatively in this way. They may *experience* cost exposure for healthcare as a setback to their welfare. They may rationally prefer that their insurance not be designed in such a way to make costs such an overt factor in their healthcare decision making, just like they may prefer to go on all-inclusive vacations where they do not have to reach for their wallets every time they want a drink or a bite.

In recent decades, there has been a remarkable trend toward greater and greater cost exposure at the point of consumption, as we have seen. How-ever, it's not clear that these changes reflect changing consumer preferences, or actually the results of political and economic ideology, as shown in Chapter 1. They might also reflect other market failures, such as principal-agent problems, between those who purchase health insurance plans and the employees who receive them. Finally, they may beg larger questions about wealth distribution, if patients choose plans with higher cost sharing, because they simply cannot individually afford the higher premiums that go with lower cost sharing.

The RAND HIE sheds some light on this question, though one has to look beyond its headline findings. Recall that the scientists randomly assigned people to plans with higher and lower cost-sharing plans and then tried to recruit people into the study and to prevent their attrition (i.e., keeping them in the study throughout the intended timeline of three to five years). Across both initial refusal rates and in-study attrition, 88% of the partici-pants exposed to no cost sharing completed the study compared to 63% in the highest cost-sharing arm.[107] These differences were statistically very sig-nificant, and analysis confirmed that it was caused by participants leaving the experiment voluntarily (not for other reasons such as death, joining the military, or becoming eligible for Medicare).[108] As we saw in Chapter 1, scholars have worried that the experiment was biased by these problems, but for our present purpose, we can simply observe people voting with their feet, trying to avoid marginal healthcare cost exposure when they can.

We also see similar trends in more recent studies. A survey of U.S. cancer patients found that three-quarters (76%) were comfortable discussing costs with their physician, but perplexingly more than half (57%) reported that they did not consider out-of-pocket costs when making treatment decisions.[109] That factor was just too difficult or dissonant to incorporate into the treatment decision.

Qualitative data confirm this point. In twenty-four focus groups with patients, researchers found that patients tended to prefer "what they perceive as the best care, regardless of expense," and expressed "inexperience with making trade-offs between health and money."[110] Memorably, one patient expressed the idea that it's fine to think about costs as a policy matter, but "in the heat of the moment, I'd be like, 'I don't care! Just fix my problem.'"[111] Another said, "That's all well and good until you actually find yourself in a life-or-death situation, and you'll really see you're not even going to be concerned about the cost."[112]

Of course, many patients are not deciding for themselves—they are choosing for loved ones, including children and aged parents. In my experience serving on an ethics committee in a major hospital, these surrogate decision makers are even less comfortable talking about the costs of care. As National Institutes of Health bioethicists Greer Donley and Marion Danis explain, these familial decision makers "may experience an emotional conflict regarding their obligation to pursue the most aggressive care to avoid feeling (or being perceived by others as) insufficiently caring."[113] A maximal approach, regardless of costs, is the best way to avoid any suggestion of blame.

Of course, if patients *are* exposed to out-of-pocket costs, then other research shows that patients want to know about those costs before treatment, and I will later argue that healthcare providers have a duty to engage those difficult conversations, as long as we continue to use cost exposure as a health policy.[114] But these sentiments show why people may prefer policies that do not include such cost exposure at all.

In this section, we have so far focused on subjective disutility caused by cost exposure, but it can also worsen objective things like patient behavior and health outcomes. Economist Katherine Baicker and colleagues have coined the term "behavioral hazard" to refer to the phenomenon of people declining to consume worthwhile healthcare.[115] Patients may be biased away from optimal decision making, due to a variety of factors. For example, patients may overweigh salient symptoms (e.g., pain) while failing to attend to other symptoms (e.g., hypertension) that require instrumentation. Patients may also act on false beliefs, whether these are faulty mental models, incomplete information, or inattention to the available evidence. They are, after all, laypersons. Even costs themselves may be irrationally weighed, as the immediate costs of care (e.g., copayments for insulin) can seem more salient than the longer-term costs (e.g., treating neuropathy for uncontrolled diabetes). The authors propose that just as cost exposure has been the principal tool to address moral hazard, we need to deploy nudges—such as reminders or framing—to mitigate behavioral hazard. Indeed, in some cases, patients may do better with zero cost exposure or negative cost sharing.

Strikingly, scholars, clinicians, and policymakers have been working for years to *increase* consumption of some healthcare. A survey by the Kaiser Family Foundation found that, even among those with health insurance, many had "put off or postponed preventative services in the past year due to cost."[116] An older survey of nearly 11,000 employees found that greater exposure to costs was associated with lower utilization of clinical preventive services, including mammograms and pap smears.[117] That is why the Affordable Care Act now requires coverage of certain preventative services without cost exposure at all. Evidence suggests that this sort of tailored approach to cost exposure can reduce spending overall.[118]

Japan's health system features a substantial reduction of cost exposure at age seventy. Hitoshi Shigeoka has found that when people cross that threshold, there are "large increases in outpatient visits for diagnoses . . . for which proper and early treatment reduces subsequent avoidable admissions."[119] Here again the evidence shows that less cost exposure may be associated with more appropriate healthcare consumption behavior.

Similarly, warfarin is an inexpensive anticoagulant (blood thinner) used to prevent blood clots and strokes. The challenge is that many patients who need to take (and pay for) the drug are asymptomatic. It's easy to remember and invest in taking a drug if it stops your headache and itching, but what if it just reduces your longer-term risk of stroke? Many patients just stop taking the drug, which scholars call an "adherence" problem. Stephen

Kimmel and colleagues sought to actually pay patients to adhere (known as "negative cost sharing"), through a lottery mechanism with a daily expected value of $3.[120] Among those patients who were having the most difficulty managing their risk, the negative cost sharing substantially and significantly improved adherence. Off-setting costs can improve decision making.

The famous RAND HIE tracked antibiotic use in particular, and found, consistent with their findings about healthcare consumption generally, that exposing patients to costs reduced consumption. Antibiotics are particularly interesting to study because they have had a transformative positive effect on public health, but overuse not only wastes money but also facilitates bacterial resistance ("superbugs"). However, the investigators reviewed medical records to distinguish low-value use of antibiotics for viral infections, where antibiotics are inappropriate, versus high-value use of antibiotics for bacterial infections, where they have had a transformative effect on public health. If exposure to costs was solving a simple moral hazard problem, we would hope and expect to see that cost exposure reduced inappropriate usage, but not appropriate usage, thereby making the healthcare economy more efficient. However, the study found that "cost sharing reduced inappropriate and appropriate . . . use to a similar degree."[121]

These studies suggest that some patients on the margins are just using cost itself as the deciding factor in a crude sort of heuristic to solve a very complicated decision task—just do whatever is cheapest right now. Of course, that is not our goal for health policy. Instead, the evidence suggests that consumers may have a better healthcare experience and make better healthcare decisions when insulated from the marginal costs of healthcare.


This chapter has shown a range of problems that arise when we use cost exposure to change the experience and behavior of patients. By asking them to serve as healthcare rationers, we complexify their choices and create risks of regret, along with stress and fear, which may undermine the quality of their decisions. Moreover, by driving them to commodify their own bodies and those of their loved ones, we may create a dissonance that rational consumers prefer to avoid. Putting a price on our healthcare might actually change the treatment relationship in ways that are not salutary. In Chapter 3, we see the financial realities that come with cost exposure.

# OUR EMPTY POCKETS

When illness or injury strikes an American family, how will they be able to afford the costs not paid by health insurance? Will they be able to divert some of their income from other spending? Will they draw down assets? Or when these efforts fail, will they turn to credit cards and other forms of medical debt? We examine whether and how substantial cost exposure is feasible as a way to pay for healthcare in the contemporary United States. And we explore the psychological evidence about how these forms of financing change consumer behavior compared to the paradigmatic notion that a person is "paying out-of-pocket." Medical debt ironically re-creates a dissociation between consuming and paying, not unlike the moral hazard of health insurance. Ultimately, we also see that the use of debt to finance healthcare has a range of downstream effects on families and the economy more generally. The evidence shows that medical debt can stand in the way of sound treatment, and even make us sicker.

---

Just today, as I am writing this chapter in Boston, a reporter covered an incident that occurred in the local subway system: "Awful scene on the orange line. A woman's leg got stuck in the gap between the train and the platform. It was twisted and bloody. Skin came off. She's in agony and weeping. Just as upsetting she begged no one call an ambulance. 'It's $3,000,' she wailed. 'I can't afford that.'"[1]

The injured woman may well have been uninsured, which puts her outside the scope of this book. But she might have been insured with a large cost exposure; which at that moment is just like being uninsured for those costs. As we have seen, it is growing increasingly common for families to have deductibles of $3,000 or more.

Although the occasional doctor's visit for allergies or a prescription for a statin might be the most salient healthcare expenses we experience on a day-to-day basis, from a policy perspective, these are dwarfed by the small proportion of patients who have extremely large healthcare expenses in a given year, getting heart surgeries, branded cancer drugs, or proton-beam therapies.

Recall the federal government report explaining that "the top 5 percent of the population accounted for 50.8 percent of total expenditures with an annual mean expenditure of $50,572."[2] Strikingly, that figure is close to the median income of American households, which allows us to observe that most health spending in the United States is by people who are spending so much in a given year that it would wipe out nearly all of a typical American's income. (Looking somewhat further into this spending data, we see that over three-quarters [76.8%] of total health spending is consumed by the one-tenth of Americans with the biggest medical expenses, averaging over $33,000 per year.) Frankly, this is why health insurance is so important for ensuring access to healthcare. If we were dealing with a $500 expense, or even a $5,000 expense, we might adopt a very different policy approach.

So, if we want to use cost exposure as a substantial tool for the large majority of all health expenses, we should be thinking about exposures in the thousands or tens of thousands of dollars. Indeed, recall that under the Affordable Care Act (ACA) employers' provisions (where most people are covered), cost exposure can be up to $15,800 per year for families, and there is no limit at all under basic Medicare. Because one of the primary goals of insurance is to spread the risk of financial catastrophe, it is sensible to focus on that worst-case scenario. We can then evaluate whether insurance is fulfilling that function.

## THE HOUSEHOLD BUDGET

### The Full Picture of Health Spending

As a reference point for a patient's worst-case scenario, we will use this $15,800 threshold, but we should acknowledge that the cap on cost exposure applies only to healthcare expenses covered by insurance, of which the patient pays a portion. Yet when a person is consuming expensive healthcare, he is also bearing many other costs.

Out-of-network care is a huge category of additional costs, not subject to the primary cap on out-of-pocket expenses, and in many health insurance plans, it is not capped at all.[3] Insurers use networks of providers (hospitals and physicians primarily) to negotiate a fee schedule of lower prices. But sometimes patients use providers outside their insurer's network, and not always voluntarily. Former *New York Times* reporter Elisabeth Rosenthal tells the story of Peter Drier, who had planned a surgery with his in-network orthopedist, at an in-network hospital, to repair his herniated disks. Nevertheless, another surgeon, whom Drier had never met, showed up to assist with the surgery and then charged him $117,000 for the service. The assisting surgeon was out-of-network, so Drier had to pay the six-figure difference between the surgeon's full charges and what his insurance covered.[4] The statutory cap on cost exposure and the lower one in his insurance contract were rendered largely irrelevant to his actual exposure.

As health insurance networks get narrower and narrower, these additional costs grow for patients. Erin Fuse Brown has surveyed the literature on this problem of surprise medical bills, which she defines as those that are "unanticipated, involuntary, and out of network."[5] In one national survey of people with private insurance and provider networks, 8% had used an out-of-network physician, and about 40% of those were involuntary.[6] In just the emergency context, a *New England Journal of Medicine* (*NEJM*) study found that nearly a quarter (22%) of visits to in-network emergency departments involved care from out-of-network physicians.[7]

Much of the most technologically advanced (and expensive) care is delivered in academic and other specialty hospitals, which will require travel—another uncovered expense. A study of cancer survivors found that nearly two-thirds paid out of pocket to travel for treatment, and about one-fourth paid for lodging as well.[8]

A review of the literature showed that breast cancer survivors spent hundreds of dollars per month on a range of other costs, such as wigs (which can cost up to $800 each), and these costs persisted even a year later.[9] Other common nonmedical expenses among cancer survivors include money spent on gifts for caregivers, driving assistance to appointments, and professional guidance on legal, employment, and financial matters (e.g., wills).[10] Families of children with cerebral palsy spend on average $2,000 per hospitalization after orthopedic surgery on *nonmedical* expenses such as food, transportation, lodging, and costs associated with lost work hours.[11] One study of women suffering from urinary incontinence found that they spent on average $750 per year on absorbent pads, diapers, laundry, and other expenses.[12] More generally, Americans spent over $30 billion on uncovered or partially reimbursed complementary therapies such as acupuncture, chiropractic manipulation, massage, natural products, osteopathy, and homeopathy.[13]

Financial Insecurity

It is also important to keep in mind that healthcare expenses, even if broadly defined, are just one item in a household budget. The Bureau of Labor Statistics estimates that for the typical American family (a married couple with children), 7% is spent on healthcare, but 32% is on housing, 17% is on transportation, 13% is on food, and 13% is on personal (nonhealth) insurance and pensions.[14] And the budgets are getting tighter. One report by a policy advocacy group has documented that "key elements of middle-class security—child care, higher education, healthcare, housing, and retirement—rose by more than $10,000 in the 12 years from 2000 to 2012, at a time when this family's income was stagnant."[15] Broad academic surveys of the American public find that six in ten (59%) have trouble paying their bills.[16]

So medical bills come into a family budget against that background of financial insecurity. A recent survey of Americans with health insurance found that 43% have difficulty with their deductibles, and 31% have trouble with their copays for prescription drugs and doctor visits.[17] What is "difficulty"? It presumably means hard choices between other spending priorities, if not an absolute privation. As a Kaiser Family Foundation survey found, among those with insurance facing problems paying medical bills,

77% report cutting back or delaying vacations or major household purchases.[18] In this sense, cost exposure causes patients and their families to make exactly the sorts of trade-offs that economic theory intends. If healthcare has more value to the consumer than does a vacation, then that trade-off promotes her welfare and aggregate social welfare.

Yet about as many families (75%) are also forced to make healthcare trade-offs that do not seem so discretionary: "reducing spending on food, clothing and basic household items." As one respondent explained, "I've cut back on just about everything for my family and the way we live." Over a third of those with insurance and having problems with medical bills "say they were unable to pay for basic necessities like food, heat, or housing as a result of medical bills." And the problems loop back to healthcare itself. As another American explained, "Charges for my insulin exceeded $1200 a month (3 times the amount of my house payment). I had to reduce the amount of insulin I took based on what I could afford; my health was negatively impacted as a result."[19]

These dynamics are the direct result of U.S. social policy choices. In a survey of 20,000 people in eleven countries, Cathy Schoen and colleagues found that Americans stood out from their counterparts in other countries. Even among the insured, 15% of Americans reported that, within the last year, they "had [a] serious problem paying or [were] unable to pay medical bills."[20] One in five (21%) of the insured Americans said that they "did not see [the] doctor when sick or did not get recommended care because of cost," and 15% of the insured "did not fill a prescription or skipped doses because of cost." In other similarly wealthy countries, such as the United Kingdom, these problems happen much more rarely: only 1% of respondents said that they had serious problems paying medical bills, 4% did not see doctors or get recommended care, and 2% passed on prescriptions.[21] Canada cuts the problems in roughly half compared to the U.S. insured population. (It bears emphasis that I am referring only to insured Americans; of course, the rates are much worse for those lacking insurance altogether.)

## INCOME AND ASSETS

To understand why even insured families are having such difficulty bearing the cost of healthcare, let's look more closely at their incomes. We need to understand both the distribution of incomes and how they can change during illness or injury.

## Income Distribution

If we break the population into five groups (quintiles), from poorest to richest in terms of annual income, the American household in the middle earned $56,400 on average.[22] When we take into account both federal taxes paid, but also federal benefits received, the Congressional Budget Office estimates that these middle Americans receive $62,300 overall in a year. In the next lower quintile, the post-tax-and-transfer average is $44,500 per year. In Figure 3.1, I have illustrated these amounts and divided them by the $15,800 cap for cost exposure under the ACA and have done likewise for the other three quintiles. This figure then shows what percentage of a family's income would have to be diverted to cover health expenses, in this worst-case-scenario year.

The story is bad enough without even looking at the bottom quintile. Concededly, many of the poorest Americans are covered by Medicaid, which has little or no cost exposure. So let's focus on middle-income Americans, and those in the next lowest quintile, as we are evaluating the current $15,800 cap and thinking about how to design good health insurance coverage.

As the figure shows, for middle Americans, even when covered by health insurance, nearly a quarter of their income (24%) could be consumed by a severe health problem, and those in the next lower quintile would have a third of their income (33%) wiped away. These financial shocks could be devastating to a family budget that was already tight.

While these figures focus on Americans with private insurance, and focus on the *potential* worst-case scenario of hitting the statutory cap on cost exposure, we see similar stories in other populations and with actual health costs. For example, in 2017, radiation oncologist Amol Narang partnered with health economist Lauren Hersch Nicholas to examine the out-of-pocket expenses of Medicare cancer patients.[23] They found that, unless patients had supplemental insurance, their out-of-pocket costs were on average 23.7% of their household income. For one-tenth of such patients, the out-of-pocket costs consumed nearly two-thirds (63.1%) of their household income.

This phenomenon—where families are exposed to more risk than they can reasonably bear—has come to be known as "underinsurance."[24] Some researchers have suggested that health insurance plans that have such high cost exposures might actually leave patients worse off than if they had stayed uninsured and avoided paying premiums for such flimsy coverage.[25]

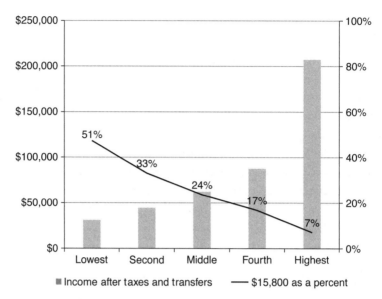

*Figure 3.1* Annual Cost-Exposure Maximum Allowed by the Affordable Care Act ($15,800 for Family Coverage) as a Percentage of Mean Annual Income (after Taxes and Transfers) for Quintiles of U.S. Population (Data source: Congressional Budget Office)

## Income Loss with Illness

This static picture of family income tells only part of the story. For working Americans, health crises present a perfect storm, not just creating surprise medical expenses, but also reducing a family's income. Generally, big medical bills come with incapacitating illnesses and big investments of time, which conflict earning income.

Healthcare is generally not a mail-order good. Need chemotherapy? Well, to have the drug pumped into your arm, you'll need to be firmly seated at the clinic—not at work. Of course, that's only a few hours a week. But how will you feel afterward? Chemotherapy causes a lack of sleep, difficulty eating, anemia, and tiredness. Some patients suffer more extreme nausea and vomiting. The American Cancer Society explains, "Some people with cancer are able to continue their normal routine, including going to work, while they're still in treatment. Others find that they need more rest or just feel too sick and cannot do as much."[26] Scholars reviewing the literature conclude that "between 40 percent and 85 percent of cancer patients stop working during initial treatment, with absences ranging from forty-five days to nearly six months."[27]

One research team followed 1,000 early-stage breast cancer patients for three years, all under the age of sixty-five.[28] Among the 746 who were employed prior to the diagnosis, about one-third of the patients were no longer working, and over half of that group wanted to be working. The sample included both breast cancer patients who received a chemo treatment and others who did not. Those receiving chemo were significantly less likely to be working.

But other expensive medical procedures are even more immobilizing than chemotherapy. Suppose you break a bone in your hand in an automotive accident or workplace injury. Scholars following a cohort of 227 workers with distal radius fracture found that 80% of those so injured lost work, and the average number of weeks was just over nine.[29] That's roughly one-fifth of a worker's annual working weeks.

Low back pain is an extremely common complaint, and lumbar disc surgery is a relatively common and expensive procedure. Research has shown that many patients never do successfully reenter the workforce, with 15%–40% remaining unemployed within one to three years after surgery, and 7%–23% remaining unemployed after seven to ten years.[30] One team of scholars following employed patients getting back surgery in Finland found that, after five years, 53% reported pain-related leave from work or early retirement.[31] For other purposes, we might want to tease apart the causal question—did the preexisting back problem cause the loss of work, or did the medical procedure do so? For the present purpose, we need only see the association between the medical procedure and the loss of work, since either causal pathway would impinge on the patient's ability to pay a substantial out-of-pocket cost exposure.

Chronic illnesses can also lead to income loss. One research team examined a range of chronic respiratory disorders, such as chronic obstructive pulmonary disease (COPD), which includes emphysema and chronic bronchitis.[32] It is hard to work when it's hard to breathe. Men suffering from chronic respiratory disorders in the prime working years (ages fifty-five to sixty-four) earned $6,879 on average less than those without the disorders. Women also suffered an income loss associated with the disease, although a bit less throughout the life span.

So far we have focused on the patient herself losing income because she is unable to work, but other members of the family might also have to stop working, or reduce their hours, in order to care for a sick loved one. In one major *Journal of the American Medical Association* (*JAMA*) paper, scholars studied 2,661 seriously ill patients discharged from the hospital. One-third of them required considerable caregiver assistance from a family member. "In 20% of cases, a family member had to quit work or make another major life change to provide care for the patient."[33] Patients with Alzheimer's disease present a particularly severe need for informal caregivers. A 1993 study of home Alzheimer's caregivers found that they spent 286 hours per month on average, which amounted to 73% of the total cost of caring for the disease, $83,205 (which I adjusted for inflation to 2018 dollars).[34]

In one of the largest and most comprehensive studies, Carlos Dobkin and colleagues used a major national economics survey to compare respondents that had been admitted to the hospital (for any non-pregnancy-related reason) in the recent year compared to those who had not been admitted.[35] One of their data sets focuses on Americans with health insurance between the ages of fifty and fifty-nine, and they found that, compared to those not hospitalized, across three years after someone is admitted to the hospital, their household experienced a 15% decline in the probability of being employed, and lost about $9,000 in income, which was 20% of their pre-hospitalization earnings.[36]

### Income-Replacement Policies

In an ideal world, the health-related income losses would be insured, either privately, by employers, or by government insurance or employer mandates. And in that world, perhaps a substantial cost exposure for health expenses could be functional. Yet the United States has quite meager policies for covering income lost to medical problems.

Congress passed the Family Medical Leave Act (FMLA) in 1993, and it provides that workers with qualified medical problems can take up to twelve weeks of leave from their jobs, without fear of being fired. However, the leave is unpaid, and employers can also require workers to substitute days of vacation or other personal leave. And this benefit does not even apply to part-time workers or to workers in businesses that have fewer than fifty employees. Accordingly, scholars have estimated that only 46% of workers are eligible for the unpaid leave guaranteed by FMLA.[37] A few states have lowered this number-of-workers threshold, and four have even enacted paid medical leave. But generally, the law does not replace income lost due to illness and often does not even guarantee that a worker can return to his job once he is well.

Among the twenty-two most economically developed countries in the world, the United States is the only one not to have a *paid* sick-leave policy.[38] The omission is striking. And, setting the scope more widely, we find 145 countries worldwide have some such guarantee.[39] (As an aside, I can't help but mention the research showing that the lack of paid sick leave in the United States causes sick workers to come back to work sooner than they otherwise would, bringing along their infectious diseases into our commercial kitchens, schools, and healthcare facilities.[40])

Notwithstanding the lack of a government mandate, many large U.S. employers do provide at least some number of paid vacation or sick-leave days, which can be about three or four weeks per year altogether.[41] About fifty million Americans are nonetheless not covered by such plans at all, and as you might expect, those with less income and less personal capital (e.g., education) are less likely to have this benefit as well.[42] Many of the largest employers also offer short-term disability insurance, which replaces 40%–60% of wages lost for, say, nine weeks or up to a year, depending on the plan.[43]

The United States does have some other programs that can help people who are out of work. Workers' compensation covers individuals who are injured on the job, and related state laws replace a portion of lost wages (e.g., two-thirds for someone 100% disabled in New York).[44]

If a person overcomes his illness such that he is then willing and able to work, but fails to find a job, then he may be eligible for unemployment insurance payments, under a joint federal-state program, which pays, for up to twenty-six weeks, a capped portion of prior income.[45] In 2013 the average recipient of unemployment received about half of her income.[46]

Workers that are permanently disabled are also eligible for federal Social Security disability payments, which is about $1,200 per month on average.[47] As the federal government explains, "That is barely enough to keep a beneficiary above the 2017 poverty level."[48]

Looking across this gamut of income-replacement policies, we see gaping holes. Accordingly, in their comprehensive study of the economic effects of hospitalization, Dobkin and colleagues found that only about 10% of the income loss that they documented was insured.[49] Of course, it need not be this way. "In Denmark, by contrast, nonfatal health shocks to households under 60 produce comparable (15–20 percent) declines in earnings, but almost 50 percent of the earnings decline is insured through various insurance programs, particularly sick pay and disability insurance."[50]

Assets

We have seen that even under the ACA, patient cost exposures may not be very affordable, given the incomes of middle Americans and the potential loss of income that comes with major medical problems. But the United States is a wealthy country. Perhaps people can draw on their assets to cover their health expenses?

The Federal Reserve Board conducts periodic surveys of consumer finances and has found that the average net worth of American families is about $692,000.[51] That amount would suggest that Americans have substantial wealth, which could be used to pay for their own healthcare. However, the distribution is key. About 35% of the wealth in the United States is held by the wealthiest 1%, and another 35% is held by the next wealthiest 9%.[52] Of course, if only the richest people were the ones consuming the most expensive healthcare, we would have no problems. However, the risk of severe illness is broadly distributed. In fact, wealthier households have lower risks, due to the health-protective factors that come with their socioeconomic situations, from safer cars to healthier diets, well-funded schools, and better air and water quality in their neighborhoods.

So, if we are thinking about cost exposure as a broad policy for the masses, the median net worth of Americans—$97,300, according to the Federal Reserve—is more meaningful than the average. Even then, however, half of Americans have less than this, and there are wild differences by ethnic group. Among the 12% of Americans who are black, and the 16% who are Hispanic or Latino, the median net worth is only $17,600 and $21,000, respectively.

Nationwide, the vast majority of net worth is tied up in housing, such that homeowners have a median net worth of $231,400, while renters have only $5,200. Even for the homeowners, we wouldn't typically expect that individuals would or could sell their houses in order to pay for healthcare. Even if one has more equity than necessary for the secured mortgage, it's not feasible to sell one-tenth of your house to pay medical bills. Nonetheless, it is some-times possible to secure a home equity line of credit. When my coauthors and I studied homeowners going through foreclosure, indeed we found that 13% of them had used home equity to pay medical bills (and in another study of people going through foreclosure a few years after the housing market had hit bottom, we found that 10% had used home equity to pay medical bills).[53]

Generally, to understand how much in medical bills Americans can bear themselves, it may be more meaningful to look at the balances in their "trans-action accounts," which include checking and savings accounts and prepaid debit cards. The Federal Reserve surveys find that people have about $4,500 on the median. The $15,800 cost-exposure maximum under federal law would thus wipe out the median American household three times over. Indeed, in the Kaiser Family Foundation survey, six in ten (59%) of those having trouble with medical bills said that they have already wiped out all or most of their savings to pay their bills.[54] Healthcare has brought them to the brink.

This finding should not be all that surprising. Policymakers and scholars have long focused on the "financial fragility" of American families, which refers to "the ability to draw upon liquid assets in the event of an unexpected loss."[55] Scholars define the term "as a lack of liquid assets equal to three months of income, or the inability to come up with $2,000 in 30 days," and estimate that financial fragility impacts 39%–46% of all U.S. households.[56] Middle Americans simply don't have large amounts of cash or cash equiva-lents, ready to throw at large and unpredictable medical expenses.

## CREDIT

When insurance plans apply such high out-of-pocket exposures that people literally cannot pay out-of-pocket (or out-of-bank), patients and their fami-lies must turn to credit instead. This is a very common move. In one study of 4,719 cancer survivors, scholars found that more than one-third (37%) reported that either they or someone in their family had gone into debt to pay for their cancer treatment.[57] We are not just talking here about credit cards or home equity lines of credit, but also payday loans, where interest rates can be exorbitant.[58] More generally, if you show up to the hospital, and they bill you for services beyond your insurance reimbursement, then you are now a debtor and the hospital a creditor. The hospital can then pursue collections, just like any other creditor.

So we can expect to find ubiquitous use of credit in this sector. But the use of credit to finance healthcare oddly undermines one of the primary purposes of imposing patient cost exposure in the first place. Recall that "moral hazard" arises from the fact that the patient stands to enjoy whatever healthcare she consumes, but the insurer, and thus the other premium payors, bear the cost of insured health spending. This problematic insurance dynamic—which dissociates the consumer from the payor—is remarkably similar to financing purchases on credit.

### The Dissociation between Buying and Paying

When one decides to purchase something on credit, he or she literally does not pay for it, at least not then, and perhaps not ever. Instead, the purchaser simply agrees (in the ideal case) that her future self *will* pay for it. In a sense then, credit allows the patient to bifurcate her consuming self from her paying self. I want to highlight two problematic aspects of this transaction.

First, the consume-now-pay-later transaction gives rise to a contract between the patient and the provider or other creditor, who facilitates the relationship. The law has for centuries depended on the notion that contracting parties express a meeting of the minds, a promise or agreement, that one person will pay in exchange for the goods or services that another supplies. But as we click through innumerable "terms of service" on webpages, sign stacks of admission documents in hospitals, and swipe our credit cards with a scribble on the electronic pad, how often are we really, consciously, agreeing and intending to meet our end of the bargain?

I do not offer this observation to support a radical notion that consumer debtors actually have no obligations to pay their debts. Under American contract law, courts will *not* attempt to look into the mind of contractors to see if they *sincerely* agree, but rather only look to their "objective" external behavior, to see if they successfully communicate something that would reasonably *appear* to be an agreement. Scribbling on the dotted line *appears* to be an agreement, right?

Contract law is actually a bit more capacious than even this. As law professor Wayne Barnes has observed, American courts even enforce putative contracts, when a seller knows quite well that the consumer is not agreeing and would not agree to the terms buried in standard-form consumer contracts.[59] Law professors and courts call these "contracts of adhesion" because the seller sticks them onto the buyer, who must take it or leave it, without the opportunity to negotiate terms. But—to be sure—the courts enforce such contracts nonetheless.

But, in the contemporary era, I do wonder how much patients in these sorts of situations *feel* like they have an obligation to pay these sorts of debts, and that is important for cost exposure to have its behavioral function for healthcare cost control. One could imagine some people having a different sort of psychological approach, one where they clicked through, flipped through, and scribbled through these "agreements" as mere thoughtless rituals associated with certain inevitable transactions. These routine scribbles might not create contingent liabilities in the patient's mind, but rather may feel like just speed-bumps that must be traversed. On this fatalistic or dissociative view, collection agencies will come, or they will not come, but our scribbling on the electronic pad has little to do with it. If the rituals associated with using credit start to lose their meaning, then they may fail to tie the current consuming self to the future paying self, in the mind of the consumer. If so, then, the use of credit to pay for healthcare may create a sense of moral hazard.

In this vein, the Aspen Institute's primer on consumer debt uses out-of-pocket medical costs as the prime example of "expenses that can push [consumers] into debt without taking out a loan. They may even be unaware of this debt or its size until negative information appears on a credit report or collection agencies call."[60] In these sorts of situations, the patient may not have even signed on the dotted line to feign agreement. She may have been wheeled into the emergency room completely unconscious, or perhaps consciously agreed to a surgery, without being fully informed of all the attendant costs or even aware of all the various entities that may try to bill her, including the hospital, the various surgeons and surgical assistants, and even the sellers of medical devices used therein. These sorts of surprise debts are clearly less salient to the purchasing decision than is suggested by the label "out-of-pocket" medical bills.

## Intertemporal Choice

There is a second major problem with credit financing. Even where the cost is salient at the moment of the consumption decision, its burden on the payor may still be dissociated from the buying decision. In the insurance setting, the buyer and the payor are actually different people, because insurance redistributes from the various premium payors to those unlucky enough to get sick. But with credit financing of healthcare, there is seemingly less of a problem. Am I not the same person as my future self? Isn't imposing a financial burden on that person the same as imposing it on myself? Perhaps not.

Of course, trivially, we have the same name and the same social security number as our future selves. But just as trivially it is also true that in a few years, almost all of the cells of our bodies will have been replaced.[61] We will then be different stuff. Neither of these trivial approaches answers the real question.

For centuries, philosophers have cogently asked, to what extent do we really share an identity with that future person? In a now-famous 1971 paper, philosopher Derek Parfit raised this profound question as the problem of "successive selves." One can conceive each moment of experience as merely overlapping with certain features of our past and future selves.[62] Parfit provocatively suggested that in fact people typically do care about their future selves, but there is no rational imperative to do so. Choosing to care about our future selves is not much different than altruism, choosing to care about other people in the world, whether presently existing or in the future. And that requires effort—a leap of imagination—to empathize with that future self or another person.

This general question of intertemporal choice has fascinated economists, since the earliest days of the field.[63] In 1889, for example, Austrian economist Eugen von Böhm-Bawerk wrote about the difficulty people have imagining the "future wants" of their future selves.[64] In 1920, English economist Arthur Pigou supposed that "our telescopic faculty is defective, and we, therefore, see future pleasures, as it were, on a diminished scale."[65] This visual analogy has inspired the use of the term "myopia" but economists also refer to this phenomenon as "discounting" of the future.

We see this dynamic in everyday life. When considering whether to eat the chocolate cake on the plate before us, it is so much easier to imagine its moist richness on the tongue than to imagine the hour of exercise that will someday be required to burn off its calories.

Although long understood by economists, this discounting theory has not featured prominently in debates about the policy of healthcare financing through consumer credit. In more recent years, however, some economists have taken an interest in the behavioral and psychological aspects of how we pay. George Loewenstein and Drazen Prelec have written about the concept of "coupling, which refers to the degree to which consumption calls to mind thoughts of payment, and vice versa. Some financing methods, such as credit cards, tend to weaken coupling, whereas others, such as cash payment, produce tight coupling."[66] One of Loewenstein's students explained the phenomenon alliteratively, noting that credit relieves much of "the pain of paying."[67]

The evidence in support of this proposition has accumulated over the last three decades. Consumer scientist Richard Feinberg reported a landmark study in 1986, which used both observational and experimental approaches to compare the behavior of those spending in cash versus those spending on credit.[68] The observational data began by simply counting the amount that restaurant customers left in tips, for comparably sized checks. Consistently across small checks and large checks, when paying by credit card, customers tipped a larger amount to their servers.

Although the field data were compelling, Feinberg needed to rule out the possibility of reverse causation, namely that more generous (or wealthier) individuals happened to be more likely to use credit cards, rather than credit cards causing them to be more generous. To solve that problem, Feinberg conducted randomized lab experiments, asking people how much they would pay for various consumer goods. The manipulation was quite subtle: in some conditions he merely displayed a credit-card logo in their field of view, using the cover story that it was from a prior experiment. Strikingly, merely seeing a card symbol caused people to say they would be willing to spend more for a consumer product, and quite substantially. For example, when a credit card was present, individuals said they would pay $33.90 on average for a dress, one that others only valued at $21.09 when no card was present. In a follow-up experiment, Feinberg found similar results when using a real money transaction, involving donations to the United Way.

More than a decade later, Drazen Prelec and Duncan Simester conducted an auction in which participants bid for tickets to major sporting events.[69] Participants were randomly assigned to conditions where the auctioneers would accept only cash or conditions where they would accept only credit cards. The authors found that use of the credit card caused a 100% increase in the price that individuals were willing to pay for the product. The size of this effect is quite striking.

The foregoing studies have not focused on the healthcare context and I am not aware of any empirical research that carefully distinguishes between those who are actually paying out of pocket versus those who must use credit. So, we have to reason by analogy.

There are some reasons to think that the effect might be even stronger in this domain. Interestingly, Prelec and Simester did not see similar effects when conducting an auction for a restaurant gift card, presumably because its value was so obvious. (Who would pay $50 for a $25 gift card?) Health-care is much more like the sports tickets, where the value is quite ambiguous, especially to the layperson patient purchasing in advance.

I have suggested that the dissociation between present and future selves explains part of these effects, which applies equally in the healthcare context. Lowenstein and O'Donoghue have explained a "second feature that can further reduce the pain of paying: when the bill comes, everything is lumped into a single payment, and so the payments become further decoupled from the purchase."[70] This bundling is already present in healthcare—when you check into the hospital, it's quite hard to decide on whether to consume this aspirin or see that specialist. But if the final bill is paid in credit, then we have a second bundling, across all of our other spending that month.

### Default

So far, we have focused on the dissociation between the spending self and the paying self, which we might call *intrapersonal moral hazard*. But the risk of default creates a more substantial problem for credit financing of healthcare—*interpersonal moral hazard*. When individuals consume healthcare that is beyond their means, the possibility that they will not *ever* actually pay undermines the core purposes of cost exposure in the first place.

Bankruptcy is a federal law (provided in the U.S. Constitution), which allows people and businesses to wipe away overwhelming amounts of debt, to get a fresh start. In recent years, about 200,000 Americans have declared bankruptcy each quarter, and the rate was about three times higher during the height of the Great Recession.[71] Economist Neale Mahoney has called bankruptcy a form of "implicit health insurance." He explains, "Households are exposed to the financial risk from medical shocks up to the level of assets that can be seized in bankruptcy, and are insured against financial risk above this level."[72]

Indeed, bankruptcy lawyers advise patients to time their bankruptcy filing to maximize its effects: "You may be able to write off more debts if you hold off on filing bankruptcy when you're expecting to incur new medical debts."[73] To illustrate this dynamic, let me just share the story offered by a bankruptcy lawyer in Louisville, Kentucky, via a blog:

> Jeremy is 30 years old, and single. He was in a car accident a year ago, resulting in serious injuries and huge medical bills. He's not yet medically stable. He was underinsured, so that a big chunk of his medical expenses were covered but a lot were not. . . . Jeremy currently owes $50,000 in medical debts, plus another $60,000 in credit cards and various other unsecured debts. In the next year or so he expects to add on another $30,000 to $40,000 in medical bills. . . .
>
> If Jeremy would file bankruptcy now, it wouldn't write off ("discharge") his upcoming $30–40,000 in medical bills. . . . His bankruptcy lawyer instead advises that he wait to file . . . until he became medically stable and had incurred most or all of his medical debts. Jeremy has limited exposure to harm by his creditors in the meantime. All of his assets are "exempt"—worth little enough to be fully protected from his creditors, even outside bankruptcy. His income is sporadic and low enough that he'd lose little if his wages were garnished. . . .
>
> So Jeremy does wait, finishes his surgeries and other medical procedures, racking up another $35,000 in medical bills, and then files a [bankruptcy] case to discharge all of his debts.[74]

Interestingly, while this sort of blogpost is protected by the First Amendment, it may be illegal for attorneys to even give their clients this sort of advice.[75] Congress would prefer patients not know the effects of bankruptcy.

Regardless, bankruptcy allows people to wipe away medical debts, completing the dissociation between consumer and payor. Our national policy of shifting costs to patients exchanges one form of moral hazard (under insurance) for another (under debt).

Prior to becoming a U.S. senator, Elizabeth Warren was a law professor with expertise in bankruptcy, and she joined with other scholars in a wave of landmark studies of people going through bankruptcy, involving both surveys of debtors and a review of their court records.[76] In order to have debts discharged, individuals must list each and every debt in an official court filing (a public record), under penalty of perjury—those records make a wonderful data set. (I was a research assistant on the project in 2008, and I remember going through the filings, marking each debt as either a medical debt [if it was to a hospital or other provider] or a nonmedical debt.) The surveys revealed that although three-quarters of the debtors had health insurance, more than one-third (34.7%) of those going through bankruptcy had medical bills of over $5,000 ($6,225 in 2018 dollars) or owed more than 10% of their annual family income in medical bills, which is a common measure of financial distress.

In addition to the one-third of filers who had more than $5,000 or 10% of their income in medical bills, the research team looked at whether the filer had mortgaged his or her home to pay medical bills (6% of filers) or had lost two weeks or more of work due to illness or to care for a family member (40% of filers).

This study was conducted in 2007 and published in 2009, prior to the ACA being passed in 2010. Although one might hope that the ACA reduced the rate of medical bankruptcies, the biggest effect of the ACA was to expand the number of people who enjoyed health insurance, and Warren's research team found problems among both the insured and the uninsured. Indeed in 2014 (as the ACA was coming into effect), one advocacy group reviewed 800 bankruptcy filings in one county in Oregon and found that 72% of filers had medical debts, and 40% of the filers owed more than $5,000 in medical-related expenses.[77] "As a whole, bankruptcies accounted for more than $5.6 million in medical debt for the year," from that county alone.

These analyses may in fact underestimate the amount of medical debts written off in bankruptcy. Law professor Melissa Jacoby and political scientist Mirya Holman compared the Warren team's survey responses with the court-record data set, and found that many people reported fewer medical debts in their bankruptcy-court filing. Further scrutiny suggested that many people charged medical bills to their credit cards, at which point the debt is no longer distinguishable in the bankruptcy records. Indeed, "respondents who reported significant out-of-pocket expenses, but had little or no detectable medical debt in their court records, reported credit card and mortgage use for medical bills at significantly higher rates than other respondents."[78]

Warren and colleagues' studies have shown that as many as two-thirds of bankruptcies have medical causes, but it's hard to isolate any one cause in such survey research, where we only observe those in bankruptcy. We need a comparison group not in bankruptcy. Other scholars offer lower estimates of how often medical problems cause bankruptcies, but it is hard to deny that there is a causal relationship. A 2013 study in one state merged medical records showing new cancer diagnoses and court records showing new bankruptcies; the scholars found that cancer patients were 2.65 times more likely to go bankrupt than people without cancer.[79] I have already mentioned the major study by Dobkin and colleagues finding that people who are hospitalized have large income losses in addition to their out-of-pocket medical expenses. Even among those with insurance, hospitalization (or the underlying medical problem that caused hospitalization) increased the risk of bankruptcy by about a third, after controlling for a range of other observable factors.[80]

Bankruptcy has been traditionally viewed as something of a failure, a shameful stigmatized act, that someone is walking away from debts instead of being responsible. Testifying before Congress in 1999, Federal Reserve Chair Alan Greenspan bemoaned that "personal bankruptcies are soaring because Americans have lost their sense of shame."[81] In the debate about the true rate of medical bankruptcies, scholars have worried that in survey research, individuals might be eager to claim that their bankruptcies have a medical cause, and less likely to admit other causes, such as a gambling problem. For that same reason, however, individuals who are blindsided by huge medical problems might also feel less stigma in wiping away their debts, since they may feel less responsible for the inevitable frailties of the human body and the exorbitant costs charged in the American healthcare system. Regardless, the sense of stigma associated with bankruptcy makes it a poor mechanism for financing healthcare.

Bankruptcy is not the only way that a person cannot pay for purchases made on credit. In 2017, accounting firm Ernst and Young performed an analysis of debt collection in the United States.[82] It found that "health care related debt (from hospitals and non-hospitals) is the leading debt category, accounting for nearly 47% of all debt collected in the industry." In contrast, credit card and retail debt are together only 2.2% of the debt collected—one-twentieth as much. Almost three-quarters of the total debt collected was "bad debt," consisting of receivables aged ninety days or more. "This debt has typically been written off by the creditor as uncollectable and is then turned over to third-party agencies for collection." On average, these third parties pay only 4.5 cents on the dollar in recognition of the low likelihood of actually collecting.[83] *Ex ante,* rational patients might likewise discount the likelihood of actually paying these debts.

Healthcare is a particularly odd domain to try to finance through credit since it involves life and death. On average, each American will spend nearly $160,000 on healthcare during the last three years of their life.[84] It is not uncommon to spend tens of thousands of dollars on a cancer treatment or a heroic surgery, knowing that, at best, it may only buy a few extra months. For insolvent patients—those left with fewer assets than liabilities—death is like an automatic bankruptcy, wiping away the debts. (The same legal term, "estate" is used in both bankruptcy and death.) And one doesn't have to die altogether destitute to get the benefit. Life insurance is paid out directly to the beneficiary, not to the deceased person's estate, where it might be accessed by creditors. Similarly, retirement accounts (e.g., IRAs and 401Ks) can pass directly to a named beneficiary, without going into the estate.

Even for patients dying with more assets than debts, death changes the situation substantially. In many states, where the assets are held in joint tenancy with a spouse, they are exempt from debt collection.[85] Moreover, thoughtful estate planning can use trusts and other vehicles to make this protection even more broad and more secure. I am not aware of any research studying how patients think about their cost exposure at the end of life, but here again, the "out-of-pocket" metaphor is unlikely to be a complete explanation.

Overall, we have seen in this section that when large cost exposures drive patients to use credit to finance their healthcare purchases it may well stimulate spending, not unlike the moral hazard effects of insurance. It does so largely because it dissociates the acts of buying and paying, not unlike insurance.

## DEBT

Debt is obviously just the flipside of credit. But in this section, I want to explore how the particular mechanism of financing healthcare through debt can have secondary effects on patients and the broader economy.

First, it is important to note that families have limited debt capacities, which may not be sufficient to bear a substantial portion of their healthcare costs. In 2016, 44% of American families held credit-card debt.[86] Yet one-fifth (20.8%) of families were considered credit constrained—"those who reported being denied credit in the past year, as well as those who did not apply for credit for fear of being denied in the past year." Generally, 13.5% are currently late on their credit payments.

Medical expenses can be paid with credit cards or even home equity loans, but in recent years a specialized product has emerged for the healthcare market in particular. Physicians and other healthcare providers may find it attractive to sell their services to patients who otherwise could not afford them, but healthcare providers do not necessarily want to bear the risks and costs of collection. CareCredit, a company with four million cardholders from 175,000 doctors' offices, explains to their physician-partners that the credit plan they provide will "increase production by enabling more patients the ability to accept, and immediately begin, recommended care without having to decline, delay or compromise treatment because of insurance benefits."[87] Doctors need only peddle the credit plans in their offices.

Patients can be particularly vulnerable credit customers, however. In 2013, GE Capital settled a complaint with the Consumer Financial Protection Bureau and refunded $34 million in fees, to resolve allegations that medical office staff placed patients in "financing plans" that appeared to be interest-free, but in fact levied 27% interest annually after an introductory period.[88]

### The Effects of Debt on Access and Outcomes

Although credit can facilitate otherwise unaffordable care in the short run, it can ironically cause patients to forego needed care in the longer run. Sociologists Lucie Kalouvsa and Sarah Bogard surveyed nearly 1,000 people in one state.[89] They found that as people had more debt, and greater ratios of debt to income or assets, patients were more likely to forego medical or dental care, and this was true even after the researchers adjusted for socioeconomic and health characteristics. Credit-card and medical debt had such effects, while housing, automobile, and student debt were not related to debtors foregoing care.

Scholars studying patients at safety-net hospitals, which serve the poorest Americans, have found that two-thirds of the patients were not only carrying debts, but that it was affecting their seeking of subsequent care: "Ironically, the reported consequences of this practice were delayed and deferred treatment for 18.6% of respondents, preferential use of emergency department services by 10.4%, and going to a different provider for care where a diagnostic work-up and evaluation would need to be repeated by 24.5% of respondents." The authors explain that "all of these scenarios increase the cost of subsequent healthcare episodes, which ultimately will be assumed by individual hospitals and providers, cost-shifted to full-pay patients, and result in unnecessary personal suffering and harm."[90] The researchers surprisingly found that medical debt had even greater effects on the health-seeking behavior of those with insurance, perhaps because these patients had more to lose. As the authors explain, medical debt creates a range of negative secondary factors.

Chronic disease is one of the largest drivers of aggregate healthcare spending, and good management can reduce those costs overall by helping patients avoid nasty outcomes, such as heart surgery or amputation. One team of researchers surveyed chronically ill patients, and their report in the *American Journal of Public Health* found that 18% of the respondents had cut back on medications that their physicians had prescribed due to cost problems, and the likelihood of them doing so was directly correlated with the size of their out-of-pocket cost exposure.[91] Ultimately, for patients with congestive heart disease, these sorts of problems can lead to a heart attack (myocardial infarction). In a *JAMA* paper mentioned already, Ali Rahimi and colleagues found that financial barriers to care were associated with worse recovery after acute myocardial infarction, more angina, poorer quality of life, and higher risk of rehospitalization.[92]

We see similar effects on kids' health. In an *NEJM* article, epidemiologist Michael Kogan's research team studied children with private insurance and found that a quarter of them were underinsured. Interestingly the privately insured population "did not differ significantly from the group of children who were never insured with respect to delayed or forgone care, lack of a medical home, [and] difficulty obtaining referrals."[93] And these access problems can impinge on health. In a paper in the journal *Pediatrics*, Donald Oswald's research team found that "children with special health care needs who were underinsured had significantly poorer outcomes than did children who were adequately insured."[94]

Oncologists have taken a special interest in this problem and have coined the term "financial toxicity." In one study, researchers asked 254 insured cancer patients at Duke Medical Center to keep personal cost diaries for four months. Forty-two percent of the patients reported that, while they were fighting for their lives, the financial burdens of care felt significant or catastrophic. The researchers found that, to cope with the financial burdens, one in five patients took less than the prescribed amount of medication, and a quarter of respondents avoided filling some of their prescriptions at all. Some skipped recommended tests or spread out chemotherapy or clinic appointments. "To the extent that cost sharing is intended to boost patient-directed decision making in health care and increase the value of health care, these findings suggest a potential for unintended adverse consequences that may result in higher downstream health care costs."[95]

I already mentioned the research in Washington State, showing that cancer increases the risk of bankruptcy, which suggests that these patients may not actually pay the costs of their healthcare. But suffering those debts may be onerous nonetheless. In follow-up research in the *Journal of Clinical Oncology*, Scott Ramsey and colleagues followed more than 250,000 cancer patients and carefully matched each one who declared bankruptcy with other similar patients who did not.[96] The team discovered that the patients who declared bankruptcy were actually 1.79 times more likely to die of their cancers.

One might worry about reverse causality: perhaps the sickest patients were more likely to declare bankruptcy, rather than bankruptcy propensity being a marker of financial insecurity, which then causes mortality. To address this concern, the research team limited their sample to patients who declared bankruptcy when their cancers were still in earlier stages, so that the cause would assuredly precede the effect. The bankruptcy rate remained unchanged compared to the full sample. As a common sense mechanism for this causal effect, the authors note a range of other research in which high out-of-pocket costs are associated with patients being unable to stay on their chemotherapy drugs.[97] As Ramsey and colleagues conclude, "Severe financial distress requiring bankruptcy protection after cancer diagnosis appears to be a risk factor for mortality."[98]

## Mental Health

The experience of medical debt can itself be onerous, as it grows with additional expenditures, interest, and fees, especially once payments begin to be missed. Most (56%) of those insured but with medical bill problems "say they've been contacted by a collection agency in the past year."[99] Other work has shown that taking on medical debt hurts credit scores and access to credit more generally, reducing options to meet other basic needs.[100] In the Kaiser Family Foundation survey, 44% of those with health insurance who carried medical debt reported that it had a "major impact" on their family.[101] The problems can drag on over time: almost half of those carrying medical debt (46%) say the illness or injury that led to the bills occurred more than one year ago. It can begin to feel oppressive, or the situation may feel precarious. As one fifty-one-year-old mother of two explained, "We're all one broken leg, one bad fall, or one case of pneumonia away from the house of cards completely falling down."[102]

Given these dynamics, it should be unsurprising that carrying debt can actually create or exacerbate mental health problems. The mechanisms of this effect should be nearly obvious: it is stressful to receive dunning calls and letters; it is stressful to make trade-offs between one basic need versus another. Moreover, debt can feel oppressive and create a sense of hopelessness, when it is out of proportion to an individual's ability to pay. In the study of 4,700 cancer patients mentioned above, two-thirds (64%) reported being worried about having to pay large bills related to their cancer.[103]

We see these effects in population studies. In one major study of 8,850 households in England, Scotland, and Wales, those in poverty were more likely to have a mental disorder, but the effect disappeared when adjusted for debt and when other sociodemographic variables were controlled. Debt was the real driver of mental illness: "The more debts people had, the more likely they were to have some form of mental disorder, even after adjustment for income and other sociodemographic variables."[104] And the number of debts formed almost a linear relationship with the risk of mental illness, which is precisely the sort of dose-response finding that supports causality.

Another study of nearly 9,000 young adult Americans found "that reporting high financial debt relative to available assets is associated with higher perceived stress and depression, worse self-reported general health, and higher diastolic blood pressure," findings that persisted even after applying regression controls.[105] Systematic reviews of the literature, covering sixty-five individual studies, affirm what these individual studies have found: debt is associated with poor mental and physical health, including obesity, drug, and alcohol abuse; neurotic disorders; psychotic disorders; and even suicide.[106]

It is hard to infer causation from such observational research (especially where there is a plausible story of reverse causation: i.e., mental health problems cause people to take on debt). Nonetheless, some research has taken advantage of exogenous shocks, such as economic crises.[107] Even at a national level, we can see economic insecurity affecting mental health, including in deaths by suicide. Historically, we saw suicide rates spike during the Great Depression, to its highest recorded rate ever, 150 per 1 million annually.[108] Thus, we should not be surprised to see micro-level shocks to a family—for example, a $10,000 bill for cancer—having similar effects.

Moreover, this link between debt and mental health is consistent with one of the largest health insurance experiments, a remarkable project in Oregon where individuals were randomly assigned to either have Medicaid coverage or not. Although the researchers did not observe major health improvements due to public insurance coverage—in part because even uninsured individuals could get care in emergency rooms—they found a clear benefit of insurance for mental health. In particular, Medicaid coverage increased respondents' self-reported mental health scores and it decreased the probability of a positive screening for depression by about 30%, as it "nearly eliminated catastrophic out-of-pocket medical expenditures" and dramatically reduced the chance of a respondent taking on medical debt or borrowing money to pay bills.[109] Because cost exposure is merely the partial lack of insurance, we should expect similar effects here. Indeed, in one study of patients with anxiety disorders, the researchers noted that the out-of-pocket exposure was so large for patients with private insurance, that they were similar to those who had no insurance at all.[110]

It is ironic that a particular mechanism for financing healthcare—medical debt—can actually cause more health problems, by impinging on mental health in particular. Whether it is undermining adherence to care or causing stress and anxiety, these disadvantages must be weighed against whatever advantages cost exposure brings as a financing mechanism.

This chapter has suggested that, as we think about debt as a mechanism for families to pay healthcare costs, the mechanism may have very different behavioral effects and health consequences than have been assumed for "out-of-pocket" healthcare expenses more generally. This is especially clear when cost exposure grows beyond the income and assets that patients can actually pay out of pocket, in a world where cost exposure is not so tailored. Recall from Chapter 2 that insurers use cost exposure to solve moral hazard.

In one sense, however, we have seen that insurance and debt are just alternative ways to finance an expense, and both of these make the cost less salient at the point of healthcare consumption. Insurance works prospectively to spread the costs of healthcare over multiple premium payments. If those premiums are individually risk-adjusted for each payor, then the primary redistribution is intertemporal, to smooth the financial shock in one month or year over many months or years. To the extent that the premiums are not individually risk-adjusted, then insurance also works to spread the risk across people, redistributing from the healthy to the sick. Debt also spreads costs intertemporally, to the extent that the patient will herself pay, or interpersonally if the patient will default. Costs are spread either way, but we have seen that debt has particular disadvantages, as it exacerbates financial fragility, impinges on access to life-saving care, and creates anxiety and physical and mental health problems. In our design of a healthcare system, our use of a large cost exposure as a financing and behavioral mechanism may be counterproductive.

# CHAPTER 4

# WHAT WE OWE

So far, we have seen that cost exposure may be a poorly motivated, inept, and infeasible mechanism for health policy, but there is also a normative element that cannot be overlooked. We start with an unreflective notion that your healthcare costs are your own responsibility, but must now thematize it and grapple directly with the philosophical question it presents. This chapter moves beyond implicit assessments and brings to bear a broader perspective, including other normative commitments, legal principles that embody those commitments, and empirical facts about whether and how our health depends on ourselves or others. Accordingly, we test ways of thinking about healthcare costs. One notion is that they should be borne individually by those who consume healthcare, or, the very least, costs should be borne individually by those who choose risky behaviors. As these approaches wither under scrutiny, we turn to notions of democratic equality, which provide a thin but compelling basis for understanding a right to access the decent minimum level of healthcare. This frame also allows us to reject the facial equality that is routinely used in existing cost-exposure mechanisms, as these forms unjustly and disproportionately impinge access for poorer citizens. This normative approach to cost exposure provides a framework for the reforms that come next.

## PAY FOR YOUR OWN HEALTHCARE

In this chapter, I aim to bring a more philosophical approach to cost exposure in an attempt to evaluate its appropriateness as a form of health policy. This is an overtly normative endeavor: to not only describe, but also assess. Yet cognitive science shows that we often start from snap judgments; only later do we try to follow with post hoc rationalizations. This is the two-stage model of first thinking fast, and only later, sometimes thinking slow.[1] Let's call out those starting points explicitly, so that they can be scrutinized.

Fortunately, we also have powers of reason and a wide range of conceptual resources to draw upon. I do not here provide or invoke a singular moral foundation or comprehensive theory of justice from which we can derive an optimal cost exposure policy. Instead, I suggest a method of synthesis from many sources of facts and values. In this spirit, Bioethicist Daniel Callahan has developed the notion of a "communitarian bioethics," one that seeks "to blend cultural judgment and personal judgment."[2] The liberal political philosopher John Rawls advanced the method of "reflective equilibrium," which synthesized our "everyday judgments" to be "in accordance" with our broader principled commitments to a theory of justice.[3] Physician-lawyer David Orentlicher has similarly argued for a back-and-forth between moral theory and practical implementation.[4] In these synthetic ways, we can arrive at moral judgments, rather than mere reactive intuitions.

### Intuitive Starting Points

Relevant to cost exposure, there is such an intuitive, perhaps obvious, appeal in the idea that every person should pay for his or her own self. No less, every person should pay for her own plumber when the toilet clogs as well as pay for her own automobile mechanic when the spark plugs need replacing.

The point almost goes without saying as it adheres in the very pronouns we use. How will Janet treat *her* cancer? Did you see that Arnold broke *his* arm? I am sorry to hear that *you* need a liver transplant. As Barack Obama said, "We've got to have the American people doing something about *their own* care."[5] Even when plural, it is the third person, *their*, rather than the first person, *our*. But the point is clear—if it's your problem, it's your attendant costs to fix the problem. As we think about allocating health costs according to some principle of justice, that would seemingly be a *re*-allocation, from the seemingly natural baseline of individual responsibility.

Against these tendencies to isolate and individualize the costs, there are clear evolutionary reasons to explain why humans would be inclined to care about the well-being of others, in relationships of kinship, reciprocal exchange, or social solidarity more generally. Whether cooperating to hunt a bison or sharing food in a time of famine, humans have thrived on such reciprocal altruism. Even human toddlers register these inclinations to collaborate and cooperate to solve problems, which are not seen in other primates in the same ways.[6] We have the capacity to empathize and, even more so, to see a common problem and solve it together.

Yet illness might be an interesting exception. Evolutionary biologists have explained why animals, including human animals, ostracize the ill, who not only pose risks of contagion but also simply have less to offer in terms of productive exchange. Thus, humans may well have developed a powerful ability to look the other way.

Of course, such evolutionary-behavioral systems are crude, not calibrated in the way that reason-based decisions can be, distinguishing real threats of contagion and the possibility of immediate exchanges from scientific reality and longer-term social policies.[7] As evolutionary psychologists Robert Kurzban and Mark Leary explain, "Seemingly irrational decisions with respect to knowledge that someone is infected with AIDS, or even cancer, might be manifestations of the operation of these hypervigilant systems."[8] In this context, false positives (shunning someone who is not in fact contagious) are less dangerous than false negatives (failing to shun someone who is contagious).

In the United States, physical disabilities and some illnesses such as HIV/AIDS have been the subject of remarkable stigma, but the phenomenon may be more ubiquitous. Nursing scholar Janet Younger writes that "ill people report that family and friends are attentive when illness begins, but as it continues involvement dwindles to a few members of the immediate family. Visible suffering typically causes friends and acquaintances discomfort because obvious suffering rips away the public, sociable presentation of self, making sociability problematic."[9] It is hard, emotional work to bear another's suffering, and it may also uncomfortably remind us of our own vulnerability and ultimate mortality. Over time, we might well learn that we are most comfortable if we keep the ill and the injured at arm's length.

As the sixteenth-century poet John Donne wrote, "As Sicknes is the greatest misery, so the greatest misery of sicknes is solitude. . . . Solitude is a torment which is not threatened in hell it selfe."[10] Literature, history, and religion are filled with such examples of spurning the ill. The biblical book of Leviticus, for example, gives remarkably detailed instructions for how to detect and then isolate those with skin disorders that were broadly conceived as "leprosy."[11] Regardless of its basis, our stigmatization or even abandonment of the sick and suffering can reinforce the notion that the costs of healthcare are also *their* own responsibility.

## Positive Law

As we think about cost-exposure policy, we can also draw from a range of legal precepts to inform our considered judgments. The Universal Declaration of Human Rights, which the United Nations adopted after the Second World War in 1948, provides that "everyone has the right to a standard of living adequate for the health and well-being of himself and of his family, including . . . medical care and necessary social services."[12] If taken seriously, the practical implications of such a right could place very heavy burdens on wealthier societies and individuals to provide for healthcare in their own or poorer countries. In a famous essay (as famous as any contemporary philosophical essay can be), Peter Singer has argued for such a universal right, on broadly utilitarian principles.[13] Ultimately, Singer argues that people in affluent societies need to alter "the whole way we look at moral issues" and reform "the way of life that has come to be taken for granted in our society."[14]

There is a somewhat less radical notion that, at the very least, within the nation-state there is a collective responsibility to provide healthcare for our compatriots. Of the 191 countries in the United Nations, 38% of their constitutions recognize such a right to medical care.[15] The UN Special Rapporteur for Health has embraced this institutional view, explaining that "the right to health can be understood as the right to an effective and integrated health system . . . accessible to all. Underpinned by the right to health, an effective health system is a core social institution, no less than a court system or a political system."[16] This approach presumes an underlying commitment of fellow nationals to take care of health needs experienced by others.

The United States has a rich body of law, which provides some material for integration into our policy judgments. Concededly, in the United States access to healthcare treatment has not been recognized as a freestanding right under the Constitution. In the context of AIDS, for example, legal scholar and bioethicist Roy Spece has reviewed a range of potential arguments for litigating a claim that the poor have a right to treatment. Although the Constitution protects interests in life, liberty, and property, all of which are implicated by illness, these have typically been viewed only as negative rights, protecting against government interference. Spece accordingly identifies this as the most controversial of possible claims: "government must provide not only subsistence but minimally adequate vital goods and services to those who cannot afford them."[17] To be sure, the foundational American legal texts provide little support for that proposition.

Within the American legal canon, the notion of self-ownership is a core commitment, which rests on a more fundamental conception of persons as autonomous individuals. The word *autonomous* comes from the ancient Greek roots for *self* and *law*, meaning that persons give to themselves their own law, or principles, or direction. In this sense, our bodies are personal, not collective, because we choose how they move and who is allowed to touch them, and under what circumstances. That same insight supports the basic principle of consent—known in the contexts of medical treatment and human subjects research, but also more generally in the laws of torts, contracts, and crime—that others are not entitled to use our bodies unless we say so.

This commitment to autonomy has special currency in today's health policy debates, especially in the United States, with its long tradition of individualism and market-based policymaking. As the health policy expert Bill Sage explains, "Nearly all progressive impulses among American health lawyers and policy makers over the past half century have sought to liberate and empower the patient. Phrases used to express this desire include 'patient autonomy,' 'patients' rights,' 'patient self-determination,' [and] 'patient preferences.'"[18] We now have a national institute, created under federal law, for "patient-centered outcomes research."

Notwithstanding this deep American legal tradition of individualism, there are instances in which the law makes others responsible for our illnesses and injuries. American tort law imposes a responsibility on those who act unreasonably, and thereby cause harm to others, to pay up, compensating their victims to make them whole. As Supreme Court Justice Oliver Wendell Holmes long ago recognized, however, such liability is the exception rather than the rule. "The general principle of our law is that loss from accident must lie where it falls. . . . The state might conceivably make itself a mutual insurance company against accidents," but as of his writing in 1881, it assuredly had not.[19] This notion of compensation proves the rule of autonomy and individual responsibility; it arises only where one has invaded the independence of another, injuring her without her consent.

Accordingly, the risks that come along with living in the corporeal world—from the stubbed toe or the broken arm to the heart attack or cancer—are each person's own problems, at least to the extent that one can bear them. In this sense, health needs and health risks seem no different than other everyday needs and risks like food, housing, plumbing, or transportation—we begin with the presumption of individual responsibility. We respect persons by leaving their own welfare to their own protection.

### The Social Phenomenon of Illness

Both our intuitive reactions and the extant legal tradition of the United States seem to reinforce an individualism about healthcare costs. Can we conceive a more profound challenge to that original framing that each person's own body is her own responsibility? Could one understand sickness as a social burden in the first instance?

Biologically, it is not clear that health is best understood at the level of the individual organism (or human person). This approach is most obvious in the domain of infectious disease.

In the sixth century, the plague spread through Northern Africa and Europe, killing 50% to 60% of the population.[20] In 1346, the plague returned, killing one-third of the European population, and over the course of 130 years, it changed politics, art, religion, and economic development in fascinating ways.[21] For just one example, even today tourists can see a line in the architecture of great European churches and cathedrals. Before the plague, churches were begun in detailed decorative style, but they were finished during the plague (if at all) in the bulkier "perpendicular" style of the later Middle Ages. Although still Gothic, these "simpler lines and masses of the new perpendicular style" can be attributed to the "lack of skilled masons and sculptors" and the "reduced expenditures" that came with the stalling and reversal of economic development.[22]

These diseases were a widespread and arguably collective problem. But the story of solutions is even more revealing. Little was done in the Middle Ages; the pandemic was left to run its course. But humankind had other chances to learn how to fight disease. Each year in the early twentieth century, smallpox afflicted 48,000 people, diphtheria struck 176,000, and polio infected 16,000 in the United States alone.[23] These illnesses infected the U.S. population as a whole, putting everyone at tangible risk, and imposing on virtually everyone an obligation to become vaccinated, once that technology became workable. At the time, eleven states had compulsory vaccination laws, but they were challenged by resisters who claimed the liberty to not have their bodies so invaded. In the landmark 1905 Supreme Court case of *Jacobson v. Massachusetts*, Justice John Marshall Harlan upheld the mandate as a form of collective action against the common enemy of disease.[24]

In 1918, a pandemic flu infected 500 million people worldwide; in some U.S. cities 30% of children did not survive to see their first birthday.[25] Mathematicians and epidemiologists still study the 1918 global pandemic, and they have found that each city had substantially different rates of death, suggesting that any individual's risk was affected by where the person was and who was nearby. No vaccine was available, but public health interventions— "including closure of schools and churches, banning of mass gatherings, mandated mask wearing, case isolation, and disinfection / hygiene measures"— also substantially reduced mortality, when introduced early and maintained throughout the pandemic.[26]

A focus on individual illness or even healthcare would miss the point of the collective action needed to solve such health problems. My health is affected by your decision to vaccinate, but more fundamentally by your ability to afford the vaccination, and by our public and private investments in research to develop that vaccine, to test it, and to distribute it. Public health interventions depend on collective action, typically through government.

Twentieth century American philosopher John Dewey argued that this sort of causal interactivity is what creates "a public," the objective basis for common political action: "the essence of the consequences which call a public into being is the fact that they expand beyond those directly engaged in producing them."[27] Economists call these phenomena "externalities," and similarly recognize that they are a primary basis for governmental intervention.

The recognition of a common problem creates the possibility of collective action to solve it, even if that means reconceiving and redistributing wealth or risks that could otherwise be conceived individually.

I have suggested that our use of pronouns can reflect and reinforce our notions of disease as a personal phenomenon of his, hers, mine, and yours. In contrast, U.S. founding documents begin with "we" statements—"we hold these truths to be self-evident . . ." and "we, the people, of the United States." Philosopher Wilfred Sellars wrote, "It is a conceptual fact that people constitute a community, a we, by virtue of thinking of each other as one of us, and by willing the common good, not under the species of benevolence—but by willing it as one of us, or from a moral point of view."[28] In terms of grammar, the "we" is in the first person, suggesting collectivity. But it is also in the nominative case—the "we" has the potential to act, not merely to be acted upon ("us"). In Continental (European) philosophy, there is a parallel, rich theory of social solidarity, which reflects this same notion that your (health) problems and my (health) problems are *our* (health) problems.[29] Accordingly, on this view, the costs of that healthcare should be borne collectively, with the risks pooled in public or private insurance programs.

Infectious disease may seem to be a special case, since it can literally spread from person to person. Nonetheless, noncommunicable diseases somehow seem to spread through communities. In Japan and the United Kingdom, for example, only about 5 people per 100,000 died in 2008 due to diabetes mellitus; in the United States the rate was triple that, at more than 15 per 100,000.[30] In Japan, fewer than 10 per 100,000 died of neuro-psychiatric conditions; in the United States the rate was more than quadruple that, at nearly 40 per 100,000.[31] Although the United States is near the worst on every such indicator, stomach cancer is a bright spot as fewer than 5 in 100,000 Americans die of stomach cancer while the rate is just below 15 for Portugal and just over 15 for Japan.[32] These patterns suggest that our nationalities, or at least our geographic locations, can substantially affect our health. Whether these differences are due to genetics, behavior, culture, economics, diet, environment, or healthcare is a broader question.

Some of these variations could be due to differences in each country's healthcare system. However, much more may depend on the national cultures, and the degree of economic inequality that is allowed to persist in each country.

In recent decades, scholars have become increasingly aware of the "social determinants of health," which are "the structural determinants and conditions in which people are born, grow, live, work and age."[33] These include education, which then affects our incomes, our neighborhoods, our habits, and our ability to withstand potential health and financial problems. In one comprehensive study, scholars compiled forty-seven high-quality research papers and performed a meta-analysis, finding that in one year "approximately 245,000 deaths in the United States in 2000 were attributable to low education, 176,000 to racial segregation, 162,000 to low social support, 133,000 to individual-level poverty, 119,000 to income inequality, and 39,000 to area-level poverty."[34] Altogether, these causes explained more than one-third of total deaths in the United States. Here again, these data challenge the notion that a person's illness is hers to bear alone.

And, of course, health is intergenerational. Our genes are passed down from our parents. And to some degree our lifestyle and habits are passed down as well. But our childhood environment is also critical. In research published in 2018, for example, scholars found that nonsmokers who grew up in households with smokers were later more likely to die of pulmonary disease. Those who were exposed to secondhand smoke as adults were also more likely to die of ischemic heart disease and stroke.[35]

Any person's chance of falling ill is affected by larger questions of social policy—how wealth is redistributed; how education is emphasized and funded; how workplace safety is regulated; how levels of environmental toxins are tolerated; how safe our roads are; how well trained the physicians, nurses, and others are in the healthcare workforce; and how much we invest in biomedical science. This recognition undermines the prima facie notion that a person's illness is her own problem and that she is obligated to pay out-of-pocket.

## PAY FOR YOUR CHOICES

The literature on social determinants of health is robust, but there are questions of causation versus mere association. People with lower incomes are also more likely to smoke, drink, eat poorly, exercise less, and not adhere to their healthcare prescriptions—all of which could be framed as individual choices.[36] Indeed, at an aggregate level, it is true that much of our health is driven by our own behaviors. Epidemiologist Farhad Islami and colleagues looked at "potentially modifiable exposures," such as "cigarette smoking; secondhand smoke; excess body weight; alcohol intake; consumption of red and processed meat; low consumption of fruits / vegetables, dietary fiber, and dietary calcium; physical inactivity; ultraviolet radiation; and 6 cancer-associated infections."[37] They found that 45% of cancer-related deaths were "attributable" to these risk factors (while at the same time conceding that causation could not be established given the current scientific record). More generally, Steve Schroeder, a physician and former president of the Robert Wood Johnson Foundation, has argued that 40% of all premature deaths are attributable to behavioral patterns (alongside the 30% he attributes to genetic disposition, 15% to social circumstances, 5% to environmental exposures, and 10% to healthcare itself).[38]

Surely, people can be made to pay for the consequences of their own decisions. This approach would suggest potentially broad or unlimited cost exposure for those costs that arise from a person's own choices. At first look, it would seem that our entire lives are driven by our choices.

### Personal Responsibility

Yascha Mounk has chronicled the way that "personal responsibility" has been central to American political discourse, especially in the late twentieth and twenty-first centuries.[39] Ronald Reagan famously said that "it is time to restore the American precept that each individual is accountable for his actions."[40] But liberals too began speaking in these terms as they reformed the modern welfare state to make benefits conditional. Most notable was the 1996 Personal Responsibility and Work Opportunity Reconciliation Act, which fulfilled President Bill Clinton's campaign promise to "end welfare as we have come to know it." The law dramatically reduced the number of Americans receiving social welfare benefits, by requiring recipients to work and imposing a lifetime limit on benefits.

In the 2017 debates over repealing the Affordable Care Act (ACA), the idea was supercharged. One Republican leader suggested that poorer individuals lack healthcare coverage because they too often buy iPhones instead.[41] In 2017 the White House budget director said that we may want to cover some healthcare costs as a society, but "that doesn't mean we should take care of the person who sits at home, eats poorly and gets diabetes."[42]

This theory fits nicely with the concept of "moral hazard," deployed by economists (and discussed in Chapter 1). As a leading expert on insurance law, Kenneth Abraham, has explained, it makes sense to pool the risks of "unavoidable activities," since the level of risk is exogenous to the choices of individuals.[43] For example, the Genetic Information Nondiscrimination Act of 2008 prohibits group health plans and insurers from denying coverage based on genetic risk, over which we have no control. If, in contrast, the risks due to our *choices* were pooled, it would invite individuals to take more such risks than would be optimal, since they can reap the benefits (e.g., the enjoyment of smoking, or not wearing a motorcycle helmet) without bearing all the costs (e.g., the subsequent healthcare bills).

There is a deep philosophical basis for this sort of thinking. Several prominent philosophers have attempted to distinguish between bad outcomes (such as illness) that result from "brute luck" (like a tornado striking a home), whose costs should arguably be shared by a fair society, versus other bad outcomes that come from individual choices and should therefore be borne individually.

Philosopher Richard Arneson has synthesized the following thesis from a range of these scholars: "it is the responsibility of society—all of us regarded collectively—to alter the distribution of goods and evils that arises from the jumble of lotteries that constitutes human life as we know it. . . . [T]he lucky should transfer some or all of their gains . . . to the unlucky."[44] Unlike tort law, which takes money from the wrongdoing defendant to compensate injured plaintiffs, this approach would compensate persons for bad luck alone, seeking to make them whole. The money would come from those who earned it due to mere good luck, since that is not a basis for them claiming the fruits as their own. But, to be sure, there is no such duty to transfer from the prudent to the imprudent.

With regard to health in particular, philosopher Ronald Dworkin argues, "If someone develops cancer in the course of a normal life, and there is no particular decision to which we can point as a gamble risking the disease, then we will say that he has suffered brute luck."[45] Compared to those who still have their healthy bodies and all the enjoyments and capabilities that go along with them, the burden of paying out-of-pocket for treatment would seem only to compound the injustice of undeserved suffering and illness.

Contrasting the point about "cancer in the course of a normal life," Dworkin says, "But if he smoked cigarettes heavily then we may prefer to say that [the person who develops cancer] took an unsuccessful gamble," and thus should bear the losses himself.[46] In the United States, as of 2010, 8.7% of healthcare spending, which amounts to $170 billion per year, could be attributed to smoking tobacco.[47] One consequence of the choice to smoke is that once cancer materializes, the patient must bear the costs of her own healthcare. In this sense, luck egalitarianism creates only a contingent obligation for a society to cover healthcare costs. It depends on whether the costs were incurred due to brute luck, or what Dworkin calls "option luck." The latter sort of bad outcome is for individuals to bear themselves.

Some countries have formally rejected the idea that the right to access treatment should be made conditional on personal responsibility. Sweden, for example, passed a 1996 amendment to a healthcare law that explicitly rejects the idea that priorities should be set based on whether a condition is self-inflicted.[48] Nonetheless, in a 2015 blind experiment, a random sample of Swedish oncologists, pulmonologists, general physicians, and members of the broad public were recruited to consider whether they would offer a novel, expensive, and marginally life-saving treatment to a lung-cancer patient, and the scenario was randomly manipulated so that the patient was either a smoker or a nonsmoker. Across each of these subgroups of respondents, when the patient was a smoker, they were much less likely to be offered the expensive treatment.[49] Remarkably, respondents split on the question about whether the patient was responsible for her own cancer, but regardless they were just as likely to refuse her the expensive care. This sort of research shows how deeply engrained these notions of personal responsibility may be—affecting our judgments, even if not fully reconciled with our conscious notions of responsibility.

## The Challenge of Evaluation

Analytically, to decide whether any particular redistribution is appropriate, luck egalitarianism requires two steps. First, one must determine who among the society is in some meaningful way worse off than others. This function divides the society into the haves and the have-nots. It is the relative difference between these persons that creates the potential for redistribution, on this view. One might worry, as philosopher Elizabeth Anderson does, that this way of slicing up a society is divisive and demeaning, as it emphasizes their material differences rather than their dignity in common solidarity.[50] Ultimately, any theory of redistributive justice will somehow identify those to whom resources should flow, but perhaps they can do so in more elegant ways.

The second step for luck egalitarianism is perhaps more difficult: to judge whether those inequalities are justifiable. Who among the have-nots is deserving of help, because they suffered bad luck (and who among the haves is deserving of envy, because they enjoyed good luck). Those who were prudent in their choices, but nonetheless unlucky, can claim a rightful redistribution. (There is a more profound problem, by the way. The luck egalitarianism theory does not tell us whether the capacity to be prudent is itself largely a result of the brute luck of our genetics, parenting, and other environmental effects.)

These sorts of assessments are tricky. Here, the smoking example assumes that the choice to smoke is not one that would be made in the "normal course of life"—it is supposed to be aberrational and unreasonable. Perhaps smoking is abnormal in the United States in 2019, but could the same be said during the 1940s, when standard military rations included cigarettes and they were glorified throughout the mass-media culture? Among men born between 1905 and 1929, nearly 80% would go on to be smokers during their lifetimes.[51] Interestingly, this figure is similar to the current rates of alcohol use. Today, 86% of Americans have consumed alcohol, and more than half have done so in the last year.[52] And we are reaching a scientific consensus that there is no safe level of alcohol use, notwithstanding its normalcy. A 2018 study found that despite its sometime beneficial effects on health, alcohol is a leading risk factor for death and disability.[53]

The theorist can say that, regardless of the popularity of smoking (or drinking), it is still an individual choice and that implies that others bear no responsibility to subsidize the bad outcomes. But life is shot through with innumerable banal choices that nonetheless affect cancer risk and many other risks as well. Must I jog every day, or just three times a week? May I jog outdoors, or must it be indoors on a treadmill to avoid the risk of being injured in traffic? Or must I do a lower-impact sport, such as an elliptical machine? Am I responsible for my own cardiovascular disease if I do not drink wine, or my own cancers, if I do? And how do I trade off all these mandates against other goals, such as time spent with family, the need to earn a living,

and the subjective experience of pleasure, which I may presumably reasonably pursue as well? If health insurance is only for he who hath not sinned,
it probably will cover no one at all.

Drinking and smoking are at least fairly discrete activities that one can
decide to partake or abstain. But they are not paradigmatic of the sorts of
ubiquitous behaviors—such as eating—which shape our health outcomes.
Consider obesity, a huge driver of health and health spending. Michelle
Mello explained that, "The notion that consumers make free choices about
eating . . . overlooks the ways in which the physical, food, and information
environments shape these decisions. For example, aggressive (and sometimes
misleading) marketing of junk foods, greater accessibility and lower price
of fast foods relative to more-healthy options in many communities, and
widespread public misunderstanding about appropriate portion size all challenge a model of rational cost-benefit decision making by informed consumers."[54] It turns out that all sorts of government policies, from schooling
and food labeling to agricultural policies and even antitrust enforcement for
food producers, shape our diets. This reality explains why obesity rates vary
so wildly, country by country.

Recognizing these sorts of challenges, Rutgers philosopher Nir Eyal has
candidly modified the theory to make more explicit that he would only exclude those guilty of "culpable" choices.[55] He defines "culpable choices" as
those that are "free and at least somewhat morally wrong."[56] Yet even with
this clarification, we need a grounding for "moral wrongs." Our paradigm
cases of moral wrongness involve harms to others, which finds little application here. And it's hard to reason by analogy, since the harm-to-others context may be preoccupied by the precept that it's wrong to cause harm *without
consent.* When we stop to imagine whether it is morally wrong for an adult
to freely (consensually) increase a risk of harm to *himself,* we lack lodestars
to do that evaluation.

Although I find it persuasive, I must admit that I am embarrassed to make
this particular argument. It generally is not fair to blame a philosopher for
the fact that their theories create difficult line-drawing problems and require
wise judgment to put into application. This is true of every theory, not just
luck egalitarianism.

Here, however, for the purposes of thinking about concrete social policy
around health insurance, the problem is not pedantic. The core analytic distinction that luck egalitarianism is supposed to leverage just collapses under

scrutiny. Wherever we draw the lines for the choices about smoking, exercise, wine, or donuts, we can be sure that, at some point, every person will at least once commit a health sin that marginally raises the risk of cancer. In this light, it is hard to know what to do with luck egalitarianism, if not conclude that *no risks* should be shared, but even luck egalitarians do not seem to endorse that conclusion. The other option is to use the insight haphazardly—as politicians are wont to do—picking out convenient scapegoats as a basis for refusing to comply with our social obligations.

Even though Americans are split by all sorts of disagreements, this sort of governmental arbitrariness should be universally abhorrent. Anderson argues that it is not "the state's business to pass judgment on the worth of the qualities of citizens that they exercise or display in their private affairs."[57] Indeed, following economist and philosopher F. A. Hayek, I would further worry that such an approach erodes the notion that there is a domain of "private affairs" at all.[58] Linking the ethos of "personal responsibility" to the redistribution of risk through health insurance implicitly imposes the state's conception of *how* we should exercise that responsibility.

For these and other reasons, many, like Harvard philosopher Daniel Wikler, have concluded that "personal responsibility for health deserves but a peripheral role in health policy."[59] Others, such as legal scholar Daniel Markovits, have sought to save luck egalitarianism by denying that its policy prescriptions must "precisely track responsibility."[60] Instead he invokes "humanitarian considerations—which are triggered by absolute need and are therefore invariant with respect to responsibility."[61] In this way, luck egalitarianism can be saved, while it is resigned to a theoretical sandbox. For present purposes, it does not answer the questions posed about who should bear the costs of healthcare.

## Epistemological Limits

Let's dig further into Dworkin's illustrative distinction between cancer "in the normal course of life" and cancer caused by smoking. Even if we focus on the paradigmatic smoker's problem of lung cancer, it is still true that about 16,000 to 24,000 *nonsmoking* Americans also die each year from lung cancer.[62] Under luck egalitarianism, it is unproblematic for those nonsmokers to claim a right to social support for their cancer costs, but their existence also creates an epistemological problem for judging the smokers. We need to know the counterfactual for each individual. For any smoker who develops lung cancer, we cannot know whether he or she may have been among the unlucky Americans who may have succumbed to cancer even if they did not smoke. To bar all smokers from enjoying full insurance for their lung cancers is overinclusive and thus unjust to a subset of them.

This is not to deny that smoking dramatically increases the risk of cancer; it is instead to emphasize that we generally can only identify these effects on the margin with aggregate data; we can identify increased risks, not individual causation. In tort litigation, this is the distinction between general causation (that smoking can cause cancer) and specific causation (that smoking caused one particular person's cancer), which can be exceedingly difficult and expensive to prove because of the multitude of individual risk factors, not all of which are known scientifically. For this reason, the Supreme Court has not allowed such cases to be litigated as class actions: each plaintiff and each defendant must fight it out in an individual jury trial, to determine whether specific causation exists in the particular case.[63] I have litigated similar cases, which can take a month-long trial, with a dozen expert witnesses from a range of fields, and millions of dollars of fees for attorneys and experts.

Symmetric to the case of unlucky non-smoking cancer patients is the fact that, even among smokers, some will be lucky to not develop lung cancer. Those who actually do get cancer are unlucky enough to have been born with genetic dispositions that dramatically increase their risk compared to other smokers, who will live to old age.[64] How does the luck egalitarian incorporate this genetic factor? In the litigation around tobacco, courts have wrestled with all these problems. "The class members were exposed to nicotine through different products, for different amounts of time, and over different time periods. Each class member's knowledge about the effects of smoking differs, and each plaintiff began smoking for different reasons. Each of these factual differences impacts the application of legal rules such as causation, reliance, comparative fault, and other affirmative defenses."[65]

As frustrating as this may be for figuring out how much a smoker owes for his cancer treatment, in practical terms of policymaking, there is a much simpler solution. Rather than trying to make individual determinations about each cancer case once it materializes *ex post*, we can simply impose a tax on tobacco *ex ante*, one that is proportionate to the additional risks caused by consumption. Those tax revenues can then supplement insurance premiums or taxes for health programs, so at the point of healthcare consumption nonsmokers, unlucky smokers, and lucky smokers can all access the needed healthcare. Indeed, this is roughly the approach taken in the United States—across state and federal taxes, about 44% of the cost of a pack of cigarettes goes to taxes, some of which are paid into the healthcare system.[66] To the extent that we want a more direct connection to healthcare costs, then health insurance premiums can be adjusted for smokers, as the ACA allows. If the inflated prices of the product and / or insurance also provide a rough signal of the risks of the product to the consumer and society, as law professor and judge Guido Calabresi has suggested, then they will also then appropriately shape behavior *ex ante*.[67] They do so while nonetheless preserving the individual liberty to choose.

As we wrestle with the broader question about whether and to what extent healthcare expenses should be borne collectively (through public or private insurance) versus individually (through cost exposure), we have waded fairly deeply into this notion of individual responsibility driven by individual choice. We have seen, however, that this theory is normatively problematic and impossible to apply in practice. The tobacco example shows the problems of trying to adjudicate individual responsibility *ex post*, once a risk materializes. Cost-exposure policy should not be motivated by such theories of moral desert. Instead, to the extent that we think a given choice presents an unreasonable risk to the healthcare system, it should be appropriately taxed *ex ante*.

## PAY AS EQUAL CITIZENS

I have so far shown the difficulty of individualizing responsibility for healthcare costs, whether generally or on the basis of personal responsibility for choices. But I have not yet given an affirmative account of why healthcare expenses should be pooled and borne collectively. In Chapter 1, we saw why rational individuals might well pay insurance premiums to spread across the course of a year, or across the course of a lifetime, their risks of having large expenses in any given period of time. And we saw that rational individuals would pay premiums to pool funds, so that any contributor could access healthcare that would be otherwise unaffordable. In addition to these premiums, these arrangements could well include some cost exposures at the point of consumption, as long as they were not so large to undermine the risk-spreading and access-guaranteeing functions that motivated the rational buyers in the first place. But these sorts of arrangements could still exclude some Americans, who are unable to afford to pay these costs, either in advance or at the point of consumption. How should we think about this heterogeneity in the ability to pay for and thus get access to healthcare?

### Why We Share

In a large, diverse society like the United States, it is challenging to get consensus on any particular economic policy, including access to healthcare. Much must be left to public debate and electoral politics. But a wide range of philosophical traditions have converged on the idea that such free debate itself presumes that some basic human capacities will be assured for all the debaters. The idea inheres in the very idea of being free and equal citizens.

Elizabeth Anderson develops this idea: "Democracy is here understood as collective self-determination by means of open discussion among equals, in accordance with rules acceptable to all."[68] This thin notion of democracy provides a neutral starting point on which people with various political ideologies may nonetheless agree. In this sense, if nothing else, Americans commit to treat each other as equals under the law. Of course, that implicates civil liberties like voting and free expression, but it also includes the preconditions for exercising those rights.

These general notions of democratic equality and fairness in distribution do not yet tell us how healthcare costs should be allocated, but they give us a frame for having that discussion. Philosopher Tom Christiano has similarly argued that, even if we reasonably disagree about redistribution of wealth more generally, it is necessary to provide all persons with "economic minimum," which includes access to healthcare, as a prerequisite to individuals being able to assert their civil liberties.[69] We can tolerate radical differences in welfare, but the very notion of democracy breaks down when some of its members are so destitute, disabled, and desperate they are unable to function as equals in the society, asserting their interests through the democratic processes.

Immanuel Kant famously argued that individuals are deserving of respect because of their capacity for rationality, as the mere force of will, to decide for oneself. Although animals and plants may also suffer, they do not demand that same sort of respect as thinking things. The conception of democratic equality is somewhat distinct, as it leverages the social fact of common citizenship. That notion of the free citizen includes freedom from private exploitation and access to a broad range of opportunities, so that people have some chance of actually doing what they want to do. As Anderson says, "The same point applies to a society in which property is so unequally distributed that some adults live in abject dependence on others, and so live at the mercy of others. Societies that permit the creation of outcasts and subordinate classes can be as repressive as any despotic regime."[70]

In my view, this commitment can be seen as a very thin one, agreeable from a broad range of political perspectives, even if some would go further to achieve greater equality in outcomes. For example, civic republicanism is focused not on achieving material equality, but on political liberty.[71] From this philosophical tradition, Phillip Pettit develops a similar point nonetheless, explaining that "Republican justice would require a rich infrastructure for social life with developmental, institutional and material aspects. It would argue for insuring people on social, medical and legal fronts."[72] Access to medical care protects people from fundamental vulnerabilities that would undermine the "exercise of some of their basic liberties."[73] The point here is not just about respecting individual persons. As legal scholar Ganesh Sitaraman has explained, this sort of broad-based material security is necessary for self-governance of a free people; otherwise "the wealthy would also begin to think that they are inherently better than the poor and they alone are worthy of the right to govern," and "without political redress from a self-satisfied opulent elite, the people might turn to a demagogue who would overthrow the government."[74]

In a minimalist spirit, philosopher Allen Buchanan has attempted to develop a libertarian case for basic welfare rights, observing that "poor nutrition and lack of health care, compounded by the cultural deprivation and inferior public education prevalent in inner cities and many rural areas, produce millions of 'citizens' who are illiterate, uninformed, and unable to communicate effectively their own interests."[75] In only the most trivial senses can we say that the disabled and destitute beggar with untreated wounds is securing the blessings of liberty, as a free and equal citizen. Much more than a century ago, Fredrick Douglass manifested this same idea, writing that "no man can be truly free whose liberty is dependent upon the thought, feeling and action of others, and who has himself no means in his own hands for guarding, protecting, defending and maintaining that liberty."[76]

To be sure, there are more ambitious approaches, which do not seek merely an overlapping consensus between liberals, libertarians, and civic republicans. Aristotle spoke in terms of what would be necessary for humans to "flourish," and contemporary philosophers like Martha Nussbaum have continued to develop this notion.[77] Nobel Prize–winning economist Amartya Sen has built a larger theory that freedom is not merely valuable as the absence of governmental restraint; it is instead concerned with the capabilities of people to do and be what they have reason to value. In that light, "health is among the most important conditions of human life and a critically significant constituent of human capabilities which we have reason to value."[78] Similarly philosopher Norm Daniels builds from the liberal theory of John Rawls, to emphasize the importance of health because it can preserve the "normal functioning" of the human species, allowing people to fully participate in all spheres of their social lives—from education and work to arts and love.[79]

Even if we do not go so far, I think we can understand a decent minimum of healthcare as a prerequisite to a free society of equal citizens. Nonetheless, in practical terms it is complicated to say whether this or that treatment is within the decent minimum. Does justice require that all persons be able to access a $2 million dollar treatment, like the one recently approved by the FDA?[80] Does it require access to patented drugs at all? The analysis could quickly devolve into case-by-case casuistry.

As a starting point, one could rely on extant insurance contracts and Medicare policies that define "medical necessity." Harvard Professor Einer Elhauge suggests that, "in rough approximation, the adequate care that society should endeavor to provide to the poor equals the level of health care actually purchased by the middle class of their society."[81] On this view, absolute equality is not the primary criterion, because wealthier individuals are free to buy more. And, notably, the actual entitlement granted to poorer people floats over time and place, along with the median healthcare consumers. Although this theory may seem stipulative, I think we will be hard pressed to do any better in the task of putting into operation the demands of democratic equality. It is at the very least grounded in the familiar.

## Can Charity Suffice?

It is now common to see desperate patients using social media, like Twitter and Facebook, and crowdfunding sites, like GoFundMe, to raise funds for medical care, which is either uncovered by insurance or covered with large cost exposures.[82] Indeed, the GoFundMe site alone claims that they have over a quarter of a million medical campaigns per year, and have raised over $650 million each year, in this healthcare category alone.[83] A spokesman for the company has said, "Every day on GoFundMe, we see the challenges Americans face with the rising costs of a broken health-care system. Their stories are often heartbreaking, and we strive to be a place where people in need can find help and support."[84]

As a mechanism for achieving democratic equality to a decent minimum of healthcare, one obvious problem with crowdfunding is that the poorest among us are also likely to have relatively impoverished social networks. Really, "crowdfunding" is a fancy word for "begging," and that is unlikely to be a systematic solution to healthcare costs, in an era when they often range into the six figures. It's thus unsurprising that 90% of crowdfunding pitches fail to reach their monetary goals.[85]

Even if begging for charity were sufficient to meet the needs of a decent healthcare minimum for all persons, it is not a fair mechanism to impose on fellow citizens. Anderson argues that democratic equality means that "goods must be distributed according to principles and processes that express respect for all. People must not be required to grovel or demean themselves[.] The basis for people's claims to distributed goods is that they are equals, not inferiors, to others."[86] Similarly, Pettit argues against a policy for meeting basic healthcare needs that would "depend on the goodwill of philanthropists," because that would debase the claimants and leave them vulnerable.[87]

In his attempt to develop a libertarian notion of a decent healthcare minimum, Buchanan has argued that although we all have a duty to provide a decent minimum of healthcare to our fellow citizens, effective charity is a "public good," in the technical sense of the term.[88] A public good is something valuable—like fresh air or national security—that is nonexcludable, meaning that providing it to one person effectively provides it to all. Public goods are nonrivalrous, meaning that when one person enjoys the good, he or she does not consume the value in a way that prevents others from enjoying it as well. These features make it hard to impose the costs of producing the good on any individual, without government intervention. Imagine one person trying to secure environmental quality or trying to protect the United States from terrorism. Similarly, when one person provides charity to help someone access expensive healthcare, other potential donors get the benefit of the need being alleviated, without themselves contributing. Yet, through charity alone, there is no way to charge those non-donors for the benefit they enjoy.

Crowdfunding has also revealed the difficulty of targeting our beneficence to those who really deserve it. As Jeremy Snyder and colleagues explain, summarizing the crowdfunding literature, "Past cases have included campaigners misusing donated funds by lying about their own illnesses, creating fake campaigns for genuinely ill friends or relatives, and using funds for other than the purpose promoted in their campaigns."[89] Instead, an institutional solution has greater hope of targeting help where it belongs.

Likewise, consider the difficulties that an individual faces when trying to make charity effective to produce true access for the poorest fellow citizens. Even if we all prefer to not see our fellow citizens dying on the street of preventable illnesses, we might as well let the next person pay the cost of saving him. Indeed, in the 1970s and 1980s, media reports highlighted the dastardly practice of hospitals dumping patients on each other, each trying to shift the burden of providing expensive, uncompensated healthcare to the next hospital. At the time, some estimated that 250,000 patients per year were shuttled from hospital to hospital, looking for one willing to take them in.[90] Some died along the way.

In 1985, Republican Senator Bob Dole sought to fix this problem and "send a clear signal to the hospital community . . . that all Americans, regardless of wealth or status, should know that a hospital will provide what services it can when they are truly in physical distress."[91] Accordingly, in 1986 Congress enacted the Emergency Treatment and Active Labor Act (EMTALA), which requires that all hospitals participating in Medicare that have emergency departments screen and provide emergency treatment to all patients, without regard for their ability to pay. The paradigmatic users of this law are uninsured people, but the same dynamics can play out for insured persons whose cost exposure is too high. EMTALA does not, however, include a direct funding mechanism to pay for that care. Nonetheless, Congress also created a Medicare payment adjustment for hospitals that provide a "disproportionate share" of treatment for low-income patients. The ACA sought to reduce the need for these transfers by instead moving toward universal health insurance.

For present purposes, this history is useful just to illustrate Buchanan's point about the important role of the state in solving the collective action problem for making charity effective; EMTALA is an example of the state intervening to coordinate the provision of care to the poor. Arguably, however, the right to a decent minimum implies more than emergency room care, which is subsequently billed to the patient at tens of thousands of dollars, driving the person into bankruptcy. Moreover, EMTALA does not directly provide access to outpatient care, prescription drugs, rehabilitation services, or a wide range of other necessary healthcare services. (In practice, however, many hospitals provide some such care, charitably or because the ailing patient will just return to the emergency room later.) By creating an incentive for people to get care in expensive emergency-room settings, EMTALA is, ironically, far from the most efficient way to satisfy our duties of beneficence.

Medicaid is instead a program that provides healthcare for the poorest among us; it reimburses hospitals and other healthcare providers for the care to the needs of fellow citizens, which we cannot refuse. And for the most part, Medicaid does so with dignity, not requiring beneficiaries to debase themselves by begging for healthcare at hospitals and clinics. To the contrary, Charles Silver and David Hyman have argued that Medicaid should be replaced by a simple cash-transfer program, supposing that poor people might be better off being able to choose how they spend the benefit (e.g., on food or housing).[92] Yet the healthcare needs will remain—people will show up at hospitals needing cancer treatments and heart transplants. The law will still require that the care be provided, and repeal seems both unlikely and unjust.

### Paying for the Decent Minimum

The foregoing has shown that a minimal notion of democratic equality presupposes that there is something like a right to a decent minimum of healthcare access, which cost exposure should not impinge. And charity cannot fill that need.

Is it nonetheless fair to demand that people pay what they can, at the point of consumption, and what would that mean in practice? As bioethicist Carla Saenz has asked, what "amount of money" *should* we reasonably expect or require "individuals to contribute toward their health insurance?"[93]

Economists have approached this question empirically, by simply looking at how much people do in fact spend on healthcare or health insurance. If people bought it, then ipso facto they could afford it. Although it reflects a certain common sense, Saenz argues that this approach is impoverished. In other moral domains, it would be laughable to answer a normative question by mere behavioral observation (a problem that philosophers have long called the "naturalistic fallacy"). We cannot use observed behavior to tell us how much people *should* pay for their own healthcare, any more than we could determine how often people *should* lie by observing how often people do in fact lie. Affordability has a normative dimension.

Admittedly, the observation that people at a certain income level are willing to voluntarily trade their money for health coverage reveals that health coverage is more valuable to them than alternative uses of the same money. Let's call this "intrapersonal value." In contrast, affordability asks a larger question of redistribution across persons throughout the society—call this "interpersonal justice." Evidence of how a single person spends the money she does in fact have cannot tell us whether our society *should* obviate the need for such trades by subsidizing her health insurance coverage. This becomes clear when we imagine profound tradeoffs—people paying for healthcare only by going hungry or homeless, or degrading and debasing themselves to make money.

Instead, Saenz argues for a "reasonable trade-off" approach to thinking about affordability. On this view, "the cost of health insurance [or cost-sharing exposure] is not excessive if it can be borne without sacrificing something of comparable value. If, on the contrary, individuals are required to make unreasonable tradeoffs in order to pay for insurance [or exposed costs], then the insurance is not affordable."[94] People should not have to forgo college, suffer foreclosure on their modest homes, or stop eating healthy foods, to pay their medical bills. As such, Saenz provides a generalized sketch of a modern state.

The "reasonable trade-off" approach seems rather vacuous and difficult to apply to any particular case. Elhauge has suggested a more fundamental premise that underlies many such commitments: "An individual's ability to pay should . . . be irrelevant to determining that individual's access to the minimum of adequate care."[95] Let's call this the Irrelevance Proviso. Once we determine that a given sort of healthcare should be accessible as part of the decent minimum, we cannot use wealth to discriminate between who has access.

The Irrelevance Proviso fits nicely into the theory of democratic equality, because we are familiar with other domains, such as voting, where wealth should not be a relevant discriminator. In the 1966 case of *Harper v. Virginia Board of Elections,* the Supreme Court confronted southern states' use of poll taxes to disenfranchise blacks. But the court initially framed the problem as not one of race or even voting, but of affluence. "We conclude that a State violates the Equal Protection Clause of the Fourteenth Amendment whenever it makes the affluence of the voter or payment of any fee an electoral standard. Voter qualifications have no relation to wealth nor to paying or not paying this or any other tax."[96] Of course, the American political system is far from perfect, as we know that wealth gives all sorts of other advantages in the political process. But we can nonetheless see the point and borrow the concept.

Similarly, we might say that "ability to walk up steps" should be irrelevant to voting, going to school, or accessing healthcare in the United States. This thesis would imply that polling places, schools, and healthcare facilities need to be adjusted so that those unable to walk could access them just as well as others. That is essentially what the Americans with Disabilities Act has done, through the concept of universal design.

## False Equality

Putting this criterion to work, I want to target one particular form of cost exposure that stands in the way of achieving access to a decent minimum of healthcare, which justice requires. As we saw in the Introduction, in the employer-based health insurance market, which covers the vast majority of nonelderly Americans, a typical plan might include a $1,000 deductible and a $5,000 cap on cost exposure for each insured household. Such a scheme equalizes exposure for all the patients within a plan. Actual payments in a given year are not equalized, since the healthiest patients will pay no health-care costs, the sicker patients will meet their deductible (paying say $1,000), and the sickest will hit their cap (paying $5,000 out-of-pocket). But from an ex ante perspective, where we lack individualized information, each person has identical exposure to costs—enjoying the assurance that they will pay no more than $5,000 in the worst case. With this facial equality, health insurance can seem fair on this dimension.

Facial equality in cost exposure is ubiquitous and seemingly banal, not unlike driving on the right side of the road or stopping for a red light. As Liam Murphy and Thomas Nagel have noted, it is difficult to get normative traction against such entrenched practices, which have "the appearance of natural forms; their conventionality becomes invisible."[97] To gain some analytical perspective, consider that other context where the norm is different—taxes.

A "head" tax—also known as a per capita tax—is one where everyone pays the same dollar amount, regardless of wealth or income. It has facial equality as to the absolute value of the levy (say, $250). Per capita taxation has not seen routine use in the developed world since the nineteenth century. Still, there are disguised head taxes. Sales taxes on basic goods—like groceries—can function like a head tax, since they are imposed on the fixed cost of being alive. For this reason, most states (all but fourteen) exempt groceries from their sales taxes.[98]

One interesting counterexample proves the rule: Margaret Thatcher's imposition of a head tax in Great Britain in 1989.[99] Property taxes had been based on imputed rental income, which thus scaled decently well with ability to pay and with notions of luck egalitarianism, since much of the land was inherited. Instead, Thatcher thought a lump-sum head tax could be both fairer and more efficient. In particular, Thatcher's Conservatives were concerned that many voters without landholdings avoided paying substantial taxes altogether, and they thereby failed to consider the costs of local policies. Giving each person skin in the game could make local government more effective.

The reform turned out to be a disaster. Most citizens experienced it as a large tax hike, as the change redistributed the burdens of local government from the wealthier to the poorer. More than 200,000 people showed up in London to protest the reform, leading to some of the worst riots in British history. Ultimately, the scandal engulfed the Thatcher administration and she resigned in 1990. Every candidate campaigning to replace Thatcher promised to repeal the tax, and when John Major was elected, he promptly did so.

In contrast to a head tax, a "flat rate," or "proportional" tax, is one where everyone pays the same percentage of income; it has facial equality as to the rate (say, 10%). Still, those with more income pay more taxes. Eight U.S.

states and several countries employ flat taxes, and every few years there is another proposal to implement such a reform at the federal level.[100]

The current U.S. federal income tax is progressive. Such a tax is paid as a percentage of adjusted income, with several tiers of increasingly higher percentages, depending on income. In 2017, for example, a married couple filing jointly with $18,650 of income paid 10%, but at the other end of the scale, those earning more than $470,700 would pay 39.6% on earnings above that level. (In practice, the progressive tax code is undermined by various exclusions, deductions, and other loopholes that can allow some very wealthy individuals to pay at a lower rate than poorer individuals.)

For taxes, progressive scaling is eminently reasonable. As legal scholars Joseph Bankman and Thomas Griffith have explained the theory of "diminishing marginal utility of money," higher incomes create more disposable wealth.[101] Those with lower income must allocate more of it proportionally to basic human needs. For this reason, among scholars, there is now broad consensus that progressivity allocates the experienced burden of taxation more equitably than a flat rate.[102] There is also a powerful argument that wealthier individuals actually extract more value from public investments in infrastructure, education, policing, courts protecting property rights, and other trappings of modern government, compared to those at lower income levels.

In this light, it should be astonishing that for healthcare cost exposure, we have flipped the rule. Instead of progressivity being the norm, U.S. employer-based plans are two steps away, using a facially-equal system that is not even flat-scaled to income. Just like a head tax, U.S. employer-based plans apply per capita cost-exposure schemes that are regressive in the sense that poorer beneficiaries must pay a larger percentage of their incomes than higher-paid beneficiaries.[103] This is false equality.

Per capita cost exposure is even worse than per capita taxes, because it also has a behavioral function. Cost exposure is specifically designed to reduce consumption of insured healthcare. As such, per capita cost exposure not only inequitably distributes the *burden* of exposed healthcare spending, but also inequitably distributes the *benefits* of *insured* health spending. It stands as a barrier to the decent minimum of healthcare, just as a poll tax stood as a barrier to voting.

As legal scholar Gregg Bloche explains, "Those who are less able and willing to pay out of pocket, outside the hospital, receive less of the high-cost care that exceeds annual maxima and is therefore insured in full. These less prosperous policyholders thus tap the insurance pool to a lesser degree."[104] In short, a patient must spend more out-of-pocket to get the full benefits from insurance. Similarly, physicians Steffie Woolhandler and David Himmelstein have called out the way in which insurance plans give wealthy workers access to tummy tucks, but deny poorer workers access to basic care.[105] This concern about perverse redistribution would be trenchant even if poorer beneficiaries were able to access a decent minimum of healthcare, but richer beneficiaries drew *even more* actuarial value from the common pool.

In fact, the evidence shows that when cost exposure is onerous, underinsured individuals behave as if they lack insurance altogether and thus fail to extract the value from the shared insurance pool. More generally, we have already seen the literature showing that underinsured children have the same sorts of challenges accessing care as those who are uninsured and that after heart attacks, underinsured patients have trouble getting follow-up care and medication.[106] Another study of individuals in high-deductible health plans focused on emergency-room visits, and distinguished between appropriate utilization for high-severity incidents and inappropriate utilization for low-severity incidents. The study found that when patients are moved to high-deductible health plans, poorer patients, but not richer patients, dramatically reduce the amount of high-severity (appropriate) emergency care they consumed.[107] The same cost-exposure thresholds can have very different effects. As a result, we see high-income employees consuming more healthcare than their lower-paid counterparts.[108]

Beyond the poll tax already mentioned, the U.S. Supreme Court has recognized that a range of civil rights cannot be conditioned on the ability to pay a user fee. In 1974, the Court held that states may not impose filing fees on indigent candidates for public office, as these could deny access to the ballot.[109] In *Mayer v. Chicago*, the Supreme Court held that filing fees could not be used to prevent petty criminal offenders from appealing their convictions.[110] In another case, the Supreme Court agreed with a litigant who argued that "the size of her pocketbook should not be dispositive when 'an interest far more precious than a property right' is at stake"—when a trial court has terminated a parent's rights, her inability to pay fees could not be used to deny her access to the courts.[111] The Supreme Court has neither recognized healthcare as a "fundamental right" like due process nor recognized poorer persons as a "protected class," like racial or religious minorities. Nonetheless, now that we have seen that the decent minimum healthcare is itself "far more precious than a property right" and a necessary component of democratic equality, it should seem objectionable to discriminate on ability to pay.

This analysis shows the complexity of applying notions of democratic equality. Since a simplistic facial equality in cost exposure can effectively block poorer Americans from accessing the decent minimum of healthcare, or make tragic trade-offs on the verge of bankruptcy if they do so, these cost-exposure profiles contravene the notion of democratic equality. Instead, we must pursue the sorts of reforms proposed in Chapter 5 or reject substantial cost exposure, as I suggest in Chapter 6.

We have laid bare the basic intuitions that individuals should pay for their own healthcare, and recognized the fatal problems with trying to distinguish between the costs caused by responsible choices of those individuals, so we could make them pay accordingly. We settled on an approach of democratic equality as a basis for guaranteeing a decent minimum of healthcare. We then found that a facial equality in cost exposures could contravene that principle, undermining the prerequisites for participation in a free and equal society, by conditioning access to a decent minimum on an irrelevant factor: the ability to pay.

# CHAPTER 5

# FIXES WE COULD TRY

M any of the foregoing observations and analyses have suggested a
range of reforms to cost exposure, and it is now time to develop
them directly. First, though, we must consider the case for any intervention at all, and this involves a review of market failures and behavioral failures. In the next Chapter, I will ultimately argue that the
United States can and should eliminate substantial cost exposure; it is
a failed experiment driven by an ill-conceived ideology, which misun-
derstands the purpose of health insurance. But here, we first consider
several incremental reforms to understand how cost exposure could at
least be optimized to serve its goals while reducing harm. Specifically,
if the policy mechanism is to guide consumption behavior, healthcare
providers need to be much more transparent in their pricing and must
guide patients in making healthcare choices in light of their cost exposures. If we want cost exposure to drive value in healthcare, it must
be so tailored, in contrast to its existing forms which indiscriminately
deter good and bad healthcare alike. To preserve the core function of
insurance to guarantee access to care, we must also scale cost exposure to income, and for large healthcare expenses use partial indemnities, a novel form of cost exposure.

## THE FALSE LURE OF LAISSEZ-FAIRE

"We believe it's appropriate to put in place a system that gives every person the financial feasibility to be able to purchase the coverage that they want for themselves and for their family."[1] So said Tom Price, President Trump's first secretary of health and human services. The Republican physician went on to say that people should choose how to insure themselves, not get "what the government forces them to buy."[2]

Similarly, health economist Mark Pauly has advocated a hands-off approach to health insurance design. He argues that this position of "aggressive neutrality" will allow people to choose "an appropriate level of health and financial protection, balancing incentives to use care with incentives to provide financial protection."[3] Pauly suggests that people should not be nudged toward health plans with high deductibles, nor should they be nudged toward plans with lower or zero deductibles. Those who prefer high deductibles can get lower premiums and vice versa—let them choose.

This sort of hands-off approach (aka laissez-faire) reflects a standard starting point for economic reasoning, inspired by Adam Smith's notion that the "invisible hand" of the market would aggregate individual rational choices in a way that served overall welfare. Indeed, we can assume that because consumers know their own situations and preferences best, laissez-faire is sensible in a wide range of applications. In the grocery market, consumers do not need the government's help in deciding between spinach or arugula (even if one has more iron, isn't so bitter, and is less expensive too). Nor does government need to decide which television brand is right for me. In these domains, at most we need government enforcement of basic disclosure and safety standards of disclosure, and then get hands-off, so consumers can decide for themselves.

Laissez-faire is a fair default rule; it's the presumptively right approach to any policy question. Consequently, before considering various reforms below, one has a burden of proof as to why health insurance, and cost exposure in particular, is different than groceries and vacations. Why not laissez-faire? Why interfere with individual choices?

### Health Insurance Is Different

Insurance takes money from a common pool (built by premiums and/or taxes) and redistributes the money to individuals who make claims on the pool as their risks materialize. That claiming function allows for a sort of opportunism in choosing the insurance plan, which does not exist in the market for spinach or televisions.

Although insurance is designed to spread the risk that any of us could fall ill and have large medical bills, that risk is not evenly distributed and is not completely opaque. As law professor Tom Baker has explained, "High-risk people tend to prefer more complete health insurance coverage, fewer restrictions on their choice of doctors, and other plan features that make it easier to consume more health care."[4] This dynamic is known as "adverse selection." And the concern is more than theoretical. In fact, people with chronic illnesses and other large bills tend to buy insurance plans with the lowest cost exposures at the point of consumption.[5] Meanwhile, those who predict that they will have less risk are fine with higher out-of-pocket exposures, because they know that it is unlikely that they will really suffer those high costs. They will happily take lower premiums in exchange for a risk that they know is largely theoretical.

This choice-based approach exploits each individual's private information about her own risk, and as health policy experts explain, it thereby "subdivides the population into discrete risk categories, which may adversely affect the future stability of the insurance plan options."[6] If all the sickest people are stuck in their own risk pool, then the premium costs of that pool will become so expensive that individuals are no longer able to afford insurance coverage at all.

This same logic explains why even market-oriented health insurance reforms (like the Heritage Foundation proposal, which later became Republican Mitt Romney's signature reform in Massachusetts and the model for Obamacare) have included a mandate for all persons to buy health insurance. If people only sign up for health insurance once their risk materializes (like homeowners buying insurance after the fire), premiums would be astronomical.

Legal scholar Russell Korobkin has noted that the market for health insurance is odd, because "the seller does not wish to retain some of its customers," namely those who are likely to have the highest costs.[7] Insurers have nonetheless had only limited abilities to discriminate against the sickest individuals, because that information was in the hands of the patients. And the Affordable Care Act (ACA) prohibited them from asking about preexisting conditions and then discriminating on that basis. However, cost exposure can be used to force patients to reveal that information.

We normally think that markets work well when consumers can vote with their feet. That is how bad products get run out of the market. For example, if a car has a propensity to explode when struck from behind, and people learn that it is not crashworthy, they will wisely stop buying that car. The carmaker is then incentivized to fix the problem. In theory, government needs only to ensure that the safety information is known to buyers, and the problem fixes itself.

Here, however, health insurers can make a bad product, with onerous cost exposures that drive people into financial devastation and undermine their need to access care, and if the sickest people vote with their feet, all the better. Specifically, the insurer is delighted if the costliest patients avoid their health insurance plans or, even better, pay premiums but drop out of the plan after a risk materializes. For example, if AIDS patients are expensive risks for an insurance company, then a company should put exceedingly high copayments on all the AIDS drugs.[8] No rational AIDS patient would select or keep such a plan. As law professor Matt Lawrence explains, "We should not expect the threat of exit by enrollees who have negative experiences with their health insurance plan" to cause health insurers to improve their products.[9] If the sickest leave, all the better!

If this approach is available to one company, then their competitors would be silly to not embrace it as well. Ultimately then, AIDS patients (and others with expensive illnesses) will have no real choice of cost-exposure plans, because no company wants to be the chump holding all the risk, which other companies have sloughed off.

## Rational Actors and Irrational Choices

I am not meaning to demonize insurance companies; we should expect people to behave rationally according to the incentives that the policy domain has established for them. But, under the laissez-faire approach, no single insurer has an interest in setting a cost-exposure policy that is sensible from a broad social point of view. Instead, they rationally compete to try to avoid insuring those who need insurance the most, and cost-exposure plans are one mechanism for doing so. In cases like this, legal scholars identify a "market failure"—it's the exceptional situation where unrestrained competition fails to produce socially acceptable outcomes, and some sort of governmental intervention is required.

One solution is to sell health insurance with a given cost exposure profile to a broad group, clustered together for nonhealth reasons. The United States has relied on large employers to perform this pooling function, covering everyone who works for the company, regardless of their health status. And they have generally embraced this idea that insurance is a group benefit. The law reinforces this norm, prohibiting individual risk rating according to each person's health.[10]

Even aside from this adverse selection problem, there are a range of other reasons for why individual choice is problematic for health insurers. Insurance contracts are very complex financial instruments, which require a certain sophistication (not unlike the choice of healthcare treatments themselves, where we have established physicians as gatekeepers). In one study of a representative sample of adults with employer health insurance, George Loewenstein and colleagues first asked respondents yes-or-no questions about whether they understood each of four basic components of traditional health insurance design. Then the team provided a multiple-choice question for each component to measure actual comprehension. As it happened, people were highly confident about their understanding of copays, deductibles, and maximum out-of-pocket costs (more than 90% saying so), but only 57% said that they understood coinsurance. But the reality was worse. "Respondents' actual understanding of concepts was lower than perceived understanding, ranging from a high of 78% for deductibles to a low of 34% for coinsurance. Only 14% of respondents answered all four questions correctly," even though they were multiple-choice questions, which allowed guessing.[11]

Loewenstein's team asked additional questions, which would require patients to actually estimate the cost of a course of treatment under a given health insurance plan. "Only 11% of respondents gave the correct response to a relatively simple fill-in-the-blank question about the cost of a 4-day hospital stay," and only 14% came within plus or minus $1,000 of the correct number.[12] This research presents a challenge to the affirmative case for cost exposure—after all, how are patients supposed to make an intelligent decision about going to the hospital if they cannot even discern its marginal costs to them?—but it also presents a challenge to the laissez-faire notion that people should choose their own health insurance plans, selecting the appropriate level of risk ex ante.

Individuals also suffer from various cognitive biases, which are especially significant in the domain of predicting future risks. People tend to be optimistic, not just as a friendly characteristic, but by actually underestimating their risk of experiencing health problems that can produce large costs. Yale law professor and economist Christine Jolls calls this an "amazingly robust finding," because it has been demonstrated in so many different social science contexts.[13] In one typical research study, 100 undergraduates were asked to rate their susceptibility to forty-five different health risks, such as alcoholism, diabetes, and glaucoma, as being above or below their average student. On average, the students thought their risk was well below average.[14] Similarly, a large body of work has shown that people have fairly accurate understandings of the aggregate risk of traffic accidents, but "they tend to believe that these aggregate estimates of risk do not apply to them personally. Most drivers consider themselves to be safer, more skillful, and less likely to be involved in an accident than the average driver."[15] These sorts of systematic biases would predictably cause individuals to purchase health insurance with greater cost exposure than they might in fact need or prefer, if they estimated their own risk accurately.

The paradigm case for health insurance is to avoid catastrophic risks, not unlike the risks of losing one's home to a natural disaster. In classic research, Howard Kunreuther and Paul Slovic interviewed more than 3,000 homeowners in flood and earthquake zones and found that, in fact, individuals seemed to have a "disinclination to worry about low-probability hazards," which may nonetheless be catastrophic.[16] In follow-up laboratory experiments, the researchers found that, even where insurance was deeply subsidized—making it a clearly rational purchase—many homeowners still declined. Instead, people seemed to focus their insurance purchases on high-probability, low-loss hazards, precisely the opposite of what economic theory would predict. Not only do we have trouble estimating how much that hospital visit will cost us out-of-pocket, but we also seem to ignore the chance that it will happen to us at all.

In contrast to the low-probability events that insurance is designed to protect against, the premium payment may seem much more salient to an insurance buyer, since it comes with 100% probability. Indeed, some research suggests that many insurers just go for the lowest premium plan, regardless of its actuarial value.[17] The premium "price is simple to evaluate, while other characteristics such as deductible and coinsurance are harder to evaluate and trade off against each other."[18]

## Why Laissez-Faire Doesn't Work

Even aside from these market failures and decisional failures, more generally, the laissez-faire approach to insurance design is unrealistic for several reasons. First, in many ways the cow is already out of the barn. Federal and state policies have created so many tax incentives, health insurance coverage mandates, and implicit redistributions that it is hard to imagine, much less construct, an Archimedean point from which an insurance consumer could choose her health insurance plan. Even aside from these government interventions in the market, healthcare decisions are often mediated by various agents, such as employers purchasing health insurance and doctors recommending and providing healthcare. Some of the following recommendations are addressed not only to government but also to these adjunct decision makers, working with and for individual consumers.

Second, as we have seen, there are externalities. When a patient declines valuable healthcare (for instance, failing to take her drugs) because of an onerous cost exposure, she may well return and consume more expensive healthcare later (such as heart surgery), which imposes costs on others in the same insurance pool. Or the patient might by then have changed jobs, or gone on to Medicare, where the increased costs of a poorly designed insurance policy are borne by others. Or, if she consumes healthcare with onerous cost exposures, she may well find herself in bankruptcy or foreclosure, which then imposes those costs on her creditors and other debtors, who pay higher interest rates or higher prices as the costs are shifted. Even more, Lawrence argues that the convoluted billing schemes prevalent in the United States are themselves an externality, imposing costs on the healthcare providers who must wrangle with not only the insurers but patients-as-payors too.[19]

Third, as we have seen, there is a normative concern. When we see fellow citizens going without healthcare, or getting bankrupted by its expenses, it strikes us somewhat differently than when we see someone make a poor choice between one television or another. Indeed, Chapter 4 showed that we have not only felt obligations, but also normatively justified obligations to ensure a decent minimum of healthcare access for our fellow citizens. For this reason, we see the allocation of social resources toward healthcare as a question for democratic policymaking, not merely one of individual rational behavior.

Altogether then, we can set aside the laissez-faire approach to health insurance design. We have seen no shortage of reasons why we cannot rely on a simplistic notion of the invisible hand in this domain. But the particular mechanisms for intervention remain open. Lawrence has compellingly argued that we should create macro-level incentives for insurers to manage and reduce the problems caused by cost exposure, and then allow insurers to innovate various mechanisms to meet those targets.[20] Some key mechanisms will be the ones proposed here, such as scaling to value or scaling to income, or perhaps even split indemnities. Alternatively, it may be appropriate for governments and insurance buyers, such as employers, to simply mandate these reforms more directly. This approach will be most obvious where poorly tailored mandates already exist, such as the mandate for coverage of preventative health services without cost exposure or the mandate for a cap on annual cost exposure. Those current policies just need to be revised. Nonetheless, I will ultimately argue that these sorts of policy tinkerings are unlikely to sufficiently solve the problems that ail cost exposure. A more straightforward path will be to pivot away from cost exposure altogether.

## COST TRANSPARENCY AND GUIDANCE

Anthropologist Howard Stein has described a "taboo in official American health culture: namely, a prohibition upon allowing the physician to appear concerned with financial matters." Perhaps connecting back to the ancient traditions of spiritual healers, physicians discussing money seems to violate "the sacred by the profane."[21] We see these sentiments echoed in the journal *Oncology*, with physicians writing that "many see the patient-physician relationship as a sacred space where discussions of money are unwelcome. Talking about finances seems to challenge the identity of the physician as compassionate caregiver, whose only responsibility is to provide the best possible care."[22]

Yet, if cost exposure will remain a primary part of the U.S. health system, physicians and healthcare providers have to do better at informing patients about those costs and guiding healthcare decisions in light of those costs. As physician-journalist Elisabeth Rosenthal concludes, "It should be

considered a doctor's obligation to provide you with financial information."[23] But we have to find a legal mechanism to make that obligation real.
For this point I want to leverage the existing common law of informed
consent and medical malpractice in provocative ways. Fundamentally, a
provider's failure to communicate such information can undermine validity
of informed consent, and the lack of guidance can cause patients to get
healthcare that is inappropriate for them and thus outside the standard
of care.

## Collections and Consent

As an example of the problem, let's revisit one of the worst practices that
leaves patients exposed to exorbitant medical bills—"drive-by doctoring."
Rosenthal has told the story of one case, in which a patient planning a surgery had carefully chosen a surgeon and a hospital, both of which were in
his insurer's network. Once he was put under anesthesia, a second surgeon
came to assist.[24] This stranger later sent the patient a six-figure bill, expecting
to be paid on top of the negotiated rates charged by the hospital and primary surgeon. For first-year law students, this fact pattern would present obvious issues of contract law. Agreement is the hallmark of any contract, and
it seems to be lacking in this case. If the patient has not made an agreement
with this assisting surgeon, the patient has no duty to pay these rates. Alternatively, we might consider this a form of "quasi-contract," which also can
impose an obligation to pay, but it seems unlikely that this patient *would*
have agreed to these rates or agreed to undergo the procedure on these terms,
if the assistant surgeon's fees had been disclosed in advance.

   In one of my first legal cases, I worked on a team representing thousands
of patients who were suing their hospitals, challenging the exorbitant prices
charged. This case was one instance in a wave of nationwide litigation. We
initially asserted that these nonprofit hospitals were violating their duties
under federal tax laws and state charity regulations, but those provisions generally do not allow private citizens to enforce them. So we also argued that
the patients had not specifically agreed to the prices charged. Although many
of them had signed a sheaf of paperwork when they entered the hospital,
including a line promising to pay for all necessary care, no prices were
listed. Thus, we reasoned that the hospitals could only demand reasonable

reimbursement under these "open-price" contracts. They could not just make up whatever ridiculous numbers they wanted to collect.

That litigation had a few notable wins, when several hospital systems agreed to adopt explicit charity care policies and stop some of the more egregious practices. Some of these reforms in how hospitals would provide a "community benefit" later became part of the ACA.

Overall, however, this litigation often failed to get recourse for patients. Courts rejected our efforts to amass hundreds of patients into the same case, so we could invest the time and money to go up against the multibillion-dollar enterprises that are modern hospitals.[25] Instead, courts held that patients would have the burden to prove the unreasonableness of each item on each medical bill, and they had to do so individually—each one hiring attorneys, recruiting expert witnesses, and gathering data to compare the prices charged by their healthcare provider versus other competitors. Ironically, these patients would have to spend tens of thousands of dollars to pay experts and lawyers in order to challenge the inflated bills charged by their healthcare providers. Although each patient had thousands of dollars at stake, an amount that was devastating for many of them, it was not enough to justify the tens of thousands of dollars of legal bills necessary to challenge those prices. The courts' refusal to aggregate the litigation left many consumers without an effective recourse to challenge their unreasonable bills.

The courts also invoked the fact that the hospitals did maintain a price list, known as the "chargemaster," which the patient could have theoretically requested. Thus, the courts refused to even consider whether the charged prices were in fact reasonable.[26]

Still, it is possible for patients to proceed alone. One father, Jeffrey Fox, reached out to me years later, to share his story of how he successfully challenged his son's medical bills. First, he paid off the charges, so that the healthcare provider would not start collections and report the bad debt. That way Mr. Fox protected his credit rating. He then sued in small claims court to demand a refund of what he had paid. Fortunately, the healthcare provider did not show up in court, so Mr. Fox just explained the basics of the open-price contract theory, which every judge has learned in law school. The judge gave Mr. Fox a default judgment, and he eventually received a refund from his son's healthcare provider, paying him the difference between the actual charges and what the judge determined would have been reasonable.

Mr. Fox protected his credit rating by paying first and then going to court. More commonly, a patient simply does not (and often cannot) pay, and after ninety days or so, the healthcare provider refers the debt to a collection agency or sells it outright. After trying phone calls and letters to extract a payment, the collector typically goes to court for a judgment, to garnish wages or seize assets. I would suggest that courts begin requiring healthcare providers to show not just that there was a contract (which debt buyers are often unable to do), but also that the prices charged are in fact reasonable. The burden should be on the party claiming a given rate and seeking a recovery. And, if courts push this point, it will also cause healthcare providers to try harder in the first place to disclose real prices and get patient consent.

Aside from contract law, exorbitant prices also raise questions about the professionalism of physicians. The law gives great deference to physicians as a learned profession, and it delegates to them substantial power to make healthcare decisions for vulnerable patients. But that trust depends on the profession, to some extent, regulating itself. Consider other professions, such as lawyers, which also have extraordinary powers, to initiate expensive legal proceedings against fellow citizens. One of the very first provisions in the American Bar Association's Model Rules of Professional Conduct, which most states have adopted nearly verbatim, is that "a lawyer shall not make an agreement for, charge, or collect an unreasonable fee."[27] This provision has teeth; courts often reduce the amount of fees charged by attorneys and sometimes discipline attorneys for demanding too much.

For physicians, there are ethics opinions saying much the same thing, but it is not clear that such rules are ever actually applied by the courts or by medical boards that are in charge of physician discipline.[28] Of course, these boards are largely run by the physicians themselves. As law professor Nadia Sawicki has articulated, "One of the most prominent criticisms of the medical profession in the 20th century has been that it is self-protective, monopolistic, and more attuned to the economic security of its members than to the welfare of the public at large."[29]

But the difference is not just in the enforcement. The rules regulating attorneys specifically require that they disclose any fees to be charged, so the client can make a decision about whether and how to proceed.[30] For physicians, there is no comparable mandate in their professional code. And physicians have historically not been very forthcoming with information for patients.

Instead, the more general doctrine of informed consent must be bent to these purposes. The law has long required that physicians must get the consent of patients before touching them, and that consent must include any information that is "material" to the patient's decision. A physician that instead proceeds to provide healthcare is thereby committing malpractice, battery, or even fraud.[31] This law exists as a counter to what Jay Katz, a physician and Yale law school professor, has called a "history of silence," or really a history of manipulation, where physicians would "shape the disclosure process so that patients will comply with their recommendations."[32]

Of course, patients can always ask about costs, or anything else, and they can decline treatment if they do not get satisfying answers. However, the legal doctrine of informed consent is not just about fraud—giving false answers to explicit patient questions. Instead, informed consent is an affirmative duty, obligating the physician to provide all "material" information, even if not explicitly asked. The burden of securing consent before touching is on the physician, and the doctrine requires *informed* consent.

As the law of informed consent has developed over the last century, it has primarily focused on the risks of the proposed treatment itself. Deciding what to disclose itself requires professional judgment to *evaluate* the magnitude of the risk, the frequency of its occurrence, and the viability of alternative therapeutic measures—all in light of a patient's capacity to receive and understand the information.

Some case law suggests that only "medical" or "health-related" risks and benefits are material to the treatment *choice*. For example, in one California Supreme Court case, the widow of a cancer patient sought to preserve a jury verdict that had ruled in her favor, finding that the physician was negligent in failing to inform her husband that, even if he underwent chemotherapy treatment, his life expectancy was very low. Had the husband and wife known that death was imminent, they could have made appropriate financial arrangements. The court overturned the jury verdict, writing "that the Court of Appeal erred in suggesting . . . that under the doctrine of informed consent, a physician is under a duty to disclose information material to the patient's nonmedical interests."[33] The court went on to reiterate a prior decision that a "physician is not the patient's financial adviser."

If U.S. policy is going to continue to impose substantial healthcare costs on patients, then this view must change. How can patients intelligently perform the cost-control function that cost exposure assigns to them if their primary advisors simply shrug?

Indeed, some courts are embracing a more capacious notion of materiality. In the landmark case of *Canterbury v. Spence,* the Federal Court of Appeals in the District of Columbia defined "material risks" as those risks a reasonable person in the patient's position would be likely to consider significant.[34] Since then we have seen courts requiring various nonmedical disclosures, including personal or economic information that may influence their judgment.[35]

So we can conceive materiality in a broader way, but it still does not establish that costs are a material factor in the informed-consent process. With coauthors, I have previously argued that a causal notion of materiality is helpful: information is material if it is likely to change the decision of a substantial number of patients.[36] We suggested and piloted an empirical method for shedding light on that question, with a randomized survey vignette experiment, where we manipulate the presence or absence of the information in question. If substantially fewer people agree to the treatment after learning the information, that suggests that the information was material, and failure to disclose it undermined informed consent.

In this domain, I do not think that such a tailored experiment is necessary, because decades of research reviewed in Chapter 1 shows that cost exposure changes patients' healthcare behavior. If the cost of the care they were consuming was immaterial, then we would see patients blithely consuming healthcare regardless of their cost exposure.

Other states follow a "reasonable physician" or "customary practice" standard for liability. Law professor Thaddeus Mason Pope notes an increasingly common practice of physicians discussing costs with patients, and guidelines from the Institute of Medicine and professional societies suggesting they do so. All this amounts to an inchoate custom to discuss costs. Thus, "Because the professional custom is to discuss costs, physicians have a legal duty to discuss costs."[37]

And this shouldn't be surprising to healthcare providers. Can you imagine if you dropped off your car for an oil change, and when you picked it up an hour later and start to pay the agreed-upon bill, they said, "Oh, yeah, you also owe our buddy $10,000 because we decided to bring him in to help."

Drive-by doctoring is an extreme case. I want to suggest that healthcare providers more generally should be proactive about communicating the costs of care with patients, and in fact they should convey the financial implications of alternative courses of care. For example, patients with heart problems face a choice between having a stent implantation surgery, with potentially a five-figure bill, or instead simply taking a range of generic prescription drugs, with minimal cost exposure. The cost implications are part of any informed choice, and physicians are in the best position to estimate those costs.

For these reasons, law professor Wendy Netter Epstein has argued that the law should impose a price of $0, where it would have been feasible for a seller to disclose the real price but declined to do so. "While $0 may seem like a harsh penalty," it is necessary "to induce requisite changes in the market."[38] This approach reflects a broader strategy, advocated by law and business scholars Ian Ayres and Robert Gertner in the 1980s, suggesting that by inferring unattractive terms, courts can create incentives for parties to better specify their own terms in advance.[39]

Healthcare providers will counter that costs are complicated and unpredictable; physicians largely do not know a lot about costs. Indeed, several studies show that physicians often have no clue about the costs of the procedures that they recommend.[40] As Elisabeth Rosenthal has explained, "Doctors are generally taught little or nothing about the cost of healthcare, [and] individual doctors often have a hard time extracting prices from the finance departments and testing centers."[41]

And information alone will not suffice. As Harvard professors Meredith Rosenthal and Anna Sinaiko have explained, "Determining the cost of medical care is different from determining the cost of other goods because it is often hard to know in advance what exact combination of services a patient will need. For this reason, the average price for a particular procedure or service, which is the most readily available information, doesn't capture a patient's actual cost of care and may be a misleading indicator of true cost differences."[42] Indeed, one court has said that the only way to inform patients would be "handing the patient an inches-high stack of papers detailing the hospital's charges for each and every conceivable service, which he or she could not possibly read and understand before agreeing to treatment."[43]

In early 2019, the U.S. Department of Health and Human Services began implementing a provision of the ACA, which caused hospitals to begin posting their prices. They were incomprehensible, filled with codes and numbers that no patient could decipher. And they were merely the "chargemaster" rate, which is only the starting point for negotiations with insurers, not necessarily the real rate that any patient actually pays.

Okay: the status quo is bad. But how can it be fixed, or more precisely, *who* will fix it? The question is, who holds the real data about actual payments and who is in the best position to make the necessary investments in making sense of the data? The hospitals and physicians are the experts and the repeat players, and they are thus in a much better position to invest in maintaining and purchasing relevant databases and generating predictive analytics to generate estimates of likely costs tailored to individual patients. Given that a physician will recommend heart stent implantation to dozens or hundreds of her patients, it is vastly more efficient to impose the duty on her, rather than the patient, who has neither the expertise, experience, nor support to do so.

Indeed, when scholars have made efforts to inform physicians about costs, it has paid off. In one study, an interactive teaching conference and a pocket guide that listed drug prices had a substantial effect on physicians even six months later, making them more likely to talk to patients about the costs of the drugs being prescribed.[44] Physician recommendations are the key drivers of healthcare consumption, so if we want to rationalize that consumption, physicians have to be made aware of those costs.

Of course, physicians work in teams, along with other professionals and office staff, increasingly as part of large hospital systems. Currently, cost questions are delegated to the front-of-office staff, as if it's two different questions—what healthcare will you get, versus how much will it cost and how will you pay for it? To make these reforms realistic may require a reorganization of the staff structure and culture of a physician's office and hospital, to make informed consent inclusive of cost considerations.

Invocation of the informed-consent doctrine is potentially transformative, tilting the scales of justice toward patients. For cases in which healthcare providers seek to collect on substantial surprise medical bills, patients should counterclaim, asserting that the healthcare provider lacked the patient's informed consent to perform the procedure, and thus should be liable for malpractice or assault. The healthcare provider would owe damages to the patient, which should offset its contract claim.

## Treatment Decisions

If patients are going to be exposed to substantial healthcare costs, then this reality should also change the physician's substantive treatment recommendations for her patients. The law of negligence generally requires that a professional should act reasonably under the circumstances. The fact that the person depending on your advice is potentially on the hook for thousands of dollars of costs is a relevant circumstance. And the patient's ability to pay those costs is a relevant circumstance as well.

These observations suggest that mere disclosure of costs and the securing of patient consent will not be sufficient for clinicians to satisfy their duties to patients. As bioethicist Art Caplan has explained, "You can consent to a course of action—say hospitalisation or the implantation of a left-ventricular assist device—without fully realizing that you are thereby consenting to a huge number of other actions that will of necessity follow. Consent is inherently limited in that no one can actually predict much less comprehend all the risk and benefit details associated with any given choice."[45] Accordingly, patients depend on physicians to present appropriate options in the first place, with a broader understanding of their likely consequences and implications for the patient.

Why do patients consult physicians in the first place? I would suggest that it is to solve a heterogeneity problem. If every illness and every patient were the same, we could simply consume the standard treatment whenever ill. But the reality is that there are thousands of potential ailments that must be differentially diagnosed and thousands of potential treatments that must be matched to the ailment, and calibrated for the patient's physiology, prognoses, tolerances, and personal preferences. Ideally, the healthcare provider solves that problem by figuring out the appropriate treatment for each patient.

Similarly, patients have very different exposures to cost, depending on their insurance coverage, and very different abilities to bear those costs, depending on their income, assets, and credit. An appropriate treatment for a wealthy, well-insured person may be inappropriate for a poor, underinsured person, and vice versa.

To the contrary, one might again argue that doctors and other healthcare providers should be concerned only with a patient's health. Yet, as we have seen, costs impinge on health. In addition to undermining a patient's adherence to drugs, cost pressures can create stress and more severe mental health problems and can worsen other social determinants of health. In this sense, scholars have recently begun to argue that costs are a side effect or a risk of treatment. Physician and behavioral scientist Peter Ubel explains, "Because treatments can be 'financially toxic,' imposing out-of-pocket costs that may impair patients' well-being, . . . physicians need to disclose the financial consequences of treatment alternatives just as they inform patients about treatments' side effects."[46] But we expect physicians to do more than merely disclose treatments' side effects. Rather, they become part of the physician's discretion about whether the treatment is a reasonable risk / benefit tradeoff to recommend it for the patient. Similarly, beyond disclosure, the different financial consequences of different treatments must also inform a physician's judgment as to which healthcare (if any) is appropriate for the patient. Cost concerns should be particularly salient in the ubiquitous situations where the costly treatment is unproven to deliver marginal benefits over the less-expensive standard of care.

If we are going to remain in the present world where policymakers use cost exposure to frame healthcare as just another economic transaction subject to consumer decisions, we must also start thinking of physicians as economic agents and economic advisors as well. The physician has to treat the whole patient, recognizing that health is just a means to a broader set of interests (ends). In some cases, patients may well have a bona fide interest in a less expensive treatment (or no treatment at all), and physicians should recognize as much. To do otherwise would be negligent.

This principle of treating the whole patient has been recognized in other domains around the margins of healthcare, such as end-of-life planning. For example, a National Institutes of Health (NIH) consensus document has explained that "outcome domains related to end of life include physical or psychological symptoms, social relationships, spiritual or philosophical beliefs, hopes, expectations and meaning, satisfaction, *economic considerations,* and caregiver and family experiences" (emphasis added).[47] Thus, even if costs were not drivers of patient health outcomes, physicians should consider them when recommending treatments or making outright treatment decisions. Oncology has come the farthest in this sense, with scholars proposing that "financial health" be a routine part of the clinical assessment and developing instruments to measure "distress," as a sixth vital sign after pain.[48]

More generally, I think that physicians think of themselves as fiduciaries, who have duties to incorporate patient-cost considerations into their recommendations for their client-patients. This would include, for example, not wasting their patients' money by recommending expensive care that lacks proven benefits or referring them to higher-cost providers whose services are indistinguishable from lower-cost providers. Although the doctor-patient relationship is the paradigm example of a fiduciary relationship, with dependency and vulnerability at its core, courts have generally not actually applied the heightened standards of conduct typically inferred by the term.[49] Even if courts begin to take the fiduciary concept more seriously in this context, it will nonetheless often be difficult for a patient to recover on such a breach, where the difference in price is a few hundred dollars. These sorts of domains are precisely where administrative regulation may be necessary.

In harder cases, a physician might need to recommend a lower-cost treatment, even if it would not be optimal for a wealthier patient. Admittedly, this is a difficult conversation to have. I would not want my doctor to say, "I usually recommend treatment X, but since your insurance imposes such a large out-of-pocket exposure, treatment Y may be a better choice for you." Yet this is precisely the sort of conversation that cost-exposure policies seek to encourage.

For a practical example, I have argued that if we are going to retain substantial cost exposure in the United States, even for patients with modest means, then we may need to import some of the lower-cost medical procedures used elsewhere in the world. In India, for example, cataracts are treated with a manual eye surgery costing $15, in contrast to the $3,500 phacoemulsification surgery used in the United States.[50] Although the high-tech and expensive approach promises slightly better outcomes, the manual procedure is undoubtedly better than nothing for patients with gigantic and unaffordable cost exposures. Less exotically, there are many situations where older generic drugs actually have the strongest evidentiary basis for safety and efficacy, but clinicians may be excited to try newer drugs, often in contexts where there is little or no reliable evidence that they are in fact any better. For poorer patients with large cost exposures, such novel treatments may be contraindicated.

It may seem unfair for physicians to recommend one treatment for a wealthy person (or one with comprehensive insurance) but recommend another treatment for a poor person (or one with thin insurance). We might well believe that there is a fundamental human right to health or believe that we owe more to our fellow citizens, points I have developed in Chapter 4. Nonetheless, when at the bedside of a sick patient who has a given health insurance policy, it does little good for a physician to pine for an altogether different healthcare system any more than it does to wish the patient did not have the disease in the first place.

In sum, the patient's ability to pay for procedures, drugs, and medical devices should be a part of the reasonable physician's medical evaluation. If a physician prescribes an expensive patented drug, which the patient ultimately stops buying due to cost, then when she suffers a bad outcome, a jury may well find that the physician's recommendation was unreasonable. If the physician had some ulterior motive for favoring the expensive treatment (e.g., a financial relationship with the drug company), the jury should hear about this too. As long as we retain a policy regime of substantial cost exposure, then the exposed costs of care are a material factor, which should shape the reasonable judgment of a physician.

## TAILORING TO VALUE

A second major category of reforms begins with the observation that cost exposure has largely been deployed indiscriminately, like a generalized tax on healthcare consumption. Instead, it should be tailored to the value of the healthcare consumed.

In the United States, we have become so hyperaware of our inflated healthcare spending that it seems as if our primary policy goal is to reduce spending for its own sake. But there are a wide range of healthcare products and services where a rational policymaker would actually want to encourage consumption. For example, cholesterol drugs are very commonly prescribed to those with a heart disease risk, because the drugs have been proven to reduce cardiac events and mortality. Thus, we generally want patients to comply with their physicians' prescriptions and take their cholesterol drugs—it's good for them and good for their insurers and those of us who pay those premiums and taxes.

Yet cost exposure can undermine this goal. In a major research study of 17,183 patients with newly diagnosed health problems, Matthew Solomon and colleagues found that for every $10 increase in copayments, medication compliance fell by 5 percentage points.[51] As drug compliance fell, patients were instead more likely to use expensive medical services, such as hospitalizations and emergency departments. The RAND Corporation, which conducted much of this work, estimated that "reducing the co-payment for these drugs to zero would lower hospitalizations by about 80,000 to 90,000 per year and emergency department visits by 30,000 to 35,000; the reductions would generate estimated aggregate savings of more than $1 billion annually."[52]

In Chapters 1 and 2, I reviewed other evidence showing that indiscriminate cost exposure cuts healthcare consumption indiscriminately—cutting out good and bad healthcare alike. Instead of thinking of cost exposure vaguely as a patient's responsibility—a flat fee or percentage of the cost—we should instead think of cost exposure as a form of choice architecture. If we use it at all, we should use it intelligently to nudge patients toward valuable care and away from poor care.

## Value-Based Insurance Design

Over the last two decades, several groups of researchers have been working on selective reductions or eliminations of cost exposure for particular high-value procedures. This movement has been called value-based insurance design (VBID). Initial work used computer simulations and models, based on historical insurance claims databases, and tested interventions like providing full insurance coverage for drugs after patients suffered heart attacks. One research team predicted that such a reform (aka giving away drugs) could save lives and reduce overall health spending by $2,500 per patient.[53] Another simulation focused on patients taking cholesterol drugs and considered the possibility of eliminating copays for high- and medium-risk patients (and offsetting it with increases on low-risk patients, to maintain par overall).[54]

More recently, employers have begun to implement VBID policies, which allows more rigorous empirical analysis. Pitney Bowes has been one of the most innovative employers in this space. For one study, it reduced copays for statins by 97%, which increased adherence significantly.[55] Several other studies of targeted cost-exposure reductions have likewise found behavioral improvements, and potentially health improvements.[56] However, this body of research is still in its infancy, and not every study has been extensive or long enough to document overall financial savings.

Plus, as one of the leading VBID research teams explains, it may be hard for any particular employer (or health insurer) to recoup the savings, even if it is real. "Although VBID may reduce aggregate healthcare spending by avoiding expensive exacerbations and complications, the financial impact on the employer is less obvious."[57] The insurance plan will take on more of the drug costs on the front end, but "a significant part of the savings in the form of avoided complications might go to Medicare once the patient retires. As long as health insurance is largely employer-based, there will be an inherent divide between employer healthcare spending and aggregate spending on a population level."[58]

This sort of collective-action problem is precisely the sort of situation that demands a role for government. For similar reasons, the 2010 ACA prohibited cost exposure for certain preventative services, including an annual wellness visit with physicians. A broader strategy could prohibit cost exposure for any procedure that is known to provide good value to patients, or if we only care about the financial impacts, to any procedure that is known to be cost-effective.

At the very least, Congress could eliminate its bias toward cost exposure. Presently, there are tax advantages (the ability to create a health savings account) linked to having a health insurance plan with a high deductible. Such a deductible can, however, interfere with the management of a chronic disease. In 2016, a bipartisan group of representatives in the U.S. Congress introduced H.R. 5652, a bill that would have permitted health plans to eliminate deductibles for medical management of chronic diseases, while still enjoying the tax advantages of being a high-deductible health plan. The bill died in committee, but similar legislation was introduced again in 2018. If we are going to continue to have cost exposure as a prominent part of U.S. health policy, these sorts of tailoring efforts are necessary and worthwhile.

Still, studies and field trials of VBID policies have been largely limited to prescription drugs linked to certain chronic illnesses, like diabetes or heart disease. These diseases are, of course, huge drivers of mortality, morbidity, and cost in our healthcare system. But we should think more broadly about value when designing patient cost-exposure policies.

### Cost-Exposure Calibration

For pharmaceuticals, an insurer will typically impose a relatively low out-of-pocket cost (say, $15) for a generic drug, and impose the highest copay on a class of "nonpreferred" patented drugs (say, $150), with a group of preferred drugs in the middle. Almost all people (91%) who receive healthcare from employers are in such tiered plans,[59] and this tactic is also common for Medicare drug plans.[60] Tiering is a form of value-based insurance. In these cases, the differential cost exposure steers a patient toward a drug that is expected to have the same benefit, but a lower cost both for the insurer and for the patient paying out-of-pocket. Here, let's outline several ways we can expand beyond the current value-based insurance innovations.

*Table 5.1*   Summary of Proposed Value-Based Reforms for Cost Exposure

| Policy for Cost Exposure | Coverage |
| --- | --- |
| Negative | Proven services that reduce health spending overall (e.g., chronic disease management, or choice of a less expensive treatment among a range of comparable options) |
| None | Services for which we have strong evidence of efficacy (e.g., U.S. Preventive Services Task Force Grades A or B, or national practice guidelines graded A or B) |
| Minimal | Services recommended by an unconflicted, licensed healthcare provider and approved by the Food and Drug Administration (FDA) for the specific use (where applicable) |
| Full | Services recommended by conflicted professionals and / or not specifically approved by the FDA for the prescribed indication (e.g., off-label) |

Physician and legal scholar David Orentlicher has expressed the motivating concept simply: "As a general matter, heath care policy should remove obstacles to desired behavior while erecting obstacles to undesired behavior."[61] These reforms include moving toward negative cost exposure, on the one hand, to eliminating or reducing cost exposures more broadly on the other hand. I will also argue for potentially enhancing cost exposure for some healthcare where we may suspect it lacks good value. These are summarized in Table 5.1.

First the idea of "negative" cost exposure suggests that rather than asking patients to contribute out-of-pocket for the healthcare they consume, in some cases we should actually pay patients to consume less expensive care. Ezekiel Emanuel, who was one of President Obama's key healthcare advisors, has written with Harald Schmidt to develop an idea that they call "inclusive shared savings." Their proposal "differs from value-based insurance design, which merely seeks to decrease or eliminate out-of-pocket costs. Inclusive shared savings financially rewards patients for selecting less costly but equally effective treatments."[62] As a precedent, Emanuel and Schmidt cite hotels that give customers a $5 credit if they decline housekeeping, and a Medicare demonstration project, in which patients were paid $275 each to receive care through the project. As a prime example, the authors point to a range of options for treating gastric cancer, where there happens to have recently been a large randomized trial showing that none of the treatments had a general efficacy advantage over the others. Why not use incentives to nudge patients toward at least trying the cheaper one first?

A related strategy is called "reference pricing." In a domain where there are equally good services but wildly different prices, an insurer can agree to pay for the lower-cost provider as a "reference price." If the patient prefers a higher-cost provider they pay the difference out of pocket. Because it guarantees access to care, this is a much more elegant solution compared to simply jacking up deductibles or copay rates, and has in fact been shown to be about three times more effective.[63]

A National Academies committee has recommended that federal health insurance plans reduce or eliminate cost exposure whenever there is evidence that adherence to a course of treatment can reduce the overall costs of care.[64] This is simply a rational move for a payor. Let's not discourage the care that should be encouraged. For example, epilepsy is one of many chronic diseases where the FDA has approved valuable drugs and where physicians can reliably determine which patients would benefit from them. When patients fail to take their drugs, bad things happen not just for the patients but for the payors. Scholars have estimated that nonadherence in this domain costs $1,500 in healthcare costs, even after accounting for the cost savings of not paying for the drugs.[65] Even a nominal copay can prevent some patients from beginning the drug regimen recommended by their doctor.[66] In these sorts of domains, policymakers should routinely waive patient cost-exposures, and perhaps also give patients other incentives to consume their medications.

A broader value-based approach to cost exposure could be worthwhile, but it would require a metric for defining value. Presently, the insurers often take a binary approach to coverage—either a treatment is covered as medically necessary, which triggers the contractual coverage requirement and the standard cost-exposure profile (say, a 20% coinsurance rate), or the insurer refuses to cover the treatment altogether (which is equivalent to a 100% coinsurance rate). The coverage determinations track a more fundamental epistemic assessment, generated by scientific research or at least expert opinion, making inferences from anecdotes and related research about whether a treatment is likely to work for the patient's disease. If so, the insurer considers it medically necessary and thus covers it.

However, there is a wide range of epistemic confidence; our knowledge about the efficacy of treatments is not binary. The U.S. Preventive Services

Task Force (USPSTF) assigns letter grades (A, B, C, or D) for each service that it evaluates.[67] These grades track both the likely benefit of a service and our epistemic confidence that the benefit is real. Scores of A or B imply that there is decent confidence of at least a moderate benefit, so a service should be provided widely. A grade of C suggests only moderate evidence and a small benefit, so the USPSTF suggests that the service be provided only based on physician judgment and patient preferences. Services with a grade of D should be discouraged, given "moderate or high certainty that the service has no net benefit or that the harms outweigh the benefits."

The ACA depends on the USPSTF (and a few other agencies) to define which preventative services should be immune from cost exposure.[68] So, for example, the law now requires that women age fifty to seventy-four receive free biennial breast cancer screenings (because the USPSTF gives the procedure a B), but insurers may make younger women pay out-of-pocket (because the USPSTF gives the procedure lower grades for them).[69] A 2019 Health Affairs study of employers that switched to high-deductible health plans, showed that patients with high deductibles were delayed by 1.6 months in getting breast imaging, 2.7 months to first biopsy, 6.6 months to breast cancer diagnosis, and 8.7 months to first chemotherapy.[70] This suggests that we need a much more comprehensive approach to cost exposure waivers, at every stage of the healthcare cascade, from screening to treatment.

Other countries use elaborate and assumption-ridden formulae for calculating the cost-effectiveness of each treatment, and some have proposed using these same mechanisms to adjust cost exposure in the United States.[71] But I think national practice guidelines provide a more straightforward approach, since they represent our best knowledge about appropriate medical care. In this domain, it is hard to argue cogently in favor of a cost exposure to cause patients to second-guess their providers. For example, imaging is a major driver of healthcare costs, and nonspecific low-back pain is a particularly elusive ailment. It would be terribly wasteful if every patient who complained to their physician about a sore back was rushed off to get an MRI. Thus, it makes some sense to expose patients to some of these costs, to put a small thumb on the scale against overuse. However, there are specific situations where imaging is highly appropriate. One national practice guideline developed by an expert committee and published in the *Annals of*

*Internal Medicine* recommends that if a physical exam shows two signs of neurological impingement, then a physician should indeed send the patient for imaging.[72] The failure to diagnose the nerve impingement expeditiously, and then resolve it with surgery, could lead to permanent disability. In this domain, patient cost exposure is unhelpful and indeed deleterious, if it drives some patients away from the imaging they need. A rational health insurance designer would rely on this guideline to waive cost exposure in this setting.

Notably, the strength of national practice guidelines vary, with the quality of the evidence found in systematic reviews. Analogous to the USPSTF rating system, scholars have developed a mechanism for grading the strength of national guidelines, from A (when the guideline is based on at least one randomized controlled trial) to B (when based on an extrapolation from a randomized trial or a quasi-experimental study), down to grades C or D (when based on descriptive studies or mere expert opinion).[73] Unfortunately, there are too few of the As and Bs. A 2009 *Journal of the American Medical Association* (*JAMA*) review found that of 2,711 practice recommendations issued by the American College of Cardiology and the American Heart Association, only 11% could be considered Grade A.[74] I would recommend that insurers eliminate cost exposure for treatments supported by a national practice guideline graded A or B, and reduce it substantially for care supported by less rigorous guidelines. Any of these are better than the mere opinion of a single prescribing physician.

Let me address a counterargument. In addition to reducing wasteful care, cost exposure also serves a different policy goal: to cause patients to be price-sensitive when selecting their healthcare provider, and to thereby force providers to compete on price. (This argument applies to coinsurance, which exposes patients to a portion of the cost but does not apply to fixed copays, e.g., $50 per office visit.) Unfortunately, when exposed to coinsurance, patients do very little price-shopping in this way.[75] People apparently do not think about healthcare purchases in the same ways that they think about their purchases of toilet paper or televisions.

As we think about whether to use cost exposure to deter healthcare consumption, it is worthwhile to remember that most healthcare is already passing through two key gateways prior to being covered by insurance. First, before a patient can consume an expensive procedure, it must be recommended by a physician or other licensed provider, who has years of education

and training and has met with the patient, and often conducted preliminary tests to determine what care would be appropriate. At least in cases
where the physician is putatively acting with the patients' best interests in
mind—rather than on the basis of the physician's own conflicting interests,
policy makers should defer to that expert's judgment.

Moreover, the drugs and devices being used in this recommended care
have already survived a regulatory gauntlet for achieving approval from the
Food and Drug Administration (FDA). In this way, our healthcare system
has already lopped off the worst of the low-value healthcare that could otherwise be consumed.

To the extent that we are attempting to use cost exposure to affect consumption behavior, we are doing so in the subset of care that has survived
these initial cuts. For this reason, we should flip the default rule. Impose, at
most, minimal cost exposure for the vast domains of healthcare that is recommended by an unconflicted and licensed physician and approved by the
FDA for the patient's specific condition.

In this vein, some states are legislating limits to cost exposure for insulin
for the management of diabetes. Colorado says that patients should not have
to pay more than $100 out of pocket.[76] I am all for helping diabetics adhere
to their drugs and thereby avoid neuropathy and amputation; using huge cost
exposures to reduce consumption of insulin was both stupid and heartless.
Scholars have estimated that the United States spends more than $5 billion
annually as a result of non-adherence to diabetes drugs, and a big portion of
that is likely due to cost exposure policies.[77]

To be sure, this legislative attack on insulin cost exposure reflects the un-
raveling of the cost exposure consensus. But more generally, this is a ludi-
crous way to set health policy—having legislatures tailor cost exposures for
one drug class at a time. A 2018 systematic review covered seventy-nine
studies across 14 disease groups, and found that nonadherence to prescribed
drugs costs health systems between $5271 and $52,341 per patient.[78] These
are not domains where we want cost exposures to reduce consumption of
FDA-approved drugs recommended by our licensed physicians.

There is nonetheless a domain where none of these reassurances apply.
The healthcare is not shown to reduce spending overall, not recommended
by national practice guidelines, and not recommended by an unconflicted
physician or approved by the FDA for the patient's specific condition. Unfortunately, as we will see in greater detail in the next Chapter, conflicted

physicians and off-label prescribing are both ubiquitous. Thus, it may be appropriate for health policy to impose cost exposure on patients in the hopes that they will second-guess the treatment. Even better? As I will argue in the next chapter, let's fix the underlying problems.

For now however, cost exposure could be heightened especially in domains where a given treatment or other intervention has been affirmatively repudiated by the literature. For example, the American Society of Clinical Oncology created a Value Task Force, which then developed consensus documents identifying certain "standard" clinical practices that provided no patient benefit.[79] More broadly, the American Board of Internal Medicine has promoted a "Choosing Wisely" campaign to "promote conversations between patients and clinicians," about low-value healthcare.[80] We might question whether patient cost exposure is the best way to get physicians to stop providing such low value healthcare, but it is at least targeting the domain of healthcare that needs to be targeted.

## TAILORING TO THE ABILITY TO PAY

First though, if cost exposure is to have any chance of really working for Americans, we must consider another fundamental reform. Paracelsus was a sixteenth-century physician, astrologer, and alchemist, who pioneered the use of chemistry as a branch of medicine. Arsenic was then known as a poison, but Paracelsus used it as a cure for certain parasites, and indeed it is still used as such today. But the dose is key to killing the parasite while saving the patient. He wrote, "In all things there is a poison, and there is nothing without a poison. It depends only upon the dose whether a poison is poison or not."[81] For a medicine, the right dose is the one that achieves the purposes of securing a health outcome while minimizing the adverse side effects.

Insurance can be seen similarly, and it can likewise be dosed by adjusting the cost-exposure, more or less. As we have seen, some cost exposure might be harmless, but as we have also seen, too much can defeat the core purposes of insurance, causing more harm than good. In the prior section, we considered dosing cost exposure to each treatment, but here let's consider dosing it to each patient.

Although deductibles, copays, and coinsurance are all important, the annual cap on cost exposure is worth special attention, because it presents the worst-case scenario for patients, which threatens to undermine the risk-protecting and access-guaranteeing functions of insurance, if set inappropriately. On this prominent dimension of cost exposure, the United States—with its common plans leaving families exposed to $5,000 per year, and a law that allows family exposure up to $15,800—is out of proportion with the rest of the world. Norway, for example, has an annual cap equal to US$223.[82] In Sweden, the cap is equal to US$123 for health services and US$246 for drugs.[83] Libertarians like to point to Switzerland as having a predominantly private healthcare delivery system that relies on patient cost exposure.[84] Although it is a relatively wealthy country, it nonetheless caps cost exposure equal to US$549 after the US$235 deductible.[85] In contrast, in the United States, caps are more than 10 times higher for individuals, and 20 times higher for families. Imagine if hospitals in the United States were giving chemotherapy at 20 times the dose that patients received in Switzerland!

As stark as these international comparisons can be, it makes little sense to set the same dose of cost exposure for every family *within* a country. Those with substantial income and assets may be able to bear a large cost exposure, unlike families of more modest means. As we saw in Chapter 4, wealthier families can satisfy the U.S. cap with only 8% of their income, so even these remarkably high U.S. caps are probably not too high for them. Meanwhile, lower-middle-class U.S. families face a risk of losing one-third or more of their income before hitting these caps. This disparity means that cost exposure is failing to really deter care by higher-income patients (leaving them "overinsured"), but such incomplete insurance is failing to really protect those at the lower end (leaving them "underinsured").

We have focused on the underinsurance problem in this book, but under the standard theory of moral hazard reviewed in Chapter 1, those who are overinsured will also be inclined to consume wasteful healthcare. There is some evidence of this happening. For example, in one recent study of 41,000 thyroid cancer cases in the United States, among fully insured patients, those who appeared to be wealthier were more likely to get a cancer diagnosis. Does money cause cancer? More likely, "overinsurance could increase access to imaging and biopsy for cancer screening and evaluation of benign thyroid conditions," which can lead to "risk for avoidable surgical complications, lifetime thyroid replacement therapy and perhaps secondary malignancies."[86] Chapter 4 showed the injustice of false equality when a per capita cost exposure prevents poorer citizens from accessing a decent minimum of health-care, but such a policy also showers so much "free" healthcare on wealthier individuals that it turns out to hurt them as well.

The solution is to tailor cost-exposure burdens to each beneficiary's ability to pay; we must titrate the dose for each patient. By scaling cost exposure to income, we can refine the behavioral function of cost exposure, helping avoid false negatives (where patients decline valuable care) and false positives (where patients consume wasteful care). We can also eliminate any injustice in which poorer individuals must pay health insurance premiums (implicitly through foregone wages) but are unable to actually access healthcare due to prohibi-tive levels of cost exposure. As we saw there, the current per-head cost-exposure mechanism implicitly redistributes to wealthier workers, who also pay premiums but are not deterred from consuming. Let's explore how that might work.

### Income Scaling

There was a time when physicians charged patients on a sliding scale based on someone's ability to pay. As Carl Schneider and Mark Hall have chroni-cled, "In 1931, one doctor's median fee for treating acute diabetes was $402, but his fees ranged almost fivefold, from $232 to $1052; X-ray treatments for severe acne could cost from $70 to $210.79. For a major operation, surgeons often charged patients one month's salary."[87] More recently, when physicians have waived copayments for their poorer patients, insurers have refused to pay for the healthcare at all.[88]

Nonetheless for insurance design, the idea of income scaling has been around since at least the 1970s, when economist Martin Feldstein argued for a government-sponsored health insurance system, which would include "an annual direct expense limit (i.e., deductible) that increased with family income."[89] Feldstein was President Reagan's chairman of the Council of Eco-nomic Advisers, and after coming to Harvard, he later fleshed out such a proposal with MIT economist Jonathan Gruber, who would become a chief advisor to President Obama's healthcare reform team.[90] In a 2006 paper looking back on the famous RAND Health Insurance Experiment (HIE), which included such a feature, Gruber argued that, "ideally, such income-related cost-sharing limits should be incorporated into health insurance more broadly."[91] He illustrated how a 5% of income cap on cost exposure could significantly improve coverage.

It is worth looking more closely at how the famous RAND HIE included a $1,000 "stop-loss" cap on cost exposure (equal to $4,308 in 2018) but scaled that cap downward for lower-income participants, based on 5%, 10%, or 15% of annual income, depending on the experimental condition.[92] While the study has been a cornerstone of health policy, this particular feature has received scant attention. Frankly, it is hard to generalize about the policy outcomes for current unscaled health insurance from such a scaled experiment. For our purposes, however, RAND HIE proves feasibility of scaling.

The concept also got a boost by the 2010 ACA, which implemented a form of income scaling for a relatively small sector of the insurance market: those households that purchase health insurance on the individual exchanges (rather than through employers or a federal program). These caps reduce cost exposure by two-thirds, one-half, or one-third for poorer individuals (up to 250% of the poverty level).[93] Insurers were supposed to be reimbursed by the federal government for these foregone revenues. These payments became the subject of legal and political battles, with the Trump administration refusing to pay insurers. As an alternative, insurers raised premiums in a way that garnered additional federal subsidies of premiums instead, creating a roundabout way to get reimbursed for the cost-exposure reductions.[94] This may be a workable solution for now. Nonetheless, only 11.8 million Americans are covered by the exchanges; about half of them received income-based cost-exposure reductions.[95]

The U.S. healthcare system shunts the poorest individuals into the Medicaid program, and within Medicaid there is only nominal or sometimes income-tiered cost exposure. So this creates an overall form of income scaling in the U.S. economy. For hospital and doctor bills, Medicare has no cap on cost exposure at all, but Congress has provided that Medicaid benefits can be used toward Medicare cost-exposure burdens, for "dual-eligibles" who are enrolled in both programs.[96] The drug benefit in Medicare Part D also uses an income and wealth test to limit cost-exposure burdens for the poorest enrollees.[97] So, here again, we see a form of scaling for many patients.

Nonetheless, the individual market, Medicaid, and Medicare do not cover the vast majority of working-age Americans—157 million—who get their health insurance from employers.[98] Oddly, for this market, the ACA imposed a flat $15,800 cap on cost exposure per household, rather than scaling to income. One ad hoc approach to scaling has been offered by pharmaceutical companies offering discount cards or "copay assistance," imperfectly targeted to lower-income patients. Employers have actually resisted these efforts to reduce effective cost exposure.[99]

Interestingly, employers could relatively easily scale cost exposure to each worker's income, as that number is readily knowable by the employer, who pays those wages. An employer would only need to multiply the wages by a simple calculation (e.g., 6%) in order to impose a new cap on overall cost exposure. One approach would be for an employer to use their current insurance plan's per capita cap on exposure (say $5,000) as a percentage of the median employee's salary (say $60,000), and scale that percentage both upward and downward, thereby maintaining the same level of aggregate cost exposure.[100]

The scaling idea gained further traction in 2016 when the American College of Physicians, with 148,000 members, released a report discussing the growing financial burdens faced by patients. The group calls for a range of reforms, including "income-adjusted cost-sharing approaches that reduce or directly subsidize the expected out-of-pocket contribution of lower-income workers to avoid creating a barrier to their obtaining needed care."[101] In the run for president, both Donald Trump and Hillary Clinton highlighted the problem of onerous cost exposure, and Clinton proposed a specific plan to create progressive refundable tax credits for people who spend more than 5% of their income out-of-pocket.[102]

Of course, income is a very rough proxy for ability to pay. We might, for example, want to expose younger people to greater costs, since they may have longer to pay them back, while a large cost late in life could be devastating.[103] Or perhaps larger families should have lower caps, given the other expenses they bear. When wrestling with the parallel question of how to scale premiums, Harvard health economist Kathy Swartz has confessed, "It is difficult to judge people's ability to afford a necessity like health insurance on the basis of simple factors such as income, age, number and age of family members, and their health status [along with] . . . 'deserving' exceptions. . . . I grudgingly began to realize that a simple percent-of-income rule was more practical and avoided moral debates that were sure to arise."[104] I agree. Compared to the per-head cap that we now have in place, an income-scaled cap is a radical improvement. We would gain little by a more complicated scheme.

## Scaling Upward

So far, most of these reforms and proposals have focused only on scaling downward to reduce cost exposure for poorer families. Strikingly, however, this mechanism could also substantially *increase* cost exposure for wealthier Americans, potentially making it self-financing. And, because incomes are highly skewed toward the wealthy, there is perhaps a lot more potential for upward scaling. For example, a 6% income cap on annual cost exposure could peg middle-income cost exposure around $3,000 per year and reduce exposure by another $1,000 in the next lower quintile. However, the cap would more than triple for those in the highest income quintile, as the cap increases to $11,000.[105] Because the cap would scale with a skewed income distribution, it could in fact increase cost exposure overall, and thus reduce premiums, even while improving coverage for poorer Americans.

Upward scaling also allows cost exposure to target the high-cost care that really matters to aggregate health spending. As Nobel laureate Paul Krugman and economist Robin Wells have argued, "When you think of the problem of health care costs, you shouldn't envision visits to the family physician to talk about a sore throat; you should think about coronary bypass operations, dialysis, and chemotherapy."[106] They go on to explain why patient cost exposure cannot be a real solution to wasteful health spending, because "nobody is proposing a consumer-directed health care plan that would force individuals to pay a large share of extreme medical expenses, such as the costs of chemotherapy, out of pocket."[107]

That is precisely what I am proposing at least for the wealthiest fifth, or maybe two-fifths, of Americans who can afford to do so. If we are going to keep cost exposure as a policy mechanism, then we should at least apply it to the patients who can afford it and to the treatments that drive aggregate health spending.

Given that most employers' cost-exposure caps are well below the current $15,800 allowed under federal law, there is substantial room to scale upward. To capture even more of the benefits of this reform, Congress could eliminate the current cap and replace it with an income-scaled cap that goes up indefinitely. I am not worried about law firm partners and tech CEOs having too much cost exposure, and it is unclear why current law protects them.

Scaling could be rational for employers, as it reduces costs of insurance overall, by shifting more of the risk back to their higher-paid employees who can bear it. In a 1985 survey, a pair of business school professors found that 7% of employers had income-scaling deductibles.[108] In the early 1990s, income scaling got its first full scholarly article, when UCLA health economist Thomas Rice and Kenneth Thorpe, who served in the Clinton administration, proposed scaling in the employer-based insurance market.[109] They also noted that about 2%–3% of employers were then using simple forms of scaling.[110]

My own research has revealed a few such cases. Pitney Bowes modified one of its health plans in 2011 so that it "sets the deductible, out-of-pocket maximum and company contribution based on salary. Hourly workers, for example, have a $1,500 deductible and $3,000 out-of-pocket maximum, while employees at the director level or higher have a $2,500 deductible and $5,000 out-of-pocket maximum."[111] Harvard University uses income scaling to reimburse employees for out-of-pocket costs, effectively capping the exposure of their lowest-paid workers at $600 per family and higher-paid workers at $4,000.[112]

Why haven't more employers already embraced scaling? Well, the executives who choose health insurance policies would perhaps rather have their healthcare costs covered by insurance, whose premiums are paid by foregone wages of the whole workforce. They can easily afford their copays and deductibles, and have no interest in making them larger. If lower paid workers have trouble accessing care, that is their problem. But, federal employee benefits law, known as ERISA, provides that employees can only enjoy nontaxable health coverage as long as "the benefits provided under the plan do not discriminate in favor of participants who are highly compensated individuals."[113] Otherwise, top-paid employees would reduce their taxable salaries to zero, but give themselves nontaxable cars, homes, and restaurant budgets as employment benefits instead. I have argued that unscaled cost exposure is actually illegal under these same provisions.[114]

Let me explain the legal analysis. We do not buy insurance for its own sake. In practical terms, for a sick employee, the insured healthcare is the employment benefit, and without paying the access fee of cost exposure, the employee does not get the benefit. If the cost exposure allows higher-paid employees to access the benefit more than lower-paid employees, the policy discriminates against the latter group. Indeed, in its regulations about this rule, the IRS has said, "Not only must a plan not discriminate on its face in providing benefits in favor of highly compensated individuals, the plan also must not discriminate in favor of such employees in actual operation."[115] That's precisely what per-capita cost exposure does. Duke law professors Barak Richman and Clark Havighurst have described the situation as a "systematic inequity" where "health insurance premiums paid on behalf of lower-income members go to subsidize the costly consumption habits of those with higher incomes."[116]

Federal law allows a private cause of action, so in theory any employee could go to court to force their employer to adopt scaling (or perhaps dramatically reduce or eliminate cost exposure, so it did not serve as a barrier for lower-income employees) if the employer preferred.[117] Concededly, I am making a fairly radical claim that, if true, would undermine a widespread economic practice in the United States—per capita cost exposure. Nonetheless, courts have been willing to strike down such long-standing policies that were facially equal, but turned out to have a discriminatory effect in practice. In the landmark race discrimination case of *Duke Power v. Griggs,* the court struck down the practice of "requiring a high school education or passing of a standardized general intelligence test as a condition of employment," which the firm had been doing for more than a decade.[118] Congress later endorsed the Court's "disparate impact" theory, codifying it into statute.[119] Similarly here, unscaled cost exposure has disparate impact on lower-income workers, who are supposed to be protected by the tax code. The courts are an attractive avenue for pushing this reform, because Congress may wrestle with tricky political questions.

I would suggest that wealthier individuals be allowed to purchase supplemental health insurance, not unlike plans currently offered to Medicare beneficiaries. But since these insurance policies are not necessary to guarantee access to care, they should not be tax-advantaged in the same way. Alternatively, as suggested in the next chapter, it could be worthwhile to simply do away with substantial cost exposure for the wealthy and poor alike and focus on other strategies for reducing wasteful health expenditures.

Here is a final word on implementation. I have suggested that the patient's annual cost-exposure maximum be scaled, because it is both simple and reflects the aggregate risk that a patient can bear, which is so directly linked to her ability to pay. In principle all the cost-exposure features could be income-scaled, from deductibles to copays to coinsurance. Healthcare providers already must consult payor databases to figure out how much patients owe for each transaction, and thus the databases need only become somewhat more dynamic. If that is still challenging, Lawrence has compellingly argued that we should switch to a model where out-of-pocket payments are made to the insurer, rather than the provider.[120]

## Paying Patients

As a policy solution, it's now clear that cost exposure has an Achilles heel. In the modern world of exorbitant healthcare costs, which can exceed six figures, patients often just do not have the funds to pay a substantial portion. Indeed, Chapter 1 showed that access to otherwise unaffordable care is one of the primary reasons we purchase health insurance in the first place. Accordingly, to preserve access, health insurance plans cap cost exposure. While the cap protects patients, it also neuters the cost-exposure policy. Simple scaling will do a better job of redistributing those caps across the population, but caps will remain, stymieing cost exposure for the large-dollar care that drives aggregate health spending.

If we thought that cost exposure was nonetheless valuable even for very high-cost care, then we will need even more radical solutions for all but the wealthiest patients. One such approach would be to maintain a cost exposure but actually pay patients in cash (or check) the amount needed to meet that exposure, if they so choose. In this way, cost exposure can be applied to large-dollar healthcare without being a barrier to that healthcare.

Paying patients in this way sounds radical, but it is really just a form of "indemnity" insurance, which is familiar in other domains such as homeowner's insurance. When a risk materializes (e.g., a storm damages the siding on your home), the indemnity insurer sends a check for the cost of the damage. The homeowner can then choose whether and how to repair the damage and, if so, which repair company provides the best bargain of service, convenience, and price. In contrast, health insurance has traditionally provided only an "in-kind" benefit, paid to the provider rather than the beneficiary. This design is peculiar, when we stop to think about it. We can instead pay (some of) the benefit to the beneficiary.

In Chapter 1, we used indemnity insurance as a conceptual tool for understanding traditional insurance. Scholars have long assumed that it would be "impossible" to actually write health insurance contracts in the form of indemnities, because it is too hard to measure the severity of illness or predict the consequent need for care, the necessary predicates for setting an indemnity amount.[121] But what about a partial indemnity? Suppose that, when a patient is eligible for very expensive healthcare (e.g., an expensive cancer drug costing upward of $100,000) the insurer instead paid an arbitrarily sized part (say, $10,000) of the insurance benefit as an indemnity. The insurer would withhold the remainder ($90,000) to be paid in-kind to the provider (as in traditional health insurance), but only if the patient chooses to consume that expensive healthcare (as in traditional health insurance). If the patient instead declines the care, he or she can save or spend the $10,000 on anything else. The insurer saves the balance ($90,000).

In prior work, my coauthors and I called this a "split benefit," because it divides the health insurance benefit payment between the provider and the patient, rather than simply paying it to the provider.[122] In its economic function, the split benefit is not unlike a traditional copay. Once the patient receives the partial indemnity, then she has the same skin in the game that she would have if she were paying from her own funds, because these now *are* her own funds, fully fungible with anything else she may prefer to do with the money. She might prefer to stick with lower-cost treatment options and put the money in savings for her children's education, for example. Unlike a traditional cost exposure, however, the split benefit guarantees healthcare access; a patient need not decline the care or go into debilitating levels of debt to meet her out-of-pocket payment.

In recent years, there has been increasing interest in paying patients to promote their own health, whether it is to stop smoking or perhaps choose less expensive healthcare options.[123] Law professor Govind Persad has pulled together many of these examples, which often involve paying patients to consume *more* valuable care, or at least purchase the care from a particular pharmacist, dentist, or other provider.[124]

But the split benefit is distinctive and has not yet been used in the field. Preliminary experiments have randomized people to imagine themselves in various scenarios, with or without split benefits, and the predicted behaviors were promising.[125] If properly targeted to high-cost, low-value healthcare, the split benefit may well reduce healthcare spending, without impinging on patient choice and access, like traditional cost exposures.

This is a good moment to revisit my larger normative framework for this book, because the split benefit nicely crystallizes these points. As we have seen, a lot of healthcare is either wasteful or epistemically ambiguous—from a policy perspective, we do not know for a particular patient whether a given healthcare expenditure really is worthwhile given its cost. That's why we defer to patients and physicians in the first place. Giving patients a reason to stop and weigh those costs—a meaningful choice—is not necessarily a bad thing. However, the book has also been critical of current cost-exposure mechanisms, because they undermine access to care, effectively discriminating against many Americans who simply cannot afford to pay a substantial portion of their own healthcare costs, without the benefit of insurance. The split benefit solves this latter problem, while continuing to serve the former goal.

I have also argued that, aside from the access problems, cost exposure creates other problems for the experience and meaning of healthcare, potentially commodifying our bodies and turning the treatment relationship into a crude quid pro quo. Admittedly, the split benefit would seem to take these problems to their extreme, almost bribing patients to *not* consume healthcare. It's like the highwayman's offer: "your money or your life."

The problem is exacerbated in the frequent situations where a patient cannot decide whether to consume a treatment and depends on a parent or next-of-kin to decide on her behalf. A split benefit payment could create or exacerbate a conflict of interest. Still, it is worth noting that traditional cost exposures (e.g., copays) already impose these sorts of dilemmas, since a parent stands to keep, or an adult child stands to inherit, funds that are not expended. Either way, the surrogate decision maker might prefer to keep the money. And, as we have seen, traditional cost exposure may deny access to the expensive care altogether, when it exceeds the families' ability to pay. The split avoids that fundamental problem.

The split benefit is a particularly attractive policy solution for very expensive healthcare and poorer beneficiaries, because traditional cost exposure would be properly stymied by income-based caps. However, some might worry about imposing even a split benefit on poorer patients. When a poorer patient is prescribed an expensive treatment and receives a $10,000 check from her insurer, it might be quite hard to rationalize spending the money on healthcare. After all, she could alternatively spend the money on other needs, like food or housing, which may feel more pressing. Even if we focused exclusively on health outcomes (rather than welfare generally), evidence is clear that investments in housing, diet, and education are often more effective than investments in expensive medical interventions. If the choice is hard, it is because the alternatives are attractive. Nonetheless, the split benefit could be designed to place the funds in an account with limited fungibility, such as a health savings account.

As we have seen, one of the primary functions of insurance is to guarantee access to care that would be otherwise unaffordable, and to protect someone from the risk of devastating health expenses. A split benefit serves those purposes, while also preserving the patient's options to pursue whatever other things may better promote her own welfare. Health insurance funds need not be irreversibly sunk in healthcare expenses. By freeing the funds, we can reduce an economic bias and enhance overall welfare. The split benefit may be the only way to really use a cost exposure mechanism for patients of modest means considering the very expensive sorts of healthcare that drive aggregate spending.

After rejecting a blithe laissez-faire approach, I have suggested three key considerations for the future of healthcare. These are steps we can take to improve cost exposure, if we cannot bring ourselves to abandon or dramatically reduce it. First, we should force healthcare providers to disclose cost information affirmatively and incorporate costs as one of the risks and consequences of care, to make reasonable treatment recommendations. Second, we should scale cost exposure to value, so it shapes consumer behavior in ways that serve health at reasonable cost, rather than indiscriminately pushing people away from healthcare. Finally, we should scale cost exposure to families' abilities to pay those costs. For the large-dollar care that drives most health spending, for all but the wealthiest families this will mean insubstantial cost exposure, unless we also deploy partial cash indemnities—which I call split benefits—to capture the advantages of cost exposure without impinging on patient access to care. These reforms present our best hope of making cost exposure work as a policy mechanism, if we are to continue using it as a primary part of the U.S. healthcare system.

# CHAPTER 6

# WHAT WE MUST DO

We have seen that cost exposure is aiming to solve the bugaboo problem of moral hazard; that it distracts, distorts, and complexifies healthcare decisions; that substantial exposure is largely infeasible for American families to pay out of pocket; and that it undermines our democratic equality as it erodes access to care. In Chapter 5, I leveraged a wide range of ideas that could potentially make cost exposure live up to its promise as a solution to wasteful spending. But in this chapter, I suggest that those reforms are not likely to come to fruition. Even if they do, cost exposure will still not solve the real drivers of wasteful spending. A more fundamental reform is required, and that is to simply turn away from substantial cost exposure as a primary mechanism of U.S. health policy. As leading companies and many other countries have proven, we can get more health and more satisfaction with complete insurance coverage.

---

## A TONIC OF REALISM

I am sympathetic to the reforms sketched in Chapter 5, perhaps because I have a bias toward clever solutions. There is something to be said for American ingenuity. And if we are to understand cost exposure as a policy mechanism, a fair assessment must consider not just its currently existing forms but also its best-potential instantiations.

It has also been worthwhile to specify what it *would* take to make cost exposure as effective as its proponents claim; it's a very heavy task, such that cost exposure would look quite different than it does now. And it might just work—these reforms have a solid basis in both theory and evidence. But a tonic of realism is in order.

The first suggested reform is greater transparency and disclosure of cost exposures by clinicians to patients; this is indeed a necessary predicate for patients to make intelligent rationing decisions and for a modicum of fairness. Whenever policy makers see a problem that they do not really have the will to solve, such transparency interventions become the milquetoast alternative, all too handy. Yet mere disclosure has been a consistent failure, in virtually every policy domain—from the stacks of forms we have to sign every time we go to the doctor's office to the tear-off tags on our pillows.[1] Yes, information is often better than nothing, but rarely does it get to the core problems. For healthcare costs in particular, disclosure is a remarkably complicated policy mechanism, and we have been plowing these fields for quite some time. In a 2018 study of healthcare providers, although half claimed to consider costs when ordering a medication, less than a third could accurately identify the price ranges of the drugs they ordered.[2] Driving information all the way down to frontline decision makers, in a way that is salient and feasible, is easier said than done. As we saw in Chapter 2, clinicians and patients have plenty else to worry about.

A larger concern is simply political. The transparency reforms target healthcare providers, potentially imposing burdensome disclosures and outright liability when they fail to embrace them. But healthcare providers are a remarkably powerful lobby—there are a million physicians in the United States, and they are both wealthy and highly mobilized to protect their interests in Congress and the state houses. They have done it before.[3] They would do it again. Healthcare providers would much more readily support a move to abolish substantial cost exposure, which just indiscriminately reduces consumption of the services they offer. A doctor does not go to medical school in dreams of someday being a bill collector.

The other key reforms, which involve scaling to value and to income, are also not likely to be attractive to either the incumbent industries or those who have championed cost exposure for decades. Tailoring exposure to value presumes that there will be public investments in the science necessary to determine value, and empowerment of a decision maker to adjust cost exposures accordingly. Of course, the industries of providers (drugs, devices, hospitals, physicians, and other clinicians) might well prefer to operate in a domain where their performance is not being robustly measured; nobody wants the risk of being on the losing side. Prior such technocratic aspirations to shape payments have failed precisely for this reason.[4]

And, even if it were politically feasible to create such a scorekeeping institution, the task is profoundly hard. It is one thing to identify value and eliminate cost exposure for a handful of well-defined preventative services, quite another to do so across the board, for a healthcare system that now consumes one-fifth of the U.S. economy. The Congressional Budget Office has surveyed the literature and estimates that "less than half of all medical care is based on or supported by adequate evidence about its effectiveness."[5] Similarly, former Food and Drug Administration (FDA) Commissioner Robert Califf has explained that "we don't have evidence on most things we do."[6] I suggested that we could use national practice guidelines that reflect current expert opinion. Yet physician-scholars Ismail Jatoi and Sunita Sah have recently shown that these guidelines vary wildly in their recommendations, in part because the U.S. guideline writers often have conflicts of interest or specialty biases.[7] It turns out that, when radiologists write guidelines about the appropriateness of medical imaging, they recommend lots of imaging. Same for surgeons and surgeries.

As to tailoring cost exposure to income, the concept has sound precedents in the individual health insurance markets under the Affordable Care Act (ACA). But these have come under political and legal attacks.[8] A broader reform for employer-based plans and Medicare, shifting the burden of cost exposure from poorer Americans to wealthier Americans, will face even more resistance. Is it feasible to expect wealthy individuals to pay large portions of their own healthcare costs out-of-pocket, even while poorer individuals are relying on insurance? For employer-based coverage, wealthier citizens, who also hold disproportionate power in corporations and Congress, might well prefer the status quo, which allows them to extract a tax subsidy for their expensive healthcare consumption behavior, even while locking out their lower-paid brethren who are unable to access as much healthcare. As scholars have recently acknowledged, "one potential solution would have employers shift benefit costs from low-wage workers to their higher-paid colleagues, . . . this reallocation approach hasn't appeared to attract employer interest, likely because of the potential negative impact on job satisfaction and retention among higher-wage workers."[9]

In Medicare, scaling might be considered a form of "means testing." Some have argued that Social Security and Medicare have been politically feasible and resilient, in a way that other social welfare programs have not been, because these are viewed as benefits for everyone rather than divisive "means-tested" handouts for the poor. For example, in 2011, when President Obama was considering whether to expand the use of means testing in Medicare, an AARP senior vice president objected, arguing that "Medicare is not a welfare program. Seniors pay into Medicare their entire working lives. . . . Applying a means test for their earned benefits would erode the popular support that has sustained these programs for years and made them so effective in helping older households."[10]

None of these reforms solve the problems discussed in Chapter 2, which involve the folly of relying on exhausted, stressed, distracted laypersons as rationers. Even worse, cost exposure imposes even more complexification of healthcare decisions and it commodifies our bodies and our treatment relationships. Indeed, the transparency and split benefit reforms will potentially exacerbate these problems as they make money all the more salient to patients. While smiting patients with costs only after they consume care seems inhumane and ineffective, overtly threatening them with looming costs while they try to figure out how to save their own lives might be even worse.

I hope that this book has crystallized both the problems and perils of cost exposure in a novel way. But frankly, to those following these issues closely, the fundamental problems are not altogether surprising and the necessary reforms are not all that novel. It's long been obvious that healthcare prices are opaque to patients. We have known for decades that cost exposure indiscriminately cuts care, but have only recently taken seriously the task of studying and legislating exceptions to protect high-value care. We have known for decades that cost exposure discriminates against those with less wealth, and scaling proposals have been floated every few years.

To be clear, cost exposure has always been driven by a free-market ideology, which only imperfectly tracks a social welfare analysis, when propped up by lots of convenient assumptions sketched in Chapter 1. Frankly, I am not sure that all the politicians who have pushed the cost-exposure agenda thus far are interested in technocratic reforms that would minimize its harms, nor are they interested in simply paying poorer patients to meet the exposed costs. If the advocates of cost exposure are not really invested in making it work for all of us, then we may simply need to outvote them and adopt a more comprehensive reform.

## BETTER TOOLS FOR COST CONTROL

Even if we could implement the reforms to cost exposure sketched in Chapter 5, we still would not have a real tool for fighting the rampant waste that infects the U.S. healthcare system. When Centers for Medicare and Medicaid Services (CMS) Administrator Donald Berwick stepped down from his post in 2011, he argued that 20%–30% of healthcare spending— more than $1 trillion a year—was waste.[11] "Much is done that does not help patients at all," Berwick said, "and many physicians know it."[12] The problem is clearly not insurance, because we know other developed countries have universal and comprehensive insurance coverage, but still spend half as much on their healthcare compared to the United States, while hitting better targets for both health outcomes and patient satisfaction.

So, if insurance is not the problem, then what *is* driving all this waste? Monopoly pricing, asymmetric information, and provider incentives are the much more important economic explanations. These real problems suggest more powerful solutions than cost exposure could ever hope to provide.

### Prices

Imagine a hurricane strikes, and your neighbor gives you money to go buy drinking water for him. The only seller of water still around demands $25 per gallon. When you pay it and return home, could the neighbor complain that you got a bad deal because you were spending his money rather than your own? That would miss the larger point that you were purchasing from a price gouger who was exploiting an effective monopoly. As Princeton health economist Uwe Reinhardt famously said, "It's the prices, stupid."[13]

The United States spends gargantuan amounts of money on healthcare and not just because Americans consume lots of healthcare. In fact, Americans go to the doctor and hospital less often than people in other OECD countries, and accordingly we have fewer physicians and hospital beds per capita.[14] Instead, we simply have higher prices for the products and services we do consume.[15] And the prices are high because of another very familiar problem for economists: lack of competition (and lack of regulation of the resulting monopolies).

Your local primary care physicians could in theory compete on prices with others in the area, but if the doctors all join together to create a huge practice, then that incentive disappears. In recent years there has been a huge wave of hospital mergers, which have also vacuumed up physicians' practices. As Berkeley scholar Brent Fulton reports, "In 2016, 90 percent of Metropolitan Statistical Areas (MSAs) were highly concentrated for hospitals, 65 percent for specialist physicians, 39 percent for primary care physicians, and 57 percent for insurers."[16]

Healthcare professionals and hospitals also benefit from government-enforced restrictions on supply, which make it illegal to practice medicine, build new hospital beds, or purchase certain medical equipment without a license. New medical products are also protected by patents and other marketing rights—monopolies protected by the government.

Without competition, sellers are free to charge whatever they can persuade desperate patients and their insurers to pay. States have tried to regulate drug prices, but have had little success in the courts.[17] Antitrust enforcement has been uneven, and does nothing where the monopoly is enforced by the government itself.[18]

So prices soar. For example, in 2013, the average price of a bypass surgery was $75,345 in the United States. That cost is nearly double the charge of the second-highest country, Australia ($42,130).[19] Notably, as I will emphasize later, Australia also has remarkably little patient cost exposure.

Drug prices fit this same pattern. A recent study of all the new drugs approved over a decade found that about "1 in 3 (30%) of all newly approved cancer medicines are not associated with any [overall survival] benefit, while 1 in 5 (20%) neither extend life nor improve [quality of life] or safety."[20] The scientific basis for even these purported benefits was rather weak. Another study examined the thirteen new cancer drugs approved in 2012, and found that only one was shown to provide survival gains that last more than two months, when tested in the carefully constructed clinical trial setting.[21] All but one of these were priced at above $100,000 per year, once they secured FDA approval. On average, then, these drugs cost about $400,000 for each additional month of life provided to patients.[22] And the problem is only getting worse; scholars have found that year over year, new drugs are priced higher even though they do not deliver better health outcomes.[23] It is hard to say what extra time alive is worth, but these numbers are not even close to reasonable estimates used elsewhere in the world. For example, the United Kingdom has a national institute that reviews drug pricing, and it requires ten times the efficacy per dollar spent, compared to these U.S. cancer drug prices.[24]

In Chapter 5, I mentioned Colorado's new $100 monthly limit on cost exposure for insulin. When Governor Jared Polis signed the bill, he claimed to "declare that the days of insulin price gouging are over in Colorado."[25] Ironically, however, the law does not actually affect the prices of insulin; just the cost exposures that patients pay out of pocket. As the news coverage noted, "the law doesn't limit what insulin manufacturers can charge insurance companies, and it's expected those insurers will pay the difference."[26] This case shows both how devastatingly large cost exposures failed to drive down the real prices in this domain where suppliers enjoy near monopolies, and it shows how tinkering with cost exposure policy will not fix what really ails the U.S. healthcare economy.

## Ignorance

We are shopping in the dark. Imagine a homebound friend sends you to the store with a shopping list and some money, with instructions to buy the healthy stuff—whole grain pasta and sauce made from organics. But when you arrive, the grocery store has a power failure. So you try to shop in the dark. While you can surely fill your cart with stuff—maybe even some pasta and sauce—you cannot read the ingredient labels or see the prices. If your friend is disappointed that you failed to get a good deal, what is the real cause?

Similarly, when patients and their doctors are making healthcare spending decisions, they are shopping in the dark. New medical technologies are the main driver of healthcare spending growth.[27] But for any such new treatment physicians and patients can largely only wonder: Does it work? Is it safe? Is it worth the price that the manufacturer is demanding? Often, nobody has done sufficient scientific research to know one way or the other.

Economists have long understood that information is a public good—neither excludable nor rivalrous.[28] If you invest in producing reliable information, it is very hard to reap the full value of that information, because others will just pass it around without chipping in. So nobody would rationally make such an investment to produce the information in the first place. That is why the United States Constitution includes a patent law system—to reward those who come up with new ideas that are potentially useful. But potentially useful is a far cry from truly safe and effective.

To be sure, no individual cancer patient, or her doctor, is in a position to spend hundreds of millions of dollars, work for many years, and recruit thousands of patients to actually determine which chemical compound is most effective for her. Even if the information would be infinitely valuable to her, she would be dead and broke long before the research was completed. Nor are the companies that make drugs and devices likely to invest in the high-stakes, rigorous research that could just as well show their products to be ineffective; marketing and cheap talk are much more reliable investments. In a famous 1970 paper, Nobel Prize–winning economist George Akerlof showed how this dynamic creates a race to the bottom, driving out high-quality products from the market, as cheap talk prevails.[29]

We cannot expect anyone to conduct this sort of expensive biomedical research about safety and efficacy (the key inputs for determining value at a given price), without a government subsidy or mandate. The FDA does perform an essential function, by forcing the makers of new diagnostics and therapies to demonstrate safety and efficacy of their product before they enter the market. In this sense, physician Victor Laurion and I have shown how the FDA's mandate causes knowledge to be produced.[30] As Rebecca Eisenberg has explained, "If a century ago the goal of drug regulation was to protect people from poisons, today drug regulation guides the development of information that turns poisons, used advisedly, into drugs."[31]

Yet we have set the bar far too low to produce the information that doctors and patients need. A recent review of new drug approvals found that in fewer than half of the cases were scientific studies comparing their product to "active controls," such as the standard of care.[32] Instead, the maker of a new drug only proves that it works better than a placebo—an inert substance that looks like a drug. I will not hold my breath waiting for drug and device sellers to begin using "better than nothing" as their advertising tagline, though it would be apt.

For medical devices, the FDA's scrutiny is even lighter. For seventy-eight "high-risk" cardiovascular devices that the FDA approved between 2000 and

2007, less than one-third had been subjected to a randomized trial, and only 5% had undergone two or more blinded randomized studies.[33] And, once a device has been approved, manufacturers typically ask the FDA to allow changes to the product, without having to actually prove that the new design is safe or effective.[34] Or the company asks for new indications, to reach broader markets for their already-approved devices. A 2017 JAMA study reviewed 83 clinical studies over a decade, which the FDA used to consider 78 of these "panel-track supplements." Less than half (45%) were randomized clinical trials, less than a third (30%) were even somewhat blinded, and only 38% were compared with controls.[35] Under these conditions, it is difficult to infer causality, that is, that the device actually provides benefits that outweigh its risks.

For example, a gastric band device was originally approved for patients with morbid obesity, but that is a relatively small market. The company instead sought to market their product for patients with Body Mass Index (BMI) greater than 30, a population of 19 million patients. Gastric bands can malfunction by eroding into the stomach or slipping down, causing obstruction, but it is hard to estimate the rate in small studies with short time for follow-up. As it happened, the FDA approved the company's application on the basis of a single-group study of 160 patients without an active control group and with only a one-year primary endpoint for measurable follow-up.[36] Subsequent research showed that nearly one fifth of the Medicare patients who received the device had to go for reoperation, suffering an average of 3.8 procedures each.[37] Medicare paid nearly half a billion dollars for lap-band surgeries during the study period, and almost half of that was for reoperations.

Randomization and blinding are key tools to mitigate biases, but these tools are still not systematically applied.[38] Just like the blank cups used in a taste test, blinding ensures the validity assessments made by patients, assessors, and analysts, so that wishful thinking does not infect the results. In a 2012 study, Asbjørn Hróbjartsson and colleagues estimated the size of the bias due to lack of blinding, and found a 36% median shift in the odds ratio toward efficacy.[39] Disconcertingly, this shift was larger than the proven effect size for most of the treatments tested.

Consider vertebroplasty, which involves injecting acrylic bone cement into fractured vertebrae. It is a treatment for a very common complication of osteoporosis. There are no figures available as to prevalence generally, but

Medicare alone covers 100,000 vertebroplasties a year, at a cost of $1 billion.[40] This procedure was initially shown to be successful on the basis of open-label trials, where the patient was aware of the procedure and with subjective outcomes self-assessed by the patients themselves.[41] On this basis, bone cement was widely marketed and widely adopted. Only later did two blinded randomized trials show that vertebroplasty was no more efficacious than placebo and conservative treatment.[42] These studies came too late to change the established clinical practice, especially since they were not backed by the sorts of marketing campaigns that caused the rapid adoption of vertebroplasty in the first place.

One would hope that when scientific research is conducted for the FDA it might show whether a drug or device actually improves health or extends life. But often not. Almost half the time (45.3%), when the FDA considers new drugs as proven effective, it is actually relying on surrogate endpoints, like blood pressure or tumor size, which are only imperfect proxies for the mortality and morbidity that we actually care about.[43] Even worse for medical devices: less than a fifth of applications for expanded marketing studied real health outcomes.[44] As former FDA Commissioner Robert Califf explains, "because of the complexity of diseases and therapies, the vast majority of biomarkers are not good surrogates for improved patient outcomes."[45] Indeed, a 2018 systematic review of cancer treatments found that the primary surrogate used—progression free survival—was not significantly associated with a health-related quality of life.[46] Whether these drugs and devices actually improve health remains unknown.

For example, in 2016, the FDA approved a new drug for Duchenne's muscular dystrophy (DMD), a heartbreaking genetic disease that largely affects boys, starting around age four.[47] Symptoms get progressively worse, until a wheelchair is required by the early teens, and the disease is almost always fatal before patients reach age forty. The drug maker submitted a pivotal study to the FDA, but it only involved twelve patients, and the research did not show that the drug actually provided a clinical benefit to patients, reducing their symptoms or extending their lives. Overruling the key scientific advisors, the FDA approved it for marketing, based on some evidence that the drug increased the amount of a protein in skeletal muscle (by 0.1% no less), which is otherwise known to help protect muscle fibers. Desperate parents applauded the victory for their sick boys. The company immediately announced that it would charge $300,000 per year for the treatment, which has not been shown to actually provide a clinical benefit for patients.[48]

For some healthcare, there is no effective FDA review at all. For a drug or medical device to be marketed in the United States, it must first be proven safe and effective, for whatever medical uses are intended by the manufacturer and listed on the label. However, the law also allows physicians to prescribe drugs and devices for other uses where the FDA has not reviewed safety and efficacy (or even if the FDA has reviewed safety and efficacy evidence but rejected a new indication). In some domains, like pediatrics, psychiatry, neurology, and oncology, these "off-label" uses are very common, accounting for substantial healthcare spending.

These drugs and devices may be quite effective for these other uses, but without the sorts of randomized trials required by the FDA it's hard to know. In one recent study, the authors reviewed 17,847 off-label uses and found that, 80.9% of the time, the uses "lacked strong scientific evidence."[49] Similarly, a 2006 national study found that one-fifth of prescriptions were off-label and three-quarters of the off-label uses had little or no scientific support.[50]

In these ways, the FDA's rather minimal legal mandate limits how much it can do to help ensure the safety, efficacy, and, ultimately, value of our medical products. But even when working squarely within its mission, the FDA suffers from institutional limitations. One problem is the revolving door, and FDA officials know it well, moving back and forth from industry and the agency.[51] Oncologist Vinay Prasad expresses the obvious worry: "If you [the regulator] know a major post-employment opportunity is on the other side of the table, you give them the benefit of the doubt. You, maybe, make things a little easier on the companies."[52] Philosopher Dennis Thompson and legal scholar Larry Lessig have each developed the term "institutional corruption" to refer to these sorts of situations where an institution (the FDA) can be bent to serve other purposes (company interests), rather than its own mission (producing knowledge and protecting patients), even if no individual person is actually corrupted.[53]

A federal law also pushes the FDA to move very fast, or it will lose funding provided by the very companies who seek FDA approval of their new products. This law (called PDUFA for the Prescription Drug User Fee Act) has sharply decreased the time that the agency takes to review new drug applications: from 19 months to review the median new drug application in 1993 to only 7.8 months in 2016.[54] This haste has been associated with drugs more often later being pulled from the market or receiving a "black box warning" due to major safety concerns.[55] Using more granular data, Daniel Carpenter and colleagues have documented how, as a PDUFA deadline approaches, reviewers rush to decide on the application, and such "just before the deadline" decisions are linked to more postmarket safety problems.[56]

Of course, the FDA is not the only mechanism for generating knowledge about safety and efficacy of our healthcare. There is a broader biomedical literature that physicians can consult to figure out what is or is not valuable for their patients. Yet that literature is distorted by commercial interests.

The National Institutes of Health provides only a small portion of the funding needed, and it understandably focuses on very early stage research, not clinical trials of the drugs and devices being used in clinics every day. Because there is so little independent money for applied scientific research, the companies can set the scientific agenda, de-prioritizing the study of unpatented medical technologies and other nontechnology interventions.[57]

When a company does find it in its interest to run a study on its own product, the Institute of Medicine has found "substantial evidence that clinical trials with industry ties are more likely to have results that favor industry."[58] Somehow, industry-funded studies are more likely to find that the studied products are safe and effective, and the abstracts describing such studies are more likely to overstate the findings buried in the back. In my own research with hundreds of physicians reviewing biomedical journal abstracts, we found that they were much more skeptical when the abstracts disclosed industry funding.[59] Yet few journals provide those disclosures in the abstracts read by busy physicians.

In 2005, Stanford professor John Ioannidis published a landmark paper, "Why Most Published Research Findings Are False."[60] Company scientists have broad discretion in "designs, definitions, outcomes, and analytical modes," which makes it easier for them to find that their products have positive effects, in accordance with their commercial interests.[61] As Ioannidis has said, "At every step of the process, there is room to distort results, a way to make a stronger claim, or to select what is going to be concluded."[62]

For these reasons, we can see that our healthcare system has generally failed to invest in a reliable and systematic approach to the production of knowledge about the efficacy of the healthcare we consume. These economic problems cast a long dark shadow on consumers, looming much larger than the fact that patients have insurance.

Providers

"Health care markets are rife with principal–agent relationships," explain law professors Peter Hammer and Bill Sage.[63] These are situations where one party (a patient) relies on another (a physician) to guide her choices, or decide on her behalf, but their interests are not aligned. Economists have long recognized that principal–agent problems, and their associated information asymmetries, are primary causes of markets failing to reach efficient outcomes. And in medicine, the information asymmetries are profound. As Meredith Rosenthal and Anna Sinaiko argue, "The lack of independent information on the quality of care may reinforce patients' tendency to rely on physicians for advice . . . , and patients may be unwilling to go against a clinician's advice in the interest of saving a few dollars."[64] Of course, patients rely on physicians to select healthcare treatments, because they are largely incompetent to do so themselves. In fact, federal and state laws generally mandate that physicians serve as gatekeepers for access to prescription drugs and other medical products and services.

In 2016, a research team published a systematic review of all the different mechanisms for fighting low-value healthcare, including patient cost exposure, but also patient education, clinical decision support tools (e.g., giving the physician an alert when she orders an inappropriate test into an electronic health record), clinician education (e.g., lectures, face-to-face visits, emails, and pocket cards teaching about evidence-based care), and providing feedback to providers (e.g., telling physicians when their treatment recommendations are failing to accord with national guidelines). While the evidence for cost exposure was mixed (as we have seen), there were twenty-two studies showing the effectiveness of clinical decision support tools, ten studies showing the effectiveness of clinician education, and seven supporting interventions that give feedback to providers when they prescribe poorly.[65] If you want to change the healthcare consumed, change the healthcare provided.

In one of the most recent studies pre-published by the National Bureau of Economic Research, Harvard health economist Michael Chernew and colleagues examined patients' choice of where to receive more than 50,000 MRIs. Although such scans are almost commodities, without substantial differentiation between providers, prices can vary by a factor of five. The research team studied a population of patients that had very substantial cost exposure but found very little evidence that they viewed their MRI as a service that they could shop for (much less haggle over). Instead, patients tended to go wherever their physician recommended. As the authors conclude, "The influence of referring physicians is dramatically greater than the effect of patient cost-sharing."[66] After all, that is why we go to physicians in the first place—we trust them to recommend the care that we need based on their expertise and judgment. So, we go where they tell us to go.

If patients drove healthcare, we should see healthcare consumption uniformly tracking the same underlying scientific reality as to what works and a homogeneous patient demand for good health. Analogously, that is why we see the same television sets being sold at Best Buys in Dubuque as well as in Plano—we all want big, crisp screens and there is a known technological way to provide them. Cancer has the same biological properties in Dubuque and Plano too. But decades of research have shown that U.S. physician treatment patterns vary widely from physician to physician, and from region to region. This phenomenon is particularly stark in Medicare claims data, where the actual prices per procedure are fixed by federal law. We see wild differences in medical practice, and geographic areas with double, or triple, the spending per patient do not produce better outcomes as a result.[67] Some healthcare providers are just a lot more wasteful.

A research group at Dartmouth University has created a cottage industry documenting these dynamics. For example, the Dartmouth group has shown wild variation in the rate of prostate screening, with some regions (like Lebanon, Ohio, and Mason City, Iowa) screening less than 6% of their eligible men, while other regions (such as Miami, Florida, and Wilmington, North Carolina) screen more than 55% of men.[68] That is a nearly tenfold difference, not likely due to differences in patient cost exposure.

When a physician interprets a PSA test in a way that seems worrisome, and a biopsy reveals cancer cells, there is more uncertainty. Some physicians and patients will choose active surveillance or hormone therapy while others proceed toward the more radical options of radiation or surgery. Here again, the Dartmouth team has documented wild geographic variations, ranging from fewer than 72 men per 1,000 receiving prostatectomy (surgery) in places like Ocala, Florida, or Tulsa, Oklahoma, versus more than 459 per 1,000 in Meridian, Mississippi, or Munster, Indiana.[69] That is a five-times difference!

The Dartmouth team describes this phenomenon of "supply-sensitive care"—"in regions where there are more hospital beds per capita, patients will be more likely to be admitted to the hospital. In regions where there are more intensive care unit beds, more patients will be cared for in the ICU. More specialists will result in more visits to specialists."[70] In the prostate example, when a hospital buys a fancy robotic surgery machine and recruits leading surgeons to use it, somebody has to pay for it. The hospital sponsors a PSA screening initiative, gets the word out to primary care physicians and urologists, and eventually use increases.

Similarly for women giving birth, the rate of Cesarean sections varies tenfold from hospital to hospital.[71] No fewer than seventeen research studies have investigated whether for-profit hospitals tend to perform C-sections more often. In fact, they do: every single study found a positive association, and a systematic review that pooled their estimates found that for-profit status was associated with a 41% increase in the adjusted odds of a mother receiving a C-section.[72] Why? Likely because hospitals receive larger reimbursements for C-sections compared to vaginal delivery, and although all hospitals face this incentive, it is apparently more acutely felt by hospitals pursuing profit at the end of the day.

It would be bad enough if physicians were merely indifferent to costs, and practiced with a huge dose of inexplicable randomness. But these dynamics demonstrate instances where physicians and hospitals affirmatively pursue costly procedures; their financial interests do not align with the interests of patients (health), much less payors (thrift). Long before we shifted more risk to patients with cost exposure, the United States should have stopped paying healthcare providers on a fee-for-service basis. As physician-lawyer David Orentlicher concludes, "Physicians should earn their compensation solely through salary or capitation fees [an amount] for [each of] the patients they serve. Similarly, hospitals should earn their compensation solely through capitation fees."[73] Our healthcare providers should not be getting commissions on sales, like salespersons on a car lot.

Drug and device companies also pay physicians as consultants or speakers, or often just give them fancy meals while telling them about their products. In a range of high-cost fields like oncology, cardiology, urology, and hematology, my coauthors and I have found that about half of the physicians supplement their clinical incomes with money from the drug and device industries.[74]

The ACA, for the first time, required companies to begin disclosing these payments as part of a national website. A major nonprofit reporting group called ProPublica matched prescribing patterns under Medicare with physicians in five medical specialties. Doctors who receive industry payments were more likely to prescribe brand-name drugs than physicians who do not take such money.[75] Indeed, the authors found a linear relationship between the amount of money that physicians take and how often they prescribe brand-name drugs from their industry sponsors. Although it is hard to figure out the direction of causation from observational studies, this study is consistent with decades of prior research using a range of methodologies, which I have surveyed with coauthors.[76]

In fields like oncology and surgery, the incentives to provide high-cost care are particularly stark, since the physicians are typically "self-referrers"— they will both be paid to decide whether the care is appropriate and then be paid to provide it. When Medicare changed its reimbursement protocols in a way that reduced payments for oncology drugs overall, and made some drugs more profitable than others, the physicians began recommending more such drugs and higher-margin drugs, in an apparent move to maintain their revenues.[77] Similarly, Georgetown economist Jean Mitchell has studied how surgeons change their clinical recommendations when they buy into specialty surgery hospitals.[78] Using a rich data set to examine one such acquisition, Mitchell looked at how often surgeons recommended simple spinal fusion surgery versus the much more remunerative (and risky) complex spinal fusion surgery. Once they stood to profit from their own recommendation, physicians were forty times more likely to recommend the expensive and risky procedure. Some commentators have labeled this dynamic "provider moral hazard."[79]

Healthcare providers are the drivers of healthcare. And their behaviors often do not align with the interests of patients or payors. Even if cost exposure made patients laser-focused on the value of their own healthcare, they would have a very hard time figuring out where that value may lie, when their advisors are leading them elsewhere. To get at real waste, one must target the real problems.

## MOVING ON

Across the broad scope of this book, I have reviewed quite a range of evidence and arguments, suggesting that the American fixation on making health insurance incomplete and leaving patients and their families exposed to large medical bills is fundamentally misguided. Notwithstanding the elegance of moral hazard as a theory, economists have now conceded that it cannot in fact explain much of the actual spending in the United States. As Harvard and Dartmouth economists Amitabh Chandra and Jonathan Skinner explain, "Typical estimates of price elasticity cannot explain more than a tiny fraction of the overall growth in healthcare cost."[80] In a leading economics journal, Gautam Gowrisankaran and colleagues have estimated that even if patient coinsurance were increased *tenfold* (which may well be infeasible), hospital prices could only be nudged down by 16%.[81]

Cost exposure is a very weak solution to the small problem of moral hazard. Given that high-cost care drives aggregate spending, we can realistically expose patients to only a tiny portion of their overall spending, and even that may bankrupt them. Even if we could expose a patient to 20% of the cost of a $100,000 surgery or chemotherapy, health insurance is still creating a four-times subsidy for consumption. For every one dollar the patient spends, the insurer will spend four more. Even on its face, and ignoring all the behavioral science about how people really make decisions, that cost-exposure mechanism cannot cause patients to weigh the benefits of the treatment against its full costs ($100,000). Instead, that price mechanism only excludes those who cannot afford to pay $20,000. As we have seen, it undermines the core purpose of health insurance: securing access to healthcare we otherwise cannot afford.

We have also seen how cost exposure changes the experience of healthcare, commodifying our bodies and converting the doctor-patient relationship into a quid pro quo, one that may even undermine trust and efficacy. We have seen that as healthcare costs have grown with new and expensive technologies, it is less and less feasible to expose patients to substantial portions of their own healthcare. They just do not have enough money. We have also seen that cost exposure can undermine democratic equality, disproportionately denying care to the poor among us, undermining life, liberty, and the pursuit of happiness.

A recent report by the National Academy of Sciences tried to grapple with the problem of high drug prices in the United States, noting that drugs often cost several times more here than abroad. The committee report described our healthcare system as a "supremely complex amalgam of regulators, developers and manufacturers, retailers, insurers, wholesalers, physicians, employers offering benefits, and intermediaries, including organizations referred to as pharmacy benefit managers. . . . Lying at the heart of this complex, and arguably having the least influence among its participants, is the patient."[82] If this is an accurate description of the healthcare system, it reveals the folly of patient cost exposure as a policy mechanism to drive down prices and optimize consumption. Why target the least influential player in this system? Instead, we need to find the real pressure points.

## The Well-Trod Path

Altogether, we would do well to move our governmental policy, group health insurance plans, and individual health insurance purchases away from patient cost exposure. Some companies are already beginning to see the wisdom of this approach. Although Comcast is one of the least-liked companies in the United States, it has become one of the most progressive to optimize the $1.3 billion it spends each year on healthcare for its 225,000 employees and their families. It has rejected the high-deductible health plans that most employers have been flocking to, and has instead lowered its annual deductible to $250 for most workers. It has nonetheless managed to constrain the growth of health spending by creating tools that help patients make smart healthcare decisions.[83]

Globally, we also see other countries have already proven the feasibility of alternative approaches. In Canada, for physician, diagnostic, and hospital services covered by public insurance (70% of all health spending), there is no patient cost exposure whatsoever.[84] Even though Canada has altogether excluded cost exposure from the core domain of its healthcare system, it manages to achieve significantly less health spending overall—only 10.5% of its GDP compared to 17.2% in the United States.

New Zealand is also a striking story. Even less than Canada, the country spends only 9.4% of its GDP on healthcare. A Commonwealth Fund report summarizes that "residents receive treatment free of charge in public hospitals, though there are some user charges, such as for crutches and other aids supplied upon discharge."[85] On average, patients spent only US$263 out of pocket per year, about one-quarter of what Americans spend out-of-pocket.

Japan likewise spent only 11.4% of its GDP on healthcare. Although Japan includes a general 30% coinsurance for services and goods received, it has monthly caps, income caps, age caps, and various waivers, so patients spent out of pocket only US$126 each year—just over one-tenth of what Americans pay.[86]

These international examples are meant to reassure readers that, although Americans have become accustomed to substantial cost exposures and may assume that they are a necessary part of any economical healthcare system, this is not the case. Indeed, in these other countries the healthcare systems get along just fine, with performance metrics that are comparable, or in some cases better, than the U.S. healthcare system. When citizens of each country are surveyed, only 19% of Americans say their healthcare system works well, compared to 35% in Canada and 41% in New Zealand.[87] Like our other descendants from the British Empire, we might well be happy with an altogether different path than the one we have chosen to date.

### Political Possibility?

All this suggests that the United States should reverse its present emphasis on patient cost exposure. I suggest aiming for zero. As Scottish health economist Cam Donaldson argues from across the pond, the idea of charging users for healthcare "is intellectually dead, but keeps coming [like a] zombie [that] has to be slain. . . . It is wrong, unfair and ineffective."[88]

Still, in the United States, the idea of eliminating, or drastically reducing, cost exposure has seemed fanciful. Perhaps, however, the tide is turning. In 2018, President Trump's first FDA commissioner, Scott Gottlieb, railed against patient cost exposure:

> Patients shouldn't be penalized by their biology if they need a drug that isn't on formulary. Patients shouldn't face exorbitant out of pocket costs, and pay money where the primary purpose is to help subsidize rebates paid to a long list of supply chain intermediaries, or is used to buy down the premium costs for everyone else. After all, what's the point of a big co-pay on a costly cancer drug? Is a patient really in a position to make an economically-based decision? Is the co-pay going to discourage overutilization? Is someone in this situation voluntarily seeking chemo? Of course not. Yet the big co-pay or rebate on the costly drug can help offset insurers' payments to the pharmacy, and reduce average insurance premiums. But sick people aren't supposed to be subsidizing the healthy.[89]

This may seem like common sense to some readers, but after fifty years of economic indoctrination, it is revolutionary to hear such talk from a senior American government official, and indeed a Republican appointee no less. Here, Gottlieb sounds not unlike democratic socialist presidential candidate Bernie Sanders, who called for a universal healthcare plan, complete with "no more copays, no more deductibles."[90] Perhaps the tide is turning.

This book has said nothing about whether insurance should be provided publicly or through private insurance, and nothing about single-payor versus managed competition. The final solution will likely be some mix of both, just as other countries have found. For the question of this book, those are orthogonal issues of healthcare organization. Instead, the point is that from wherever we get our insurance coverage, we might as well make it complete.

With health and wealth being such foundational aspects of our lives, it behooves us to innovate ways to minimize, if not eliminate, the risk that one will be diminished at the expense of the other in our times of greatest need. The most straightforward way to do that is to reject the cost-exposure consensus and embrace complete insurance coverage. Meanwhile, let's pursue meaningful reforms to fight the real drivers of healthcare waste: monopoly prices, institutional ignorance, and the misaligned incentives of our healthcare providers.

# EPILOGUE

This book has tried to do four things. It may be useful to recapitulate them here.

First, I have highlighted the problem of cost exposure among the insured. By thematizing this issue, as distinct from the long-standing goal of achieving universal health insurance coverage, I hope to help set the agenda for the next wave of reform in the U.S. healthcare system. We can think about not just whether to insure Americans, but how to insure them. This is important for several reasons, including a political one. Most American voters have health insurance. Speaking with them about the quality of their coverage may be an essential part of achieving other public policies that advance health and the general welfare.

Second, I have revealed some of the implicit philosophical problems in this domain of health policy. The field of health economics has long devalued the choices of patients and their physicians under health insurance, but we must start from a position of profound epistemic humility concerning the efficacy, safety, and ultimate value of healthcare. Economics, with its theoretical models and regression coefficients, smuggles in big teleological assumptions about why we buy insurance in the first place and how we should interpret the consumption behavior we observe. As for causation, the right counterfactual is key for understanding the effects of insurance. Even in the domain of phenomenology, we have seen that exposing patients to costs may shape the meaning and experience of healthcare, forcing difficult choices, commodifying our bodies, and pushing our healers away as arm's-length commercial transactions instead. And the use of credit to finance health-care forces us to account for what we owe our future selves. Finally, of course, there are larger questions of distributive justice, which we have grappled with directly, considering whether health should be viewed individually or collectively, what we owe our fellow citizens, and how much we can expect them to pay.

Third, this book has had a synthetic empirical agenda. As it happens, we know quite a lot about patient cost exposure, but this knowledge is scattered in disparate academic disciplines—from psychology to sociology and from economics to health services research—over half a century. The goal and challenge is to bridge across the interdisciplinary divide, to communicate these findings to and from the academic disciplines. Pulling together this literature tells a coherent story about how cost exposure affects healthcare consumption and health outcomes, but also access to healthcare and the experience of healthcare. Such a rich understanding belies simplistic economic models or political ideologies, which suggest that overall welfare can be improved if we simply dial down health insurance coverage.

Fourth, this book has offered solutions. I have not attempted to systematically review all possible, or even all the good, reform proposals for health insurance. Given the peculiar political ideology of the United States, it is perhaps to be expected that cost exposure will remain a primary part of healthcare. So, the reforms I have suggested—leveraging information and consent, scaling to value, and scaling to income—are each promising reforms. However, notwithstanding our bias toward ingenuity, it is past time that we take seriously the idea that cost exposure has been a failed experiment in health policy—it simply does not do what we hoped it would, and it wreaks havoc in the process. So now we can, and should, take a large step away from cost exposure, as part of a broader reform of healthcare in America.

The United States has too long embraced cost exposure unreflectively, trafficking in simplistic notions of personal responsibility and economic efficiency, while the world is much more complicated (and interesting). We have suffered accordingly, with illness, inefficiency, and injustice. But as this national experiment has run its course, it has also paved the way for better approaches, calibrated to achieve our policy goals. We can embrace the inexpensive and comprehensive healthcare that the rest of the developed world enjoys, with little or no cost exposure.

# NOTES

## INTRODUCTION

1. Emily M. Mitchell and Steven R. Machlin, "Statistical Brief #506: Concentration of Health Expenditures and Selected Characteristics of High Spenders, U.S. Civilian Noninstitutionalized Population, 2015," Medical Expenditure Panel Survey (December 2017), https://meps.ahrq.gov/data_files/publications /st506/stat506.shtml.

2. "The Impact of Third-Party Debt Collection on the US National and State Economies in 2016," prepared for ACA International by Ernst & Young (November 2017), https://www.acainternational.org/assets/ernst-young/ey-2017-aca -state-of-the-industry-report-final-5.pdf.

3. "Poll: Nearly 1 in 4 Americans Taking Prescription Drugs Say It's Difficult to Afford Their Medicines, including Larger Shares Among Those with Health Issues, with Low Incomes and Nearing Medicare Age," Kaiser Family Foundation (March 1, 2019), https://www.kff.org/health-costs/press-release/poll-nearly-1-in-4 -americans-taking-prescription-drugs-say-its-difficult-to-afford-medicines-including -larger-shares-with-low-incomes/.

4. Kirnvir K. Dhaliwal, Kathryn King-Shier, Braden J. Manns, Brenda R. Hemmelgam, James A. Stone, and David J. T. Campbell, "Exploring the Impact of Financial Barriers on Secondary Prevention of Heart Disease," *BMC Cardiovascular Disorders* 17, no. 1 (2017): 61.

5. Michael D. Kogan et al., "Underinsurance among Children in the United States," *New England Journal of Medicine* 363, no. 9 (August 2010): 841–851.

6. "Premiums for Employer-Sponsored Family Health Coverage Rise 5% to Average $19,616; Single Premiums Rise 3% to $6,896," Kaiser Family Foundation (October 3, 2018), https://www.kff.org/health-costs/press-release/employer -sponsored-family-coverage-premiums-rise-5-percent-in-2018/.

7. "Key Facts about the Uninsured Population," Kaiser Family Foundation (December 7, 2018), at https://www.kff.org/uninsured/fact-sheet/key-facts-about-the-uninsured-population/.

8. Jeffrey M. Jones and R. J. Reinhart, "Americans Remain Dissatisfied with Healthcare Costs," Gallup (November 28, 2018), https://news.gallup.com/poll/245054/americans-remain-dissatisfied-healthcare-costs.aspx.

9. "Ipsos/Amino Poll: 63% of Americans Think a Large Medical Bill That They Can't Afford Is Worse Than or Equal to a Serious Illness," Amino (March 21, 2017), http://www.marketwired.com/press-release/ipsos-amino-poll-63-americans-think-large-medical-bill-that-they-cant-afford-is-worse-2204179.htm.

10. Ashley Kirzinger, Liz Hamel, Bianca DiJulio, Cailey Muñana, and Mollyann Brodie, KFF Election Tracking Poll: Health Care in the 2018 Midterms (October 18, 2018), https://www.kff.org/health-reform/poll-finding/kff-election-tracking-poll-health-care-in-the-2018-midterms/.

11. This and subsequent statistics about coverage in this section are from "Health Insurance Coverage of the Total Population," Henry J. Kaiser Family Foundation, http://kff.org/other/state-indicator/total-population/?currentTimeframe=0&sortModel=%7B%22colId%22:%22Location%22,%22sort%22:%22asc%22%7D (reflecting 2017 data).

12. "Reduce Tax Subsidies for Employment-Based Health Insurance," Congressional Budget Office (December 13, 2018), https://www.cbo.gov/budget-options/2018/54798.

13. "National Health Expenditure Data," Centers for Medicare and Medicaid Services, https://www.cms.gov/research-statistics-data-and-systems/statistics-trends-and-reports/nationalhealthexpenddata/nationalhealthaccountshistorical.html.

14. Kayla Fontenot, Jessica Semega, and Melissa Kollar, "Income and Poverty in the United States: 2017," United States Census Bureau, https://www.census.gov/library/publications/2018/demo/p60-263.html.

15. "National Health Expenditures per Capita, 1960–2023," Henry J. Kaiser Family Foundation, http://kff.org/health-costs/slide/national-health-expenditures-per-capita-1960-2023/.

16. "NHE Fact Sheet," Centers for Medicare and Medicaid Services, https://www.cms.gov/research-statistics-data-and-systems/statistics-trends-and-reports/nationalhealthexpenddata/nhe-fact-sheet.html.

17. "Technological Change and the Growth of Health Care Spending," Congressional Budget Office (January 31, 2008), 5, https://www.cbo.gov/publication/24748.

18. Robert Pear, "Reagan Has Achieved Many Goals, but Some Stir Opposition," New York Times (August 20, 1984), p. A18 (quoting Margaret Heckler).

19. OECD, "Health at a Glance 2017" (Paris: OECD Publishing, 2017), https://www.oecd-ilibrary.org/sites/health_glance-2017-en/1/2/7/2/index.html

?itemId=/content/publication/health_glance-2017-en&_csp_=a2ae54f57e835a070f
ed1d8fd9a56f53&itemIGO=oecd&itemContentType=book#sect-72.

20. See figure 2B of Joseph Dieleman et al., "Evolution and Patterns of Global Health Financing 1995–2014: Development Assistance for Health, and Government, Prepaid Private, and Out-of-Pocket Health Spending in 184 Countries," *Lancet* 389 (May 20, 2017): 1981–2004.

21. Congressional Budget Office, "Technological Change," 8, 10.

22. Congressional Budget Office, "Technological Change," 8, 10. For a more recent source, see Joseph L. Dieleman et al., "Factors Associated with Increases in US Health Care Spending, 1996–2013," *JAMA* 318, no. 17 (November 2017): 1668–1678.

23. "2018 Employer Health Benefits Survey, Summary of Findings." Kaiser Family Foundation. (October 3, 2018), https://www.kff.org/report-section/2018 -employer-health-benefits-survey-summary-of-findings/.

24. "2018 Employer Health Benefits Survey, Report." Kaiser Family Foundation. (October 3, 2018), https://www.kff.org/report-section/2018-employer-health -benefits-survey-section-8-high-deductible-health-plans-with-savings-option/.

25. Paul Fronstin, "Health Savings Account Balances, Contributions, Distributions, and Other Vital Statistics, 2017: Statistics from the EBRI HSA Database," Employee Benefit Research Institute (October 15, 2018), https://www.ebri.org /content/health-savings-account-balances-contributions-distributions-and-other -vital-statistics-2017-statistics-from-the-ebri-hsa-database.

26. Liz Hamel et al., "Kaiser Family Foundation / LA Times Survey Of Adults With Employer-Sponsored Health Insurance," Henry J. Kaiser Family Foundation (May 2019), http://files.kff.org/attachment/Report-KFF-LA-Times-Survey-of -Adults-with-Employer-Sponsored-Health-Insurance.

27. "Cost-Sharing for Plans Offered in the Federal Marketplace for 2019." Kaiser Family Foundation (December 5, 2018), https://www.kff.org/health -reform/fact-sheet/cost-sharing-for-plans-offered-in-the-federal-marketplace-for -2019/.

28. "Medicare 2019 Costs at a Glance," Medicare.gov, https://www.medicare .gov/your-medicare-costs/medicare-costs-at-a-glance.

29. "Kaiser Commission on Medicaid and the Uninsured," Policy Brief, Henry J. Kaiser Family Foundation (February 2013), https://kaiserfamilyfoundation.files .wordpress.com/2013/02/8416.pdf.

30. "2018 Employer Health Benefits Survey."

31. "2018 Employer Health Benefits Survey."

32. "2018 Employer Health Benefits Survey."

33. "2018 Employer Health Benefits Survey."

34. "Medicare 2019 Costs at a Glance," https://www.medicare.gov/your -medicare-costs/medicare-costs-at-a-glance.

35. "Change the Cost-Sharing Rules for Medicare and Restrict Medigap Insurance," Congressional Budget Office (December 8, 2016), https://www.cbo.gov /budget-options/2016/52235.

36. "Kaiser Commission on Medicaid and the Uninsured."

37. See James C. Robinson and Timothy T. Brown, "Increases in Consumer Cost-Sharing Redirect Patient Volumes and Reduce Hospital Prices for Orthopedic Surgery," *Health Affairs* 32, no. 8 (August 2013): 1392–1397.

38. "2018 Employer Health Benefits Survey."

39. "Out-of-Pocket Maximum / Limit," HealthCare.gov, https://www .healthcare.gov/glossary/out-of-pocket-maximum-limit/.

40. "2018 Employer Health Benefits Survey."

41. "2018 Employer Health Benefits Survey."

42. "Explaining Health Care Reform: Questions about Health Insurance Subsidies," Henry J. Kaiser Family Foundation (November 20, 2018), https://www.kff .org/health-reform/issue-brief/explaining-health-care-reform-questions-about-health/.

43. Katie Keith, "Insurers Can Continue Silver Loading for 2019," HealthAffairs .com (June 13, 2018), https://www.healthaffairs.org/do/10.1377/hblog20180613 .293356/full/.

44. This paragraph is a close paraphrase from Christopher T. Robertson, "Scaling Cost-Sharing to Wages: How Employers Can Reduce Health Spending and Provide Greater Economic Security," *Yale Journal of Health Policy Law and Ethics* 14, no. 2 (2014): 239–295.

45. See Karen Pollitz et al., "Coverage When It Counts: How Much Protection Does Health Insurance Offer and How Can Consumers Know?," Center for American Progress Action Fund (May 2009), 6, http://cdn.americanprogress.org /wp-content/uploads/issues/2009/05/pdf/CoverageWhenItCounts.pdf.

46. David Lazarus, "When Your Insurer Denies a Valid Claim Because of 'Lack of Medical Necessity,'" *Los Angeles Times* (January 23, 2018) (quoting Chuck Idelson, the spokesman for the California Nurses Association).

47. "Autism and Insurance Coverage | State Laws," National Conference of State Legislatures (August 8, 2018), http://www.ncsl.org/research/health/autism -and-insurance-coverage-state-laws.aspx.

48. Martin S. Andersen, Christine Buttorff, and G. Caleb Alexander. "Impact of HIE Drug Formularies on Patient Out-of-Pocket Costs," *American Journal of Pharmacy Benefits* 8, no. 6 (2016): 220.

49. Sabrina Corlette et al., "Narrow Provider Networks in New Health Plans: Balancing Affordability with Access to Quality Care," Center on Health Insurance Reforms and Urban Institute (May 29, 2014), https://www.rwjf.org/en/library /research/2014/05/narrow-provider-networks-in-new-health-plans.html.

50. Jack Hoadley, Sandy Ahn, and Kevin Lucia, "Balance Billing: How Are States Protecting Consumers from Unexpected Charges?," Center on Health

Insurance Reforms and Robert Wood Johnson Foundation (June 2015), http://www
.insurance.pa.gov/Documents/Balance%20Billing/Kevin%20Lucia.pdf.

## 1. YOUR HEALTHCARE, THEIR MONEY

1. Louis Nelson, "Trump: 'There's Nothing like Doing Things with Other
People's Money,'" *Politico* (September 20, 2016), https://www.politico.com/story
/2016/09/donald-trump-other-peoples-money-228434.

2. Nicholas Bagley and Abbe R. Gluck, "Trump's Sabotage of Obamacare Is
Illegal," *New York Times* (August 14, 2018).

3. James Kwak, *Economism: Bad Economics and the Rise of Inequality* (New
York: Pantheon, 2017).

4. Kenneth J. Arrow, "Uncertainty and the Welfare Economics of Medical
Care," *American Economic Review* 53, no. 5 (December 1963): 941–973.

5. Mark V. Pauly, "The Economics of Moral Hazard: Comment," *American
Economic Review* 58, no. 3, part 1 (June 1968): 531–537.

6. Deborah Stone, "Behind the Jargon: Moral Hazard," *Journal of Health
Politics, Policy, and Law* 36, no. 5 (2011): 887–891.

7. Pauly, "Economics of Moral Hazard," 534.

8. Tom Baker, "On the Genealogy of Moral Hazard," *Texas Law Review* 75,
no. 2 (December 1996): 239.

9. Pauly, "Economics of Moral Hazard," 534.

10. "CMS History Project President's Speeches," Centers for Medicare and
Medicaid Services, 35, https://www.cms.gov/About-CMS/Agency-Information
/History/downloads/CMSPresidentsSpeeches.pdf.

11. "CMS History Project President's Speeches," 36.

12. Richard Zeckhauser, "Medical Insurance: A Case Study of the Tradeoff
between Risk Spreading and Appropriate Incentives," *Journal of Economic Theory* 2,
no. 1 (1970): 10.

13. Zeckhauser, "Medical Insurance," 10.

14. "CMS History Project President's Speeches," 60.

15. Martin S. Feldstein, "The Welfare Loss of Excess Health Insurance,"
*Journal of Political Economy* 81, no. 2 (1973): 276–277.

16. Feldstein, "Welfare Loss of Excess Health Insurance," 251.

17. Feldstein, 251.

18. Martin S. Feldstein, "A New Approach to National Health Insurance,"
*Public Interest* 23 (Spring 1971): 93–105; Martin Feldstein and Jonathan Gruber,
"A Major Risk Approach to Health Insurance Reform," in *Tax Policy and the
Economy*, vol. 9, ed. James M. Poterba (Cambridge, MA: MIT Press, 1995),
103–104 (calculating welfare effects of the proposal, arguing that it could "reduce
aggregate health spending by nearly 20 percent"); Martin S. Feldstein, "The High

Cost of Hospitals and What to Do about It," *Public Interest* 48 (Summer 1977): 40–54.

19. "CMS History Project President's Speeches," 82.

20. "CMS History Project President's Speeches," 97.

21. "CMS History Project President's Speeches," 98.

22. See Joseph P. Newhouse et al., "Some Interim Results from a Controlled Trial of Cost Sharing in Health Insurance," *New England Journal of Medicine* 305, no. 25 (December 1981): 1501–1507; Newhouse, *Free for All?*, 19, 24.

23. Jonathan Gruber, "The Role of Consumer Copayments for Health Care: Lessons from the RAND Health Insurance Experiment and Beyond," Henry J. Kaiser Family Foundation (October 2, 2006), 8; see also Aviva Aron-Dine, Liran Einav, and Amy Finkelstein, "The RAND Health Insurance Experiment, Three Decades Later," *Journal of Economic Perspectives* 27, no. 1 (Winter 2013): 197–222.

24. Newhouse, *Free for All?*, 6, 401–402.

25. See, e.g., Frank A. Sloan and Chee-Ruey Hsieh, *Health Economics* (Cambridge, MA: MIT Press, 2012), 102.

26. "CMS History Project President's Speeches," 120.

27. "CMS History Project President's Speeches," 125.

28. Daniel C. Cherkin, Louis Grothaus, and Edward H. Wagner, "The Effect of Office Visit Copayments on Utilization in a Health Maintenance Organization," *Medical Care* 27, no. 7 (July 1989): 669–679.

29. Cherkin et al., "Effect of Office Visit Copayments," 676.

30. Roger Feldman and Bryan Dowd, "A New Estimate of the Welfare Loss of Excess Health Insurance," *American Economic Review* 81, no. 1 (March 1991): 300.

31. "CMS History Project President's Speeches," 153.

32. "CMS History Project President's Speeches," 153.

33. Victor R. Fuchs, "Economics, Values, and Health Care Reform," *American Economic Review* 86, no. 1 (March 1996): 1–24.

34. Willard G. Manning and M. Susan Marquis, "Health Insurance: The Tradeoff between Risk Pooling and Moral Hazard," *Journal of Health Economics* 15, no. 5 (October 1996): 609–639.

35. "CMS History Project President's Speeches," 305.

36. David U. Himmelstein et al., "Illness and Injury as Contributors to Bankruptcy," *Health Affairs* 24 (2005): w63–w73.

37. Christopher Tarver Robertson, Richard Egelhof, and Michael Hoke, "Get Sick, Get Out: The Medical Causes of Home Foreclosures," *Health Matrix* 18, no. 1 (February 2008): 65–104.

38. Christina A. Cutshaw et al., "Medical Causes and Consequences of Home Foreclosures," *International Journal of Health Services* 46, no. 1 (2016): 36–47.

39. See, e.g., David Dranove and Michael L. Millenson, "Medical Bankruptcy: Myth versus Fact," *Health Affairs* 25, no. 2 (2006): w74–w83.

40. Barack Obama, "Address to Joint Congressional Session" (September 9, 2009), http://www.cbsnews.com/news/transcript-obamas-health-care-speech/.

41. Barack Obama, "Remarks by the President on Health Care Reform," White House (March 3, 2010), https://www.whitehouse.gov/the-press-office/remarks -president-health-care-reform.

42. Charles Silver and David A. Hyman, *Overcharged: Why Americans Pay Too Much for Health Care* (Washington, DC: Cato Institute, 2018), 21.

43. Peter Sullivan, "Trump Officials Consider Allowing Medicaid Block Grants for States," *The Hill* (January 11, 2019), https://thehill.com/policy/healthcare /424988-trump-officials-consider-allowing-medicaid-block-grants-for-states.

44. Zarek C. Brot-Goldberg, Amitabh Chandra, Benjamin R. Handel, and Jonathan T. Kolstad. "What does a deductible do? The impact of cost-sharing on health care prices, quantities, and spending dynamics." *The Quarterly Journal of Economics* 132, no. 3 (2017): 1288.

45. Michael Chernew, Zack Cooper, Eugene Larsen-Hallock, and Fiona Scott Morton, "Are Health Care Services Shoppable? Evidence from the Consumption of Lower-Limb MRI Scans," NBER Working Paper No. 24869 (January 2019).

46. Mark V. Pauly, "Medicare Drug Coverage and Moral Hazard," *Health Affairs* 23, no. 1 (January / February 2004): 114.

47. Pauly, 115.

48. John A. Nyman, *The Theory of Demand for Health Insurance* (Stanford, CA: Stanford University Press, 2003), xiii.

49. Emily M. Mitchell and Steven R. Machlin, "Statistical Brief #506: Concentration of Health Expenditures and Selected Characteristics of High Spenders, U.S. Civilian Noninstitutionalized Population, 2015," Medical Expenditure Panel Survey (December 2017), https://meps.ahrq.gov/data_files/publications /st506/stat506.shtml.

50. Melissa D. Aldridge and Amy S. Kelley, "The Myth Regarding the High Cost of End-of-Life Care," *American Journal of Public Health* 105, no. 12 (December 2015): 2411–2415.

51. Aldridge and Kelley, 2412.

52. Mitchell and Machlin, "Statistical Brief."

53. M. Gregg Bloche, "Consumer-Directed Health Care and the Disadvantaged," *Health Affairs* 26, no. 5 (September / October 2007): 1325.

54. Timothy Jost, *Health care at risk: a critique of the consumer-driven movement.* (Durham, NC: Duke University Press, 2007).

55. Christopher Tarver Robertson, "From Free Riders to Fairness: A Cooperative System for Organ Transplantation," *Jurimetrics* (2007): 1–41.

56. Avraham Stoler et al., "Incentivizing organ donor registrations with organ allocation priority." *Health Economics* 26, no. 4 (2017): 500–510.

57. Newhouse, *Free for All?*, 7.

58. Aron-Dine et al., "RAND Health Insurance Experiment," 197–222.

59. Aron-Dine et al., 202.

60. Newhouse, *Free for All?*, 366.

61. Nyman, *Theory of Demand*, 165.

62. Dana P. Goldman et al., "Pharmacy Benefits and the Use of Drugs by the Chronically Ill," *JAMA* 291, no. 19 (May 19, 2004): 2344–2350.

63. Ali R. Rahimi et al., "Financial Barriers to Health Care and Outcomes after Acute Myocardial Infarction," *JAMA* 297, no. 10 (March 2007): 1063–1072.

64. Teresa B. Gibson, "Cost Sharing, Adherence, and Health Outcomes in Patients with Diabetes," *American Journal of Managed Care* 16, no. 8 (August 2010): 589–600.

65. J. Frank Wharam et al., "Diabetes Outpatient Care and Acute Complications before and after High-Deductible Insurance Enrollment: A Natural Experiment for Translation in Diabetes (NEXT-D) Study," *JAMA Internal Medicine* 177, no. 3 (March 2017): 358–368.

66. J. Frank Wharam et al., "Low-Socioeconomic-Status Enrollees in High-Deductible Plans Reduced High-Severity Emergency Care," *Health Affairs* 32, no. 8 (August 2013): 1398–1406.

67. Kenneth E. Thorpe, Lindsay Allen, and Peter Joski, "Out-of-Pocket Prescription Costs under a Typical Silver Plan Are Twice as High as They Are in the Average Employer Plan," *Health Affairs* 34, no. 10 (October 2015): 1695–1703.

68. Kathryn Swartz, "Cost-Sharing: Effects on Spending and Outcomes," Robert Wood Johnson Foundation Research, Research Synthesis Report no. 20 (December 2010): 1.

69. Sloan and Hsieh, *Health Economics,* 143. See also Sloan and Hsieh, 512 (describing Nyman's theory in passing, but not in the chapter on demand for healthcare and moral hazard).

70. Sander Kelman and Albert Woodward, "John Nyman and the Economics of Health Care Moral Hazard," *ISRN Economics* 2013 (March 2013): 1–8. Compare Amy Finkelstein, *Moral Hazard in Health Insurance* (New York: Columbia University Press, 2014) (ignoring Nyman's theory).

71. Thomas Kuhn, *The Structure of Scientific Revolutions* (Chicago: University of Chicago Press, 1962).

72. See, generally, Victor Laurion and Christopher Robertson. "Ideology Meets Reality: What Works and What Doesn't in Patient Exposure to Health Care Costs," *Indiana Health Law Review* 15 (2018): 43.

73. Nyman, *Theory of Demand,* 165.

74. Silver and Hyman, *Overcharged,* 21.

75. See Frank D Gianfrancesco, "A Proposal for Improving the Efficiency of Medical Insurance," *Journal of Health Economics* 2, no. 2 (1983): 175–184; Robert F. Graboyes, "Our Money or Your Life: Indemnities vs. Deductibles in Health Insurance," Federal Reserve Bank of Richmond (Working Paper No. 00–04, August 2000), http://www.richmondfed.org/publications/research/working_papers /2000/pdf/wp00-4.pdf; Mark V. Pauly, "Indemnity Insurance for Health Care Efficiency," *Economics and Business Bulletin* 24 (1971): 53–59.

76. See, e.g., the Massachusetts insurance regulation at 211 CMR 123.05. See also Susan Feigenbaum, "'Body Shop' Economics: What's Good for Our Cars May Be Good for Our Health," *Regulation: Cato Review of Business and Government* 15, no. 4 (Fall 1992): 25–31.

77. California Insurance Code §2051.5(c).

78. Joshua M. Wiener and Alison Evans Cuellar, "Public and Private Responsibilities: Home- and Community-Based Services in the United Kingdom and Germany," *Journal of Aging and Health* 11, no. 3 (August 1999): 438.

79. John A. Nyman, Cagatay Koc, Bryan E. Dowd, Ellen McCreedy, and Helen Markelova Trenz, "Decomposition of Moral Hazard," *Journal of Health Economics* 57 (2018): 168–178, 177.

80. Christopher Robertson, Andy Yuan, Wendan Zhang, and Keith Joiner, "Distinguishing Moral Hazard from the Access Function of Insurance for Expensive Healthcare" (unpublished manuscript, available from the authors).

81. Spencer C. Evans et al., "Vignette Methodologies for Studying Clinicians' Decision-Making: Validity, Utility, and Application in ICD-11 Field Studies," *International Journal of Clinical and Health Psychology* 15, no. 2 (2015): 160–170; Jens Hainmueller, Dominik Hangartner, and Teppei Yamamoto, "Validating Vignette and Conjoint Survey Experiments against Real-World Behavior," *Proceedings of the National Academy of Sciences* 112, no. 8 (2015): 2395–2400; Lisa Wallander, "25 Years of Factorial Surveys in Sociology: A Review," *Social Science Research* 38, no. 3 (2009): 505–520.

82. Kathryn Zeiler, "Cautions on the Use of Economics Experiments in Law," *Journal of Institutional and Theoretical Economics* 166, no. 1 (2010): 184.

83. Wayne Drash, "When Insurance Wouldn't Pay, Parents Funded Cancer Patient's $95,000 Lifesaving Treatment," CNN.com (August 17, 2018), https://www .cnn.com/2018/08/15/health/cancer-survivor-insurance-denial-battle/index.html.

## 2. HOW WE EXPERIENCE EXPOSURE

1. Nir Eyal, Paul L. Romain, and Christopher Robertson, "Can Rationing through Inconvenience Be Ethical?," *Hastings Center Report* 48, no. 1 (January–February 2018): 10–22.

2. Alison K. Hoffman, "Health Care's Market Bureaucracy," *UCLA Law Review* 66 (forthcoming, draft as of May 27, 2019), available at https://papers.ssrn.com/sol3/papers.cfm?abstract_id=3394970.

3. Charles J. Hobson et al., "Stressful Life Events: A Revision and Update of the Social Readjustment Rating Scale," *International Journal of Stress Management* 5, no. 1 (January 1998): 1–23.

4. J. E. McGrath, "Stress and Behavior in Organizations," in *Handbook of Industrial and Organizational Psychology,* ed. M. Dunette (Chicago: Rand McNally, 1976), 1352.

5. See generally Daniel Kahneman, *Thinking, Fast and Slow* (New York: Farrar, Straus and Giroux, 2011); Thomas Gilovich, Dale W. Griffin, and Daniel Kahneman, *Heuristics and Biases: The Psychology of Intuitive Judgment* (Cambridge: Cambridge University Press, 2002).

6. Sendhil Mullainathan and Eldar Shafir, *Scarcity: Why Having Too Little Means So Much* (New York: Times Books, 2013).

7. Hobson et al., "Stressful Life Events," 1–23.

8. S. Yousuf Zafar et al., "The Financial Toxicity of Cancer Treatment: A Pilot Study Assessing Out-of-Pocket Expenses and the Insured Cancer Patient's Experience," *Oncologist* 18, no. 4 (April 2013): 381–390.

9. Fay J. Hlubocky et al., "Financial Burdens (FB), Quality of Life, and Psychological Distress among Advanced Cancer Patients (ACP) in Phase I Trials and Their Spousal Caregivers (SC)," *Journal of Clinical Oncology* 30, no. 15 suppl. (May 20, 2012): 6117.

10. Gustav Schelling et al., "Exposure to High Stress in the Intensive Care Unit May Have Negative Effects on Health-Related Quality-of-Life Outcomes after Cardiac Surgery," *Critical Care Medicine* 31, no. 7 (July 2003): 1971–1980.

11. Richard S. DeFrank and John M. Ivancevich, "Stress on the Job: An Executive Update," *Academy of Management Executive* 12, no. 3 (August 1998): 55–66; James Campbell Quick et al., *Preventive Stress Management in Organizations* (Washington, DC: American Psychological Association, 1997).

12. Bruce S. McEwen, "Central Effects of Stress Hormones in Health and Disease: Understanding the Protective and Damaging Effects of Stress and Stress Mediators," *European Journal of Pharmacology* 583, no. 2–3 (April 2008): 174–185.

13. Eva Pool, Sylvain Delplanque, Géraldine Coppin, and David Sander, "Is Comfort Food Really Comforting? Mechanisms Underlying Stress-Induced Eating," *Food Research International* 76 (2015): 207–215.

14. Mara Mather and Nichole R. Lighthall, "Risk and Reward Are Processed Differently in Decisions Made under Stress," *Current Directions in Psychological Science* 21, no. 1 (February 2012): 36–41.

15. Paul S. Appelbaum, Loren H. Roth, Charles W. Lidz, Paul Benson, and William Winslade, "False Hopes and Best Data: Consent to Research and the Therapeutic Misconception," *Hastings Center Report* 17, no. 2 (1987): 20–24.

16. Katrina Starcke and Matthias Brand, "Effects of Stress on Decisions under Uncertainty: A Meta-analysis," *Psychological Bulletin* 142, no. 9 (2016): 909–933.

17. See, for instance, Kaileigh A. Byrne, Astin C. Cornwall, and Darrell A. Worthy, "Acute Stress Improves Long-Term Reward Maximization in Decision-Making under Uncertainty," *Brain and Cognition* (2019, forthcoming) (finding that acute stress, e.g., immersing a hand in ice water, can improve goal-oriented learning).

18. B. Ann Hilton, "Quantity and Quality of Patients' Sleep and Sleep-Disturbing Factors in a Respiratory Intensive Care Unit," *Journal of Advanced Nursing* 1, no. 6 (1976): 453–468.

19. Sharon K. Inouye, Sidney T. Bogardus Jr., Peter A. Charpentier, Linda Leo-Summers, Denise Acampora, Theodore R. Holford, and Leo M. Cooney Jr., "A Multicomponent Intervention to Prevent Delirium in Hospitalized Older Patients," *New England Journal of Medicine* 340, no. 9 (1999): 669–676.

20. William D. S. Killgore, "Effects of Sleep Deprivation on Cognition," in *Progress in Brain Research,* ed. G. A. Kerkhof and H. P. A. Van Dongen, vol. 185 (Oxford: Elsevier, 2010), 114.

21. Killgore, "Effects of Sleep Deprivation on Cognition."

22. Pennie S. Seibert and Henry C. Ellis, "Irrelevant Thoughts, Emotional Mood States, and Cognitive Task Performance," *Memory and Cognition* 19, no. 5 (September 1991): 507–513.

23. Mary Frances Luce, James R. Bettman, and John W. Payne, "Choice Processing in Emotionally Difficult Decisions," *Journal of Experimental Psychology: Learning, Memory, and Cognition* 23, no. 2 (March 1997): 387.

24. Luce, Bettman, and Payne, 387.

25. George F. Loewenstein et al., "Risk as Feelings," *Psychological Bulletin* 127, no. 2 (March 2001): 267–286.

26. Anandi Mani et al., "Poverty Impedes Cognitive Function," *Science* 341, no. 6149 (August 30, 2013): 976–980.

27. Mani et al., 976.

28. Mani et al., 980.

29. Mani et al., 976.

30. Mani et al., 980.

31. See Jelte M. Wicherts and Annemarie Zand Scholten, "Comment on 'Poverty Impedes Cognitive Function,'" *Science* 342, no. 6163 (December 6, 2013): 1169; Anandi Mani et al., "Response to 'Comment on "Poverty Impedes Cognitive Function,"'" *Science* 342, no. 6163 (December 6, 2013): 1169.

32. Bruce Vladeck, "The Market v. Regulation: The Case for Regulation," *Milbank Quarterly* 59 (1981): 209.

33. Cass R. Sunstein, "Incommensurability and Kinds of Valuation: Some Applications in Law," in *Incommensurability, Incomparability, and Practical Reason,* ed. Ruth Chang (Cambridge, MA: Harvard University Press, 1998), 234, 238.

34. Margaret Jane Radin, "Market-Inalienability," *Harvard Law Review* 100, no. 8 (June 1987): 1849–1937; see also Margaret Radin, *Contested Commodities* (Cambridge, MA: Harvard University Press, 1996).

35. Keith A. Joiner and Robert F. Lusch, "Evolving to a New Service-Dominant Logic for Health Care," *Innovation and Entrepreneurship in Health* 3, no. 3 (January 2016): 25–33.

36. Richard A. Epstein, "Are Values Incommensurable, or Is Utility the Ruler of the World?," *Utah Law Review* 1995, no. 3 (1995): 683–715.

37. Michael J. Sandel, *What Money Can't Buy: The Moral Limits Of Markets* (New York: Farrar, Straus and Giroux, 2012).

38. Christopher Robertson et al., "The Appearance and the Reality of Quid Pro Quo Corruption: An Empirical Investigation," *Journal of Legal Analysis* 8 no. 2 (May 23, 2016): 375–438.

39. I. Glenn Cohen, "The Price of Everything, the Value of Nothing: Reframing the Commodification Debate," *Harvard Law Review* 117, no. 2 (December 2003): 689–710.

40. Gilbert Ryle, *The Concept of Mind* (Chicago: University of Chicago Press, 1949).

41. David Mechanic and Mark Schlesinger, "The Impact of Managed Care on Patients' Trust in Medical Care and Their Physicians," *JAMA* 275, no. 21 (1996): 1693–1697.

42. Robert J. Blendon et al., "Understanding the Managed Care Backlash: Regardless of How Well Their Plans Perform Today, People in Managed Care Have Greater Fears Than Their Traditionally Insured Peers Do That Their Plan Will Fall Short When They Really Need It," *Health Affairs* 17, no. 4 (1998): 80–94.

43. David Schenck and Larry Churchill, *Healers: Extraordinary Clinicians at Work* (New York: Oxford University Press, 2012), 42.

44. Mark A. Hall, *Making Medical Spending Decisions: The Law, Ethics, and Economics of Rationing Mechanisms* (New York: Oxford University Press, 1997).

45. Akshay R. Rao and Kent B. Monroe, "The Effect of Price, Brand Name, and Store Name on Buyers' Perceptions of Product Quality: An Integrative Review," *Journal of Marketing Research* 26, no. 3 (August 1989): 351–357.

46. Baba Shiv, Ziv Carmon, and Dan Ariely, "Placebo Effects of Marketing Actions: Consumers May Get What They Pay For," *Journal of Marketing Research* 42, no. 4 (November 2005): 383.

47. Thomas Kramer et al., "The Effect of a No-Pain, No-Gain Lay Theory on Product Efficacy Perceptions," *Marketing Letters* 23, no. 3 (February 2012): 517–529.

48. Rebecca L. Waber et al., "Commercial Features of Placebo and Therapeutic Efficacy," *JAMA* 299, no. 9 (April 2008): 1016–1017.

49. W. H. Shrank, "Patients' Perceptions of Generic Medications," *Health Affairs* 28, no. 2 (March / April 2009): 546–556.

50. Aaron S. Kesselheim et al., "Variations in Patients' Perceptions and Use of Generic Drugs: Results of a National Survey," *Journal of General Internal Medicine* 31, no. 6 (June 2016): 609–614.

51. Anna D. Sinaiko, Ateev Mehrotra, and Neeraj Sood, "Cost-Sharing Obligations, High-Deductible Health Plan Growth, and Shopping for Health Care." *JAMA Internal Medicine* 176, no. 3 (March 2016): 395–397.

52. See also Alfredo R. Paloyo, "Co-Pay and Feel Okay: Self-Rated Health Status after a Health Insurance Reform," *Social Science Quarterly* 95, no. 2 (June 2014): 507–522; Adriana Samper and Janet A. Schwartz, "Price Inferences for Sacred versus Secular Goods: Changing the Price of Medicine Influences Perceived Health Risk," *Journal of Consumer Research* 39, no. 6 (April 2013): 1343–1358.

53. See James F. Childress and Mark Siegler, "Metaphors and Models of Doctor-Patient Relationships: Their Implications for Autonomy," *Theoretical Medicine* 5, no. 1 (February 1984): 17–30.

54. Analee E. Beisecker and Thomas D. Beisecker, "Using Metaphors to Characterize Doctor-Patient Relationships: Paternalism versus Consumerism," *Health Communication* 5, no. 1 (1993): 41–58.

55. Leo G. Reeder, "The Patient-Client as a Consumer: Some Observations on the Changing Professional-Client Relationship," *Journal of Health and Social Behavior* 13, no. 4 (December 1972): 406–412.

56. *Schloendorff v. Society of New York Hospital*, 105 N.E. 92 (N.Y. 1914).

57. 409 U.S. 1064, 93 S. Ct. 560, 34 L. Ed. 2d 518 (U.S. Nov. 1, 1972).

58. Jochanan Benbassat, Dina Pilpel, and Meira Tidhar, "Patients' Preferences for Participation in Clinical Decision," *Behavioral Medicine* 24, no. 2 (Summer 1998): 81–88.

59. Beisecker and Beisecker, "Using Metaphors," 51; Stephen Barrett, *Consumer Health: A Guide to Intelligent Decisions,* 2nd ed. (Maryland Heights, MO: C. V. Mosby, 1980).

60. Beisecker and Beisecker, "Using Metaphors," 51.

61. Matthew J. B. Lawrence, "The Social Consequences Problem in Health Insurance and How to Solve It," *Harvard Law and Policy Review* 13 (forthcoming).

62. Zelda Di Blasi et al., "Influence of Context Effects on Health Outcomes: A Systematic Review," *Lancet* 357, no. 9258 (March 10, 2001): 757.

63. Arch G. Mainous III et al., "The Relationship between Continuity of Care and Trust with Stage of Cancer at Diagnosis," *Family Medicine* 36, no. 1 (January 2004): 35–39.

64. Mohammadreza Hojat et al., "Physicians' Empathy and Clinical Outcomes for Diabetic Patients," *Academic Medicine* 86, no. 3 (March 2011): 359–364.

65. Hojat et al., 362.

66. John D. Piette et al., "The Role of Patient-Physician Trust in Moderating Medication Nonadherence Due to Cost Pressures," *Archives of Internal Medicine* 165, no. 15 (August 2005): 1749–1755.

67. Fred Hirsch, *The Social Limits to Growth* (Cambridge, MA: Harvard University Press, 1976), 87, 92, 93.

68. Hirsch, 86.

69. Ellery Chih-Han Huang, Christy Pu, Yiing-Jenq Chou, and Nicole Huang, "Public Trust in Physicians—Health Care Commodification as a Possible Deteriorating Factor: Cross-Sectional Analysis of 23 Countries," *Inquiry: The Journal of Health Care Organization, Provision, and Financing* 55 (2018): 1–11.

70. Peter J. Cunningham, "High Medical Cost Burdens, Patient Trust, and Perceived Quality of Care," *Journal of General Internal Medicine* 24 no. 3 (March 2009): 418.

71. Cunningham, 416.

72. Cunningham, 419.

73. Larry R Churchill, Joseph B. Fanning, and David Schenck, *What Patients Teach: The Everyday Ethics of Health Care* (New York: Oxford University Press, 2013), 33–34, table 2.1.

74. Cass Sunstein and Richard Thaler, *Nudge* (New Haven, CT: Yale University Press, 2008), 8.

75. George Loewenstein et al., "Can Behavioural Economics Make Us Healthier?," *British Medical Journal* 344 (May 2012): 1–3.

76. Sarah Kliff, "In Health Care, Determining What's Unnecessary," *Washington Post Wonkblog* (January 19, 2012), http://www.washingtonpost.com/blogs/wonkblog/post/in-health-care-determining-whats-unnecessary/2012/01/19/gIQAGo2mAQ_blog.html.

77. See Victoria Craig Bunce and J. P. Wieske, "Health Insurance Mandates in the States 2010," Council for Affordable Health Insurance (2010), 1, https://www.senatorpatrickcolbeck.com/wp-content/uploads/2013/06/MandatesintheStates2010.pdf.

78. Mark A. Hall, "State Regulation of Medical Necessity: The Case of Weight-Reduction Surgery," *Duke Law Journal* 53, no. 2 (2003): 653–672.

79. Eduardo Porter, "The More Choice the Better: Yes, No or Maybe?," *New York Times* (March 29, 2005).

80. Bruce C. Vladeck, "The Market vs. Regulation: The Case for Regulation," *Milbank Memorial Fund Quarterly Health and Society* 59, no. 2 (1981): 212.

81. See generally Barry Schwartz, *The Paradox of Choice, Why More Is Less* (New York: HarperCollins, 2004).

82. Sheena S. Iyengar, Gur Huberman, and Wie Jiang, "How Much Choice Is Too Much? Contributions to 401(k) Retirement Plans," in *Pension Design and Structure: New Lessons from Behavioral Finance,* ed. Olivia S. Mitchell and Stephen P. Utkus (New York: Oxford University Press, 2004), 83–95.

83. Donald A. Redelmeier and Eldar Shafir, "Medical Decision Making in Situations That Offer Multiple Alternatives," *JAMA* 273, no. 4 (January 25, 1995): 302.

84. Benjamin Scheibehenne, Rainer Greifeneder, and Peter M. Todd, "Can There Ever Be Too Many Options? A Meta-Analytic Review of Choice Overload," *Journal of Consumer Research* 37, no. 3 (October 2010): 409–425.

85. Eric J. Johnson and Daniel G. Goldstein, "Do Defaults Save Lives?," *Science* 302, no. 5649 (November 21, 2003): 1338–1339.

86. Ilana Ritov and Jonathan Baron, "Outcome Knowledge, Regret, and Omission Bias," *Organizational Behavior and Human Decision Processes* 66, no. 2 (November 1995): 119–228.

87. Ziv Carmon, Klaus Wertenbroch, and Marcel Zeelenberg, "Option Attachment: When Deliberating Makes Choosing Feel Like Losing," *Journal of Consumer Research* 30, no. 1 (June 2003): 15–29.

88. Maya Bar-Hillel and Efrat Neter, "Why Are People Reluctant to Exchange Lottery Tickets?," *Journal of Personality and Social Psychology* 70, no. 1 (January 1996): 17–27.

89. Terry Connolly and Jochen Reb, "Regret Aversion in Reason-Based Choice," *Theory and Decision* 73, no. 1 (July 2012): 35–51 (reviewing studies).

90. Janet Landman, *Regret: The Persistence of the Possible* (New York: Oxford University Press, 1993), 45.

91. Terry Connolly and Jochen Reb, "Regret in Cancer-Related Decisions," *Health Psychology* 24, no. 4 suppl. (August 2005): S31.

92. Connolly and Reb, S31.

93. Richard Thaler, "Toward a Positive Theory of Consumer Choice," *Journal of Economic Behavior and Organization* 1, no. 1 (March 1980): 53.

94. Matthew K. Wynia et al., "Do Physicians Not Offer Useful Services Because of Coverage Restrictions?," *Health Affairs* 22, no. 4 (July / August 2003): 190–197.

95. Jack A. Clark, Nelda P. Wray, and Carol M. Ashton, "Living with Treatment Decisions: Regrets and Quality of Life among Men Treated for Metastatic Prostate Cancer," *Journal of Clinical Oncology* 19, no. 1 (January 2001): 72–80.

96. Thomas Gilovich and Victoria Husted Medvec, "The Experience of Regret: What, When, and Why," *Psychological Review* 102, no. 2 (May 1995): 379–395.

97. Connolly and Reb, S29–S34.

98. Itamar Simonson, "The Influence of Anticipating Regret and Responsibility on Purchase Decisions," *Journal of Consumer Research* 19, no. 1 (June 1992): 105–118.

99. Youngmee Kim et al., "Serotonin Transporter Polymorphism, Depressive Symptoms, and Emotional Impulsivity among Advanced Breast Cancer Patients," *Supportive Care in Cancer* 26, no. 4 (October 2017): 1185.

100. See Stacey L. Sheridan, "Shared Decision Making about Screening and Chemoprevention," *American Journal of Preventive Medicine* 26, no. 1 (January 2004): 56–66.

101. See Marco Boeria et al., "The Role of Regret Minimisation in Lifestyle Choices Affecting the Risk of Coronary Heart Disease," *Journal of Health Economics* 32, no. 1 (January 2013): 253–260.

102. Thaler, "Toward a Positive Theory," 53.

103. Cruise Lines International Association, "2017 Cruise Industry Outlook" (December 2016), https://www.cruising.org/docs/default-source/research/clia-2017 -state-of-the-industry.pdf?sfvrsn=0.

104. Scott Mayerowitz, "Paying to Pee: Have the Airlines Gone Too Far?," *ABC News* (April 13, 2010), https://abcnews.go.com/Travel/Green/paying-pee-airlines -critics-call-ryanairs-fee-inhumane/story?id=10355139.

105. Herb Weisbaum, "Consumers Will Spend Almost $800 Billion on Holiday Shopping," *NBC News* (October 18, 2016), http://www.nbcnews.com/business /consumer/consumers-will-spend-almost-800-billion-holiday-shopping-n667646.

106. Jennifer Pate Offenberg, "Markets: Gift Cards," *Journal of Economic Perspectives* 21, no. 2 (Spring 2007): 227–238.

107. Aviva Aron-Dine, Liran Einav, and Amy Finkelstein, "The RAND Health Insurance Experiment, Three Decades Later," *Journal of Economic Perspectives* 27, no. 1 (Winter 2013): 197–222.

108. Joseph P. Newhouse, *Free for All? Lessons from the RAND Health Insurance Experiment* (Cambridge, MA: Harvard University Press, 1996), 19, 24.

109. Andrea J. Bullock et al., "Understanding Patients' Attitudes toward Communication about the Cost of Cancer Care," *Journal of Oncology Practice* 8, no. 4 (July 1, 2012): e50–e58.

110. Roseanna Sommers et al., "Focus Groups Highlight That Many Patients Object to Clinicians' Focusing on Costs," *Health Affairs* 32, no. 2 (February 2013): 338.

111. Sommers et al., 343.

112. Sommers et al., 343.

113. Greer Donley and Marion Danis, "Making the Case for Talking to Patients about the Costs of End-of-Life Care," *Journal of Law, Medicine and Ethics* 39, no. 2 (2011): 190.

114. Marion Danis et al., "Exploring Public Attitudes towards Approaches to Discussing Costs in the Clinical Encounter," *Journal of General Internal Medicine* 29, no. 1 (July 2013): 223–229.

115. Katherine Baicker, Sendhil Mullainathan, and Joshua Schwartzstein, "Behavioral Hazard in Health Insurance," *Quarterly Journal of Economics* 130, no. 4 (November 2015): 1623–1667.

116. "Preventive Services Covered by Private Health Plans under the Affordable Care Act," Henry J. Kaiser Family Foundation (August 4, 2015), http://kff.org /health-reform/fact-sheet/preventive-services-covered-by-private-health-plans/.

117. Geetesh Solanki and Helen Halpin Schauffler, "Cost-Sharing and Utilization of Clinical Preventive Services," *American Journal of Preventive Medicine* 17, no. 2 (August 1999): 127–133.

118. Susan H. Busch, Colleen L. Barry, Sally J. Vegso, Jody L. Sindelar, and Mark R. Cullen, "Effects of a Cost-Sharing Exemption on Use of Preventive Services at One Large Employer," *Health Affairs* 25, no. 6 (2006): 1529–1536.

119. Hitoshi Shigeoka, "The Effect of Patient Cost Sharing on Utilization, Health, and Risk Protection," *American Economic Review* 104, no. 7 (2014): 2154.

120. Stephen E. Kimmel et al., "Randomized Trial of Lottery-Based Incentives to Improve Warfarin Adherence," *American Heart Journal* 164, no. 2 (August 2012): 268–274.

121. Betsy Foxman et al., "The Effect of Cost Sharing on the Use of Antibiotics in Ambulatory Care: Results from a Population-Based Randomized Controlled Trial," *Journal of Chronic Diseases* 40, no. 5 (1987): 429.

## 3. OUR EMPTY POCKETS

1. Editorial Board, "This Tweet Captures the State of Health Care in America Today," *New York Times* (July 2, 2018).

2. Emily M. Mitchell and Steven R. Machlin, "Statistical Brief #506: Concentration of Health Expenditures and Selected Characteristics of High Spenders, U.S. Civilian Noninstitutionalized Population, 2015," Medical Expenditure Panel Survey (December 2017), https://meps.ahrq.gov/data_files/publications /st506/stat506.shtml.

3. Julie Appleby, "2016 PPO Plans Remove Out-of-Network Cost Limits, a Costly Trap for Consumers," *Kaiser Health News* (December 3, 2015), https://khn .org/news/2016-ppo-plans-remove-out-of-network-cost-limits-a-costly-trap-for -consumers/.

4. Elisabeth Rosenthal, "After Surgery, Surprise $117,000 Medical Bill from Doctor He Didn't Know," *New York Times* (September 20, 2014).

5. Erin C. Fuse Brown, "Consumer Financial Protection in Health Care," *Washington University Law Review* 95, no. 1 (2017): 137.

6. Kelly A. Kyanko, Leslie A. Curry, and Susan H. Busch, "Out-of-Network Physicians: How Prevalent Are Involuntary Use and Cost Transparency?," *Health Services Research* 48, no. 3 (June 2013): 1154–1172.

7. Zack Cooper and Fiona Scott Morton, "Out-of-Network Emergency-Physician Bills—an Unwelcome Surprise," *New England Journal of Medicine* 375, no. 20 (November 17, 2016): 1915–1918.

8. Matthew P. Banegas et al., "For Working-Age Cancer Survivors, Medical Debt and Bankruptcy Create Financial Hardships," *Health Affairs (Millwood)* 35, no. 1 (January 2016): 54–61 (see Exhibit 3).

9. Maria Pisu et al., "The Out of Pocket Cost of Breast Cancer Survivors: A Review." *Journal of Cancer Survivorship* 4, no. 3 (September 2010): 202–209.

10. "Managing the Cost of Cancer Care," *American Society of Clinical Oncology*, https://www.cancer.net/sites/cancer.net/files/cost_of_care_booklet.pdf.

11. Judith A. Vessey et al., "Impact of Non-Medical Out-of-Pocket Expenses on Families of Children with Cerebral Palsy Following Orthopaedic Surgery," *Journal of Pediatric Nursing* 37 (November–December 2017): 101–107.

12. Leslee L. Subak et al., "High Costs of Urinary Incontinence among Women Electing Surgery to Treat Stress Incontinence," *Obstetrics and Gynecology* 111, no. 4 (April 2008): 899–907.

13. "Paying for Complementary and Integrative Health Approaches," National Institutes of Health, https://nccih.nih.gov/health/financial.

14. "Consumer Expenditures—2016," Bureau of Labor Statistics, Economic News Release, https://www.bls.gov/news.release/cesan.nr0.htm.

15. Jennifer Erickson, ed., "The Middle-Class Squeeze," Center for American Progress, https://www.americanprogress.org/issues/economy/reports/2014/09/24/96903/the-middle-class-squeeze/.

16. Stacia West and Gary Mottola, "A Population on the Brink: American Renters, Emergency Savings, and Financial Fragility," *Poverty and Public Policy* 8, no. 1 (March 2016): 56–71.

17. Bianca DiJulio et al., "Data Note: Americans' Challenges with Health Care Costs," Henry J. Kaiser Family Foundation (March 2, 2017), https://www.kff.org/health-costs/poll-finding/data-note-americans-challenges-with-health-care-costs/.

18. Liz Hamel et al., "The Burden of Medical Debt: Results from the Kaiser Family Foundation / *New York Times* Medical Bills Survey, Section 3," Henry J. Kaiser Family Foundation (January 5, 2016), https://www.kff.org/report-section/the-burden-of-medical-debt-section-3-consequences-of-medical-bill-problems/.

19. Hamel et al.

20. Cathy Schoen et al., "Access, Affordability, and Insurance Complexity Are Often Worse in the United States Compared to Ten Other Countries," *Health Affairs* 32, no. 12 (December 2013): 2207.

21. Schoen et al., 2207.

22. "Average Household Income, by Income Source and Income Group, 1979 to 2014," Congressional Budget Office, http://cbo.gov/about/products/major -recurring-reports. (Scroll to the section titled "Distribution of Household Income and Federal Taxes"; select "March 2018"; scroll to and select "Supplemental Data (Single Excel File)"; and select "3. Avg HH Income.")

23. Amol K. Narang and Lauren Hersch Nicholas, "Out-of-Pocket Spending and Financial Burden among Medicare Beneficiaries with Cancer," *JAMA Oncology* 3, no. 6 (June 2017): 757–765.

24. See, e.g., Cathy Schoen et al., "How Many Are Underinsured? Trends among Adults, 2003 and 2007," *Health Affairs* 27, no. 4 (June 2008): w298–w309.

25. Paul D. Jacobs and Gary Claxton, "Comparing the Assets of Uninsured Households to Cost Sharing under High-Deductible Health Plans," *Health Affairs* 27, no. 3 (April 2008): w214–w221.

26. "Going to Work during Cancer Treatment," American Cancer Society, https://www.cancer.org/latest-news/going-to-work-during-cancer-treatment.html.

27. Scott Ramsey et al., "Washington State Cancer Patients Found to Be at Greater Risk for Bankruptcy than People without a Cancer Diagnosis," *Health Affairs (Millwood)* 32, no. 6 (June 2013): 1143.

28. Reshma Jagsi et al., "Impact of Adjuvant Chemotherapy on Long-Term Employment of Survivors of Early-Stage Breast Cancer," *Cancer* 120, no. 12 (June 2014): 1854–1862.

29. Joy C. MacDermid, James H. Roth, and Robert McMurtry, "Predictors of Time Lost from Work Following a Distal Radius Fracture," *Journal of Occupational Rehabilitation* 17, no. 1 (March 2007): 47–62.

30. I have taken the ranges of employment summarized in the prior literature by Puolakka and colleagues, and I then subtracted them from 100% to show the rates of unemployment. K. Puolakka et al., "Risk Factors for Back Pain-Related Loss of Working Time after Surgery for Lumbar Disc Herniation: A 5-Year Follow-Up Study," *European Spine Journal* 17, no. 3 (2008): 386–392.

31. Puolakka et al., 386–392.

32. Marcia M. Ward et al., "Lost Income and Work Limitations in Persons with Chronic Respiratory Disorders," *Journal of Clinical Epidemiology* 55, no. 3 (March 2002): 260–268.

33. K. E. Covinsky et al., "The Impact of Serious Illness on Patients' Families. SUPPORT Investigators. Study to Understand Prognoses and Preferences for Outcomes and Risks of Treatment," *JAMA* 272, no. 23 (December 1994): 1839.

34. Dorothy P. Rice et al., "The Economic Burden of Alzheimer's Disease Care," *Health Affairs* 12, no. 2 (Summer 1993): 164–176.

35. Carlos Dobkin et al., "The Economic Consequences of Hospital Admissions," *American Economic Review* 108, no. 2 (February 2018): 308–352.

36. Dobkin et al., 308–352.

37. Wen-Jui Han and Jane Waldfogel, "Parental Leave: The Impact of Recent Legislation on Parents' Leave-Taking," *Demography* 40, no. 1 (February 2003): 191–200.

38. Jody Heymann et al., "Contagion Nation: A Comparison of Paid Sick Day Policies in 22 Countries," Center for Economic Policy Research (May 2009), http://www.cepr.net/documents/publications/paid-sick-days-2009-05.pdf.

39. Xenia Scheil-Adlung and Lydia Sandner, "The Case for Paid Sick Leave," World Health Organization, World Health Report Background paper 9 (2010).

40. LeaAnne DeRigne, Patricia Stoddard-Dare, and Linda Quinn, "Workers without Paid Sick Leave Less Likely to Take Time Off for Illness or Injury Compared to Those with Paid Sick Leave," *Health Affairs* 35, no. 3 (March 2016): 520–527.

41. "SHRM Survey Findings: Paid Leave in the Workplace," Society for Human Resource Management (October 6, 2016), https://www.shrm.org/hr-today /trends-and-forecasting/research-and-surveys/Documents/2016-Paid-Leave-in-the -Workplace.pdf.

42. Rachel O'Connor, Jeff Hayes, and Barbara Gault, "Paid Sick Days Access Varies by Race/Ethnicity, Sexual Orientation, and Job Characteristics," Institute for Women's Policy Research (July 18, 2014), https://iwpr.org/publications/paid -sick-days-access-varies-by-raceethnicity-sexual-orientation-and-job-characteristics/.

43. Susan Nathan, "Short Term Disability Basics," Balance Careers, https:// www.thebalancecareers.com/short-term-disability-basics-1177839.

44. "Workers' Compensation (On-the-Job Injury or Illness), Workers' Compensation Benefits," New York State Workers' Compensation Board, http://www.wcb .ny.gov/content/main/onthejob/wcBenefits.jsp.

45. Chad Stone and William Chen, "Introduction to Unemployment Insurance," Center on Budget and Policy Priorities (July 30, 2014), https://www.cbpp .org/research/introduction-to-unemployment-insurance.

46. Stone and Chen, "Introduction to Unemployment Insurance."

47. "The Facts about Social Security's Disability Program," Social Security Administration (2018), https://www.ssa.gov/pubs/EN-05-10570.pdf.

48. "Facts about Social Security's Disability Program."

49. Dobkin et al., "Economic Consequences," 309.

50. Dobkin et al., 309, citing Fadlon, Itzik, and Torben Heien Nielsen, "Family Labor Supply Responses to Severe Health Shocks," National Bureau of Economic Research Working Paper 21352.

51. "Changes in U.S. Family Finances from 2013 to 2016: Evidence from the Survey of Consumer Finances," *Federal Reserve Bulletin* 103, no. 3: 1–42, https://www.federalreserve.gov/publications/files/scf17.pdf.

52. "Changes in U.S. Family Finances," 1–42.

53. Christopher Tarver Robertson, Richard Egelhof, and Michael Hoke, "Get Sick, Get Out: The Medical Causes for Home Mortgage Foreclosures," *Health Matrix: The Journal of Law—Medicine* 18, no. 1 (2008): 65–104; Christina A. Cutshaw et al., "Medical Causes and Consequences of Home Foreclosures," *International Journal of Health Services* 46, no. 1 (2016): 36–47.

54. Liz Hamel et al., "The Burden of Medical Debt: Results from the Kaiser Family Foundation / New York Times Medical Bills Survey, Section 1," Henry J. Kaiser Family Foundation (January 5, 2016), https://www.kff.org/report-section /the-burden-of-medical-debt-section-1-who-has-medical-bill-problems-and-what -are-the-contributing-factors/.

55. West and Mottola, "Population," 56.

56. West and Mottola, 58.

57. Banegas et al., "For Working-Age Survivors," 54–61.

58. Trey Bickham and Younghee Lim. "In sickness and in debt: do mounting medical bills predict payday loan debt?," *Social Work in Health Care* 54, no. 6 (2015): 518–531.

59. Wayne Barnes, "The Objective Theory of Contracts," *University of Cincinnati Law Review* 76 (2008): 1119–1158.

60. "Consumer Debt: A Primer," Aspen Institute, https://assets.aspeninstitute .org/content/uploads/2018/03/ASPEN_ConsumerDebt_06B.pdf.

61. Adam Cole, "Does Your Body Really Refresh Itself Every 7 Years?," National Public Radio (June 28, 2016), https://www.npr.org/sections/health-shots /2016/06/28/483732115/how-old-is-your-body-really.

62. Derek Parfit, "Personal Identity," *Philosophical Review* 80, no. 1 (January 1971): 3–27.

63. Shane Frederick, George Loewenstein, and Ted O'Donoghue, "Time Discounting and Time Preference: A Critical Review," *Journal of Economic Literature* 40, no. 2 (June 2002): 351–401.

64. Frederick et al., 354, citing Eugen Von Böhm-Bawerk, *Capital and Interest* (1889; South Holland: Libertarian Press, 1970).

65. Frederick et al., 354, note 2, citing Arthur C. Pigou, *The Economics of Welfare* (London: Macmillan, 1920).

66. Drazen Prelec and George Loewenstein, "The Red and the Black: Mental Accounting of Savings and Debt," *Marketing Science* 17, no. 1 (February 1998): 4.

67. Ofer Zellermayer, "The Pain of Paying," unpublished dissertation, Department of Social and Decision Sciences, Carnegie Mellon University,

Pittsburgh, PA (1996). See also George Loewenstein and Ted O'Donoghue, "'We Can Do This the Easy Way or the Hard Way': Negative Emotions, Self-Regulation, and the Law," *University of Chicago Law Review* 73, no. 1 (2006): 183–206 (developing this idea).

68. Richard A. Feinberg, "Credit Cards as Spending Facilitating Stimuli: A Conditioning Interpretation," *Journal of Consumer Research* 13, no. 3 (December 1986): 348–356.

69. Drazen Prelec and Duncan Simester, "Always Leave Home without It: A Further Investigation of the Credit-Card Effect on Willingness to Pay," *Marketing Letters* 12, no. 1 (February 2001): 5–12.

70. Loewenstein and O'Donoghue, "'We Can Do This,'" 196.

71. "Quarterly Report on Household Debt and Credit, 2017:Q4," Center for Microeconomic Data (February 2018), https://www.newyorkfed.org/medialibrary/interactives/householdcredit/data/pdf/HHDC_2017Q4.pdf.

72. Neale Mahoney, "Bankruptcy as Implicit Health Insurance," *American Economic Review* 105, no. 2 (2015): 711.

73. "Bankruptcy Timing with New Medical Debts," Wasson Thornhill: Bankruptcy Blog (September 20, 2017), https://wassonthornhill.com/bankruptcy-timing-new-medical-debts/.

74. "Bankruptcy Timing with New Medical Debts."

75. See *Milavetz, Gallop & Milavetz, P.A. v. United States*, 559 U.S. 229, 243 (2010) (holding that federal law "prohibits a debt relief agency only from advising a debtor to incur more debt because the debtor is filing for bankruptcy, rather than for a valid purpose" but not addressing the question of whether the law is valid under the First Amendment).

76. David U. Himmelstein et al., "Medical Bankruptcy in the United States, 2007: Results of a National Study," *American Journal of Medicine* 122, no. 8 (August 2009): 741–746.

77. "In the Red for a Hospital Bed: Medical Debt and Household Bankruptcies in Lane County," Act Now for a Healthy Oregon, http://acthealthyoregon.org/wp-content/uploads/2015/12/LaneCountyMedicalDebt.pdf.

78. Melissa B. Jacoby and Mirya Holman, "Managing Medical Bills on the Brink of Bankruptcy," *Yale Journal of Health Policy Law and Ethics* 10, no. 2 (2010): 242.

79. Ramsey et al., "Washington State Cancer Patients," 1143–1152.

80. Dobkin et al., "Economic Consequences," 308–352.

81. Quoted in Igor Livshits, "Recent Developments in Consumer Credit and Default Literature," *Journal of Economic Surveys* 29, no. 4 (August 2015): 598.

82. "The Impact of Third-Party Debt Collection on the US National and State Economies in 2016," prepared for ACA International by Ernst and Young

(November 2017), https://www.acainternational.org/assets/ernst-young/ey-2017-aca
-state-of-the-industry-report-final-5.pdf.

83. "The Structure and Practices of the Debt Buying Industry," Federal Trade
Commission (2013), http://www.ftc.gov/os/2013/01/debtbuyingreport.pdf.

84. Eric B. French et al., "End-of-Life Medical Spending in Last Twelve
Months of Life Is Lower Than Previously Reported," *Health Affairs* 36, no. 7
(July 2017): 1211–1217.

85. Johanna M. Novak and Erica E. L. Huddas, "Collection of Unpaid Medical
Expenses after a Patient's Death," Foster Swift Health Care Law Report
(July 2008), https://www.fosterswift.com/communications-Unpaid-Medical
-Expenses-After-Death.html.

86. "Changes in U.S. Family Finances."

87. Jim Hawkins, "Toward Behaviorally Informed Policies for Consumer
Credit Decisions in Self-Pay Medical Markets," in *Nudging Health,* ed. I. Glenn
Cohen, Holly Fernandez Lynch, and Christopher T. Robertson (Baltimore, MD:
Johns Hopkins University Press, 2017), 173 (quoting a contract).

88. Alan Zibel, "GE Capital to Refund Up to $34 Million over CareCredit
Medical Credit Cards," *Wall Street Journal* (December 10, 2013), https://www.wsj
.com/articles/ge-capital-to-pay-34-million-in-creditcard-case-1386700414.

89. Lucie Kalousova and Sarah A. Burgard, "Debt and Foregone Medical
Care," *Journal of Health and Social Behavior* 54, no. 2 (April 2013): 204–220.

90. Thomas P. O'Toole, Jose J. Arbelaez, and Robert S. Lawrence,
"Medical Debt and Aggressive Debt Restitution Practices: Predatory Billing
among the Urban Poor," *Journal of General Internal Medicine* 19, no. 7
(July 2004): 776.

91. John D. Piette, Michele Heisler, and Todd H. Wagner, "Cost-Related
Medication Underuse among Chronically Ill Adults: The Treatments People Forgo,
How Often, and Who Is at Risk," *American Journal of Public Health* 94, no. 10
(October 2004): 1782–1787.

92. Ali R. Rahimi, John A. Spertus, and Kimberly J. Reid, "Financial Barriers
to Health Care and Outcomes after Acute Myocardial Infarction," *JAMA* 297,
no. 10 (March 2007): 1063–1072.

93. Michael D. Kogan et al., "Underinsurance among Children in the United
States," *New England Journal of Medicine* 363, no. 9 (August 2010): 847.

94. Donald P. Oswald et al., "Underinsurance and Key Health Outcomes for
Children with Special Health Care Needs," *Pediatrics* 119, no. 2 (February 2007):
e341.

95. S. Yousuf Zafar et al., "The Financial Toxicity of Cancer Treatment: A Pilot
Study Assessing Out-of-Pocket Expenses and the Insured Cancer Patient's Experience," *Oncologist* 18, no. 4 (April 2013): 385.

96. Scott D. Ramsey et al., "Financial Insolvency as a Risk Factor for Early Mortality among Patients with Cancer," *Journal of Clinical Oncology* 34, no. 9 (March 2016): 980–986.

97. Stacie B. Dusetzina et al., "Cost Sharing and Adherence to Tyrosine Kinase Inhibitors for Patients with Chronic Myeloid Leukemia," *Journal of Clinical Oncology* 32, no. 4 (February 2014): 306–311; Nantana Kaisaeng, Spencer E. Harpe, and Norman V. Carroll, "Out-of-Pocket Costs and Oral Cancer Medication Discontinuation in the Elderly," *Journal of Managed Care and Specialty Pharmacy* 20, no. 7 (July 2014): 669–675.

98. Ramsey, "Financial Insolvency," 980.

99. Hamel, "Burden of Medical Debt, . . . Section 1."

100. Mark Rukavina, "Medical Debt and Its Relevance When Assessing Creditworthiness," *Suffolk University Law Review* 46, no. 4 (2013): 967–982.

101. Hamel, "Burden of Medical Debt, . . . Section 1."

102. Peter J. Cunningham, Carolyn Miller, and Alwyn Cassil, "Living on the Edge: Health Care Expenses Strain Family Budgets," Center for Studying Health System Change, Research Brief No. 10 (December 2008): 4.

103. Banegas et al., "For Working-Age Survivors," 54–61.

104. Rachel Jenkins et al., "Debt, Income and Mental Disorder in the General Population," *Psychological Medicine* 38, no. 10 (February 2008): 1485–1493, 1485.

105. Elizabeth Sweet et al., "The High Price of Debt: Household Financial Debt and Its Impact on Mental and Physical Health," *Social Science and Medicine* 91 (August 2013): 94.

106. Thomas Richardson, Peter Elliott, and Ronald Roberts, "The Relationship between Personal Unsecured Debt and Mental and Physical Health: A Systematic Review and Meta-Analysis," *Clinical Psychology Review* 33, no. 8 (December 2013): 1148–1162.

107. See generally "Impact of Economic Crises on mental health," World Health Organization (2011): 1–23; Rachel Jenkins et al., "Recession, Debt and Mental Health: Challenges and Solutions," *Mental Health in Family Medicine* 6, no. 2 (June 2009): 85–90; Athina Economou, Agelike Nikolaou, and Ioannis Theodossiou, "Are Recessions Harmful to Health after All? Evidence from the European Union," *Journal of Economic Studies* 35, no. 5 (2008): 368–384; and Antti Uutela, "Economic Crisis and Mental Health," *Current Opinion in Psychiatry* 23, no. 2 (March 2010): 127–130.

108. Elizabeth MacBride, "Suicide and the Economy," *Atlantic* (September 26, 2013).

109. Katherine Baicker et al., "The Oregon Experiment—Effects of Medicaid on Clinical Outcomes," *New England Journal of Medicine* 368, no. 18 (May 2013): 1713–1722.

110. Klariz Tucker, Tyra Dark, and Jeffrey S. Harman, "Variation in Out of Pocket Health Care Costs for Individuals with Anxiety Disorders by Type of Insurance Coverage," *Journal of Anxiety Disorders* 58 (August 2018): 18–22.

## 4. WHAT WE OWE

1. Daniel Kahneman and Patrick Egan, *Thinking, Fast and Slow, Vol. 1* (New York: Farrar, Straus and Giroux, 2011).

2. Daniel Callahan, "Bioethics: Private Choice and Common Good," *Hastings Center Report* 24 (May–June 1994): 31.

3. John Rawls, *Theory of Justice* (Cambridge, MA: Belknap Press, 1999), 46.

4. David Orentlicher, *Matters of Life and Death: Making Moral Theory Work in Medical Ethics and the Law* (Princeton, NJ: Princeton University Press, 2001), 2–3.

5. Dhruv Khullar, "You're Sick. Whose Fault Is That?," *New York Times* (January 10, 2018).

6. Kyle P. Stanford, "The Difference between Ice Cream and Nazis: Moral Externalization and the Evolution of Human Cooperation," *Behavioral and Brain Sciences* 41 (2018): 1–57.

7. Joshua David Greene, *Moral Tribes: Emotion, Reason, and the Gap between Us and Them* (New York: Penguin, 2014).

8. Robert Kurzban and Mark R. Leary, "Evolutionary Origins of Stigmatization: The Functions of Social Exclusion," *Psychological Bulletin* 127, no. 2 (2001): 198.

9. Janet B. Younger, "The Alienation of the Sufferer," *Advances in Nursing Science* 17 no. 4 (July 1995): 54.

10. John Donne, *John Donne: Selected Prose,* ed. Neil Rhodes (London: Penguin, 1987), 106.

11. Leviticus 13.

12. "Universal Declaration of Human Rights: Article 25," United Nations, http://www.un.org/en/universal-declaration-human-rights/.

13. Peter Singer, "Famine, Affluence, and Morality," *Philosophy and Public Affairs* 1, no. 3 (Spring 1972): 229–243.

14. Singer, 230.

15. Jody Heymann et al., "Constitutional Rights to Health, Public Health and Medical Care: The Status of Health Protections in 191 Countries," *Global Public Health* 8, no. 6 (July 2013): 639–653.

16. "Fact Sheet: The Right to Health," World Health Organization and Office of the UN High Commissioner for Human Rights (August 2007), http://www.who.int/mediacentre/factsheets/fs323_en.pdf.

17. Roy G. Spece Jr., "AIDS: Due Process, Equal Protection, and the Right to Treatment," *Issues in Law and Medicine* 4, no. 3 (1988): 290.

18. William M. Sage, "Patient-Centered Law and Ethics: Should the Patient Conquer?," *Wake Forest Law Review* 45 (2010): 1505.

19. Oliver Wendell Holmes, *The Common Law,* ed. Mark DeWolfe Howe (Boston: Little, Brown, 1963), 76–78.

20. Thomas V. Inglesby et al., "Plague as a Biological Weapon: Medical and Public Health Management," *JAMA* 283, no. 17 (May 2000): 2281–2290.

21. Inglesby et al., 2281–2290.

22. Joseph Patrick Byrne, *Encyclopedia of Black Death, Vol. 1* (Santa Barbara, CA: ABC-CLIO, 2012), 27.

23. "Achievements in Public Health, 1900–1999 Impact of Vaccines Universally Recommended for Children—United States, 1990–1998," table 2, *MMWR Weekly,* Centers for Disease Control (April 2, 1999), https://www.cdc.gov/mmwr/preview /mmwrhtml/00056803.htm.

24. 197 U.S. 11, 25 S. Ct. 358, 49 L. Ed. 643 (1905).

25. "The Great Pandemic, the United States in 1918–1919," Internet Archive Wayback Machine, https://web.archive.org/web/20161026180557/http://www.flu .gov/pandemic/history/1918/life_in_1918/health/index.html.

26. Martin C. J. Bootsma and Neil M. Ferguson, "The Effect of Public Health Measures on the 1918 Influenza Pandemic in US Cities," *Proceedings of the National Academy of Sciences* 104, no. 18 (2007): 7588.

27. John Dewey, *The Public and Its Problems* (Athens, GA: Swallow Press, 1954), 27.

28. Wilfrid Sellars, *Science and Metaphysics: Variations on Kantian Themes* (London: Routledge, 1968).

29. See, e.g., Emile Durkheim, *The Division of Labor in Society* (New York: Free Press, 1984).

30. "Explore Findings from the New Report: 'U.S. Health in International Perspectives,' Mortality Rates: How the U.S. Compares: Diabetes Mellitus," National Academy of Sciences, Engineering, and Medicine, Committee on Population, http://sites.nationalacademies.org/dbasse/cpop/dbasse_080393#diabetes -mellitus.

31. "Explore Findings from the New Report: 'U.S. Health in International Perspectives,' Mortality Rates: How the U.S. Compares: Neuropsychiatric Conditions," National Academy of Sciences, Engineering, and Medicine, Committee on Population, http://sites.nationalacademies.org/dbasse/cpop/dbasse_080393#neuro psychiatric-conditions.

32. "Explore Findings from the New Report: 'U.S. Health in International Perspectives,' Mortality Rates: How the U.S. Compares: Stomach Cancer," National Academy of Sciences, Engineering, and Medicine, Committee on Population, http://sites.nationalacademies.org/dbasse/cpop/dbasse_080393#stomach-cancer.

33. Michael Marmot et al., "Closing the Gap in a Generation: Health Equity through Action on the Social Determinants of Health," *Lancet* 372, no. 9650 (November 8, 2008): 1661.

34. Sandro Galea et al., "Estimated Deaths Attributable to Social Factors in the United States," *American Journal of Public Health* 101, no. 8 (August 2011): 1456.

35. Ryan W. Diver et al., "Secondhand Smoke Exposure in Childhood and Adulthood in Relation to Adult Mortality among Never Smokers," *American Journal of Preventive Medicine* 55, no. 3 (September 2018): 345–352.

36. John W. Lynch, George A. Kaplan, and Jukka T. Salonen, "Why Do Poor People Behave Poorly? Variation in Adult Health Behaviours and Psychosocial Characteristics by Stages of the Socioeconomic Lifecourse," *Social Science and Medicine* 44, no. 6 (March 1997): 809–819.

37. Farhad Islami et al., "Proportion and Number of Cancer Cases and Deaths Attributable to Potentially Modifiable Risk Factors in the United States," *CA: A Cancer Journal for Clinicians,* 68, no. 1 (January 2018): 31.

38. Steven A. Schroeder, "We Can Do Better—Improving the Health of the American People," *New England Journal of Medicine* 357, no. 12 (September 2007): 1221–1228.

39. Yascha Mounk, *The Age of Responsibility: Luck, Choice, and the Welfare State* (Cambridge: Harvard University Press, 2017).

40. Ronald Reagan, excerpts of a speech by Governor Ronald Reagan, Republican National Convention, Miami, FL (July 31, 1968), Ronald Reagan Library, Simi Valley, California.

41. Eugene Scott, "Chaffetz Walks Back Remarks on Low-Income Americans Choosing Health Care over iPhones," CNN Politics, http://www.cnn.com/2017/03/07/politics/jason-chaffetz-health-care-iphones/.

42. Jason Easley, "Trump White House Says Diabetics Don't Deserve Health Care," PoliticusUSA, http://www.politicususa.com/2017/05/13/trump-white-house-diabetics-deserve-health-care.html.

43. See, e.g., Kenneth Abraham, *Distributing Risk: Insurance, Legal Theory, and Public Policy* (New Haven, CT: Yale University Press, 1986), 28–29.

44. Richard Arneson, "Rawls, Responsibility, and Distributive Justice," in *Justice, Political Liberalism, and Utilitarianism: Themes from Harsanyi,* ed. Maurice Salles and John A. Weymark (Cambridge: Cambridge University Press, in press).

45. Ronald Dworkin, *Sovereign Virtue: The Theory and Practice of Equality* (Cambridge: Harvard University Press, 2002), 73–74.

46. Dworkin, 78.

47. Xin Xu et al., "Annual Healthcare Spending Attributable to Cigarette Smoking: An Update," *American Journal of Preventive Medicine* 48, no. 3 (2015): 326–333.

48. Socialdepartementet (Ministry of Health and Social Affairs), *Prioritering-sutredningens slutbetänkande. Vårdens svåra val* [The difficult choice facing health services] (Sweden: Statens offentliga utredningar SOU, 1995), 5.

49. Joar Björk, Niels Lynøe, and Niklas Juth, "Are Smokers Less Deserving of Expensive Treatment? A Randomised Controlled Trial That Goes beyond Official Values," *BMC Medical Ethics* 16, no. 1 (2015): 28.

50. Elizabeth S. Anderson, "What Is the Point of Equality?," *Ethics* 109, no. 2 (January 1999): 287–337.

51. David M. Burns et al., "Chapter 2: Cigarette Smoking Behavior in the United States," in National Cancer Institute, Monograph 8: Changes in Cigarette-Related Disease Risks and Their Implications for Prevention and Control (February 1997), 25, figure 7, https://cancercontrol.cancer.gov/Brp/tcrb/monographs/8/index.html.

52. "Alcohol Facts and Statistics," National Institute on Alcohol Abuse and Alcoholism, https://www.niaaa.nih.gov/alcohol-health/overview-alcohol-consumption/alcohol-facts-and-statistics.

53. GBD 2016 Alcohol Collaborators, "Alcohol Use and Burden for 195 Countries and Territories, 1990–2016: A Systematic Analysis for the Global Burden of Disease Study" *Lancet* 392, no. 10152 (August 23, 2018): 1015–1035.

54. Michelle M. Mello, "Obesity—Personal Choice or Public Health Issue?," *Nature Reviews Endocrinology* 4, no. 1 (2007): 2–3.

55. See Nir Eyal, "Egalitarian Justice and Innocent Choice," *Journal of Ethics and Social Philosophy* 2, no. 1 (January 2007): 1–18.

56. Eyal, 6.

57. Anderson, "What Is the Point?," 306.

58. Friedrich August von Hayek, *The Constitution of Liberty* (Chicago: University of Chicago Press, 1960), 95–97.

59. Daniel Wikler, "Personal and Social Responsibility for Health," Ethics & International Affairs 16, no.2 (October 2002): 47. See also Daniel Wikler, "Who Should Be Blamed for Being Sick?," *Health Education and Behavior* 14, no. 1 (March 1, 1987): 11–25.

60. Daniel Markovits, "Luck Egalitarianism and Political Solidarity," *Theoretical Inquiries in Law* 9, no. 1 (2008): 271.

61. Markovits, 281.

62. Jonathan M. Samet et al., "Lung Cancer in Never Smokers: Clinical Epidemiology and Environmental Risk Factors," *Clinical Cancer Research* 15, no. 18 (September 15, 2009): 5626–5645.

63. See *Amchem Prod., Inc. v. Windsor*, 521 U.S. 591, 624, 117 S. Ct. 2231, 2250, 138 L. Ed. 2d 689 (1997).

64. Maria N. Timofeeva et al., "Influence of Common Genetic Variation on Lung Cancer Risk: Meta-Analysis of 14,900 Cases and 29,485 Controls," *Human Molecular Genetics* 21, no. 22 (November 15, 2012): 4980–4995.

65. *Castano v. Am. Tobacco Co.*, 84 F.3d 734, 743 (5th Cir. 1996).

66. Colin Cook, "How High Are Cigarette Tax Rates in Your State?," Tax Foundation (January 25, 2018), https://taxfoundation.org/state-cigarette-tax-rates -2018/.

67. Guido Calabresi, "Some Thoughts on Risk Distribution and the Law of Torts," *Yale Law Journal* 70 (1960): 499.

68. Anderson, "What Is the Point?," 313.

69. Thomas Christiano, *The Constitution of Equality: Democratic Authority and Its Limits* (Oxford: Oxford University Press, 2008), 273–275.

70. Anderson, "What Is the Point?," 315.

71. Frank Lovett, "Republicanism," *Stanford Encyclopedia of Philosophy* (Summer 2018 edition), ed. Edward N. Zalta, https://plato.stanford.edu/archives /sum2018/entries/republicanism.

72. Phillip Pettit, *On the People's Terms: A Republican Theory and Model of Democracy* (Cambridge: Cambridge University Press, 2012), 299.

73. Pettit, *On the People's Terms*, 112.

74. Ganesh Sitaraman, *The Crisis of the Middle-Class Constitution: Why Economic Inequality Threatens Our Republic* (New York: Knopf, 2017), 12.

75. Allen Buchanan, "Deriving Welfare Rights from Libertarian Rights," in *Rights and Duties: Welfare Rights and Duties of Charity,* vol. 5, ed. Carl Wellman (New York: Routledge, 2002), 112.

76. Jesse S. Crisler, ed., "Life and Times of Frederick Douglass," in *The Frederick Douglass Papers: Autobiographical Writings* (New Haven, CT: Yale University Press, 2012), 295.

77. Martha C. Nussbaum, "Human Functioning and Social Justice: In Defense of Aristotelian Essentialism," *Political Theory* 20, no. 2 (1992): 202–246.

78. Amartya Sen, "Why Health Equity?," *Health Economics* 11 (2002): 660.

79. Norman Daniels, "Justice, Health, and Healthcare," *American Journal of Bioethics* 1, no. 2 (2001): 2–16. See also Norman Daniels, *Just Health: Meeting Health Needs Fairly* (Cambridge: Cambridge University Press, 2008); and Brendan Saloner and Norman Daniels, "The Ethics of the Affordability of Health Insurance," *Journal of Health Politics, Policy and Law* 36, no. 5 (October 2011): 815–827.

80. Associated Press, "At $2M, Priciest Ever Medicine Treats Fatal Genetic Disease," *New York Times*, May 24, 2019, https://www.nytimes.com/aponline/2019 /05/24/health/ap-us-med-fda-most-expensive-medicine.html.

81. Einer Elhauge, "Allocating Health Care Morally," *California Law Review* 82, no. 6 (December 1994): 1449–1544, 1492.

82. Ford Vox, Kelly McBride Folkers, Angela Turi, and Arthur L. Caplan, "Medical Crowdfunding for Scientifically Unsupported or Potentially Dangerous Treatments," *JAMA* 320, no. 16 (2018): 1705–1706.

83. "Get Help with Medical Fundraising," GoFundMe.com (visited February 18, 2019).

84. Andrew Kershner, "The Desperate Michigan Woman Who Used Go-FundMe to Help Pay for a Heart Transplant Is Far from Alone," *MarketWatch* (November 28, 2018).

85. Lauren S. Berliner and Nora J. Kenworthy, "Producing a Worthy Illness: Personal Crowdfunding amidst Financial Crisis," *Social Science and Medicine* 187 (2017): 233–242.

86. Anderson, "What Is the Point?," 314.

87. Pettit, *On the People's Terms,* 299.

88. Allen E. Buchanan, "The Right to a Decent Minimum of Health Care," *Philosophy and Public Affairs* 13, no. 1 (Winter 1984): 55–78.

89. Jeremy Snyder, Annalise Mathers, and Valorie A. Crooks, "Fund My Treatment!: A Call for Ethics-Focused Social Science Research into the Use of Crowdfunding for Medical Care," *Social Science and Medicine* 169 (2016): 28.

90. Howard S. Berliner, "Patient Dumping—No One Wins and We All Lose," *American Journal of Public Health* 78, no. 10 (1988): 1279–1280.

91. 131 *Congressional Record* S13904 (daily ed., October 23, 1985).

92. Charles Silver and David A. Hyman, *Overcharged: Why Americans Pay Too Much for Health Care* (Washington, DC: Cato Institute, 2018), 420.

93. Carla Saenz, "What Is Affordable Health Insurance? The Reasonable Tradeoff Account of Affordability," *Kennedy Institute of Ethics Journal* 19, no. 4 (December 2009): 402.

94. Saenz, 407.

95. Elhauge, "Allocating Health Care Morally," 1455.

96. 383 U.S. 663, 666 (1966).

97. Liam Murphy and Thomas Nagel, *The Myth of Ownership: Taxes and Justice* (New York: Oxford University Press, 2002), 9.

98. Gerald Prante, "Which States Tax Groceries?," Tax Foundation, https://taxfoundation.org/which-states-tax-groceries/.

99. Simon James, "The Importance of Fairness in Tax Policy: Behavioral Economics and the UK Experience," *International Journal of Applied Behavioral Economics* 3, no. 1 (January–March 2014): 1–12; John Meadowcroft, "The Failure of the Poll Tax and Classical Liberal Political Economy: Lessons for the Future," *Economic Affairs* 26, no. 1 (2006): 25–30.

100. Martin Sullivan, "Economic Analysis: Thinking Flat, Going Global," *Tax Notes* 109 (October 11, 2005), 157, http://taxprof.typepad.com/taxprof_blog/files/sullivan_10.pdf.

101. Joseph Bankman and Thomas Griffith, "Social Welfare and the Rate Structure: A New Look at Progressive Taxation," *California Law Review* 75, no. 6 (December 1987): 1905–1967.

102. See, e.g., Joel Slemrod and Jon Bakija, *Taxing Ourselves,* 3rd ed. (Cambridge, MA: MIT Press, 2004), 62–64.

103. See Clark C. Havighurst and Barak D. Richman, "Distributive Injustices in American Health Care," *Law and Contemporary Problems* 69 (Autumn 2006): 7–82.

104. M. Gregg Bloche, "Consumer-Directed Health Care and the Disadvantaged," *Health Affairs* 26 no. 5 (September/October 2007): 1322.

105. Steffie Woolhandler and David U. Himmelstein, "Consumer Directed Healthcare: Except for the Healthy and Wealthy It's Unwise," *Journal of General Internal Medicine* 22, no. 6 (June 2006): 879–881.

106. Michael D. Kogan et al., "Underinsurance among Children in the United States," *New England Journal of Medicine* 363, no. 9 (August 2010): 841–851; Ali R. Rahimi et al., "Financial Barriers to Health Care and Outcomes after Acute Myocardial Infarction," *JAMA* 297, no. 10 (March 2007): 1063–1072.

107. J. Frank Wharam et al., "Low-Socioeconomic-Status Enrollees in High-Deductible Plans Reduced High-Severity Emergency Care," *Health Affairs* 32, no. 8 (August 2013): 1398–1406.

108. Bruce W. Sherman, Teresa B. Gibson, Wendy D. Lynch, and Carol Addy, "Health Care Use and Spending Patterns Vary by Wage Level in Employer-sponsored Plans," *Health Affairs* 36, no. 2 (2017): 250–257.

109. *Lubin v. Panish*, 415 U.S. 709 (1974).

110. 404 U.S. 189, 195–196 (1971).

111. *M.L.B. v. S.L.J.*, 519 U.S. 102, 106 (1996) (quoting *Santosky v. Kramer*, 455 U.S. 745, 758–759 [1982]).

## 5. FIXES WE COULD TRY

1. James Downie, "Tom Price and Bernie Sanders Show Just How Tough the Obamacare Fight Is for Republicans," *Washington Post* (January 19, 2017).

2. Downie, "Tom Price and Bernie Sanders."

3. Mark V. Pauly, "The Truth about Moral Hazard and Adverse Selection," Policy Brief, Center for the Study of Policy Research, Syracuse University (March 1, 2007), https://ssrn.com/abstract=1822442.

4. Tom Baker, "Health Insurance, Risk, and Responsibility after the Patient Protection and Affordable Care Act," *University of Pennsylvania Law Review* 159, no. 6 (June 2011): 1610.

5. See Melinda B. Buntin et al., "Consumer-Directed Health Care: Early Evidence about Effects on Cost and Quality," *Health Affairs* 25, no. 6 (November/December 2006): w516–w530; James M. Naessens et al., "Effect of Premium, Copayments, and Health Status on the Choice of Health Plans," *Medical*

*Care* 46, no. 10 (October 2008): 1033–1040; Wynand P. M. M. Van de Ven and Bernard M. S. Van Praag, "The Demand for Deductibles in Private Health Insurance: A Probit Model with Sample Selection," *Journal of Econometrics* 17, no. 2 (November 1981): 229–252.

6. Naessens et al., "Effect of Premium," 1033.

7. Russell Korobkin, "Efficiency of Managed Care Patient Protection Laws: Incomplete Contracts, Bounded Rationality, and Market Failure," *Cornell Law Review* 85 (1999): 42.

8. Douglas B. Jacobs and Benjamin D. Sommers, "Using Drugs to Discriminate—Adverse Selection in the Insurance Marketplace," *New England Journal of Medicine* 372 no. 5 (2015): 399–402.

9. Matthew J. B. Lawrence, "The Social Consequences Problem in Health Insurance and How to Solve It," *Harvard Law and Policy Review* 13 (forthcoming).

10. 29 U.S.C.A. § 1182(b)(1) (West 2014).

11. George Loewenstein et al., "Consumers' Misunderstanding of Health Insurance," *Journal of Health Economics* 32, no. 5 (June 2013): 855.

12. Loewenstein et al., 850–862.

13. Christine Jolls, "Behavioral Economics Analysis of Redistributive Legal Rules," *Vanderbilt Law Review* 51, no. 6 (November 1998): 1659.

14. Neil D. Weinstein, "Unrealistic Optimism about Susceptibility to Health Problems," *Journal of Behavioral Medicine* 5, no. 4 (December 1982): 441–460.

15. David M. DeJoy, "The Optimism Bias and Traffic Accident Risk Perception," *Accident Analysis and Prevention* 21, no. 4 (August 1989): 333.

16. Howard Kunreuther and Paul Slovic, "Economics, Psychology, and Protective Behavior," *American Economic Review* 68, no. 2 (May 1978): 67.

17. See generally Keith Marzilli Ericson and Amanda Starc, "Heuristics and Heterogeneity in Health Insurance Exchanges: Evidence from the Massachusetts Connector," *American Economic Review* 102, no. 3 (May 2012): 493–497 (observing that "approximately 20 percent of enrollees choose the cheapest plan available to them," 494).

18. Ericson and Starc, 494. But see Eric J. Johnson et al., "Can Consumers Make Affordable Care Affordable? The Value of Choice Architecture," *PLoS ONE* 8 no. 12 (December 2013): e81521158 (finding that consumers overweigh out-of-pocket burdens when choosing plans).

19. Lawrence, "Social Consequences Problem."

20. Lawrence.

21. Howard F. Stein, "The Money Taboo in American Medicine," *Medical Anthropology* 7, no. 4 (Fall 1983): 1–15 (emphasis omitted).

22. S. Yousuf Zafar, James A. Tulsky, and Amy P. Abernethy, "It's Time to Have 'the Talk': Cost Communication and Patient-Centered Care," *Oncology* 28, no. 6 (June 2014): 479.

23. Elisabeth Rosenthal, *An American Sickness: How Health Care Became Big Business and How You Can Take It Back* (New York: Penguin, 2017), 254.

24. Elisabeth Rosenthal, "After Surgery, Surprise $117,000 Medical Bill From Doctor He Didn't Know," *New York Times* (September 20, 2014).

25. For an example of one such case, see *Maldonado v. Ochsner Clinic Found.*, 493 F.3d 521 (5th Cir. 2007).

26. For an example of such a case in accordance with "courts across the country", see *Pitell v. King Cty. Pub. Hosp. Dist. No. 2*, 423 P.3d 900, 901 (Wash. Ct. App. 2018).

27. American Bar Association (ABA), Model Rules of Professional Conduct, rule 1.5(a) (1983).

28. American Medical Association (AMA), Code of Medical Ethics Opinion 11.3.1, https://www.ama-assn.org/delivering-care/ethics/fees-medical-services. See also Mark A. Hall and Carl E. Schneider, "Learning from the Legal History of Billing for Medical Fees," *Journal of General Internal Medicine* 23, no. 8 (2008): 1257.

29. Nadia N. Sawicki, "Character, Competence, and the Principles of Medical Discipline," *Journal of Health Care Law and Policy* 13 (2010): 316.

30. ABA, Model Rules, rule 1.5(b).

31. See Grant H. Morris, "Dissing Disclosure: Just What the Doctor Ordered," *Arizona Law Review* 44, no. 2 (Summer 2002): 313–371.

32. For a history of physician-patient disclosures, see Jay Katz, *The Silent World of Doctor and Patient* (Baltimore, MD: Johns Hopkins University Press, 1984), 1, 3, 26.

33. *Arato v. Avedon*, 858 P. 2d 598, 599–600 (Cal. 1993).

34. 464 F.2d 772, 785 (D.C. Cir. 1972).

35. *Moore v. Regents of the Univ. of Cal.*, 793 P. 2d 479, 483 (Cal. 1990).

36. Roy Spece et al., "An Empirical Method for Materiality: Would Conflict of Interest Disclosures Change Patient Decisions?," *American Journal of Law and Medicine* 40, no. 4 (October 2014): 253–274.

37. Thaddeus Mason Pope, "Informed Consent and the Oncologist: Legal Duties to Discuss Costs of Treatment," *ASCO Post* (November 15, 2017), https://www.ascopost.com/issues/november-25-2017/informed-consent-and-the -oncologist-legal-duties-to-discuss-costs-of-treatment/.

38. Wendy Netter Epstein, "Price Transparency and Incomplete Contracts in Health Care," *Emory Law Journal* 67 (2017): 1, 8.

39. Ian Ayres and Robert Gertner, "Filling Gaps in Incomplete Contracts: An Economic Theory of Default Rules," *Yale Law Journal* 99, no. 1 (1989): 87–130.

40. G. Michael Allan, Joel Lexchin, and Natasha Wiebe, "Physician Aware-ness of Drug Cost: A Systematic Review," *PLoS Medicine* 4, no. 9 (September 2007): e283; G. Michael Allan and Joel Lexchin, "Physician Awareness of Diagnostic and Nondrug Therapeutic Costs: A Systematic Review," *Interna-tional Journal of Technology Assessment in Health Care* 24, no. 2 (April 2008): 158–165.

41. Rosenthal, *American Sickness,* 244.

42. Anna D. Sinaiko and Meredith B. Rosenthal, "Increased Price Transpar-ency in Health Care—Challenges and Potential Effects," *New England Journal of Medicine* 364, no. 10 (2011): 892.

43. *DiCarlo v. St. Mary's Hosp.,* No. 05-1665, 2006 WL 2038498, at *4 (D.N.J. July 19, 2006).

44. Lisa M. Korn et al., "Improving Physicians' Knowledge of the Costs of Common Medications and Willingness to Consider Costs When Prescribing," *Journal of General Internal Medicine* 18 no. 1 (January 2003): 31–37.

45. Arthur L. Caplan, "Why Autonomy Needs Help," *Journal of Medical Ethics* 40, no. 5 (2014): 301.

46. Peter A. Ubel, Amy P. Abernathy, and S. Yousuf Zafar, "Full Disclosure—Out-of-Pocket Costs as Side Effects," *New England Journal of Medicine* 369, no. 16 (October 2013): 1484.

47. "NIH State-of-the-Science Conference Statement on Improving End-of-Life Care," NIH Consensus and State-of-the-Science Statements 21, no. 3 (De-cember 2004), 6, http://consensus.nih.gov/2004/2004EndOfLifeCareSOS024PDF .pdf.

48. Pricivel M. Carrera, Hagop M. Kantarjian, and Victoria S. Blinder, "The Financial Burden and Distress of Patients with Cancer: Understanding and Stepping Up Action on the Financial Toxicity of Cancer Treatment," *CA: A Cancer Journal for Clinicians* 68, no. 2 (2018): 153–165.

49. See for example, *Thomas v. Archer,* 384 P.3d 791, 797 (Alaska 2016) (holding that "Dr. Archer's alleged promise that she would obtain preauthorization for the transport costs from the Thomases' insurance providers and that the costs would otherwise be covered by the hospital . . . did not stem from Dr. Archer's special expertise as a physician").

50. Christopher Robertson, "Should Patient Responsibility for Costs Change the Doctor-Patient Relationship," *Wake Forest Law Review* 50 (2015): 363.

51. Matthew D. Solomon et al., "Cost Sharing and the Initiation of Drug Therapy for the Chronically Ill," *Archives of Internal Medicine* 169, no. 8 (April 27, 2009): 740–748.

52. "Prescription Drug Cost Sharing: A Powerful Policy Lever to Use with Care," *RAND, Published Research, Research Briefs,* RB-9474, https://www.rand.org /pubs/research_briefs/RB9474/index1.html.

53. N. K. Choudhry et al., "Cost-Effectiveness of Providing Full Drug Coverage to Increase Medication Adherence in Post–Myocardial Infarction Medicare Beneficiaries," *Circulation* 117, no. 10 (March 2008): 1261–1268.

54. Dana P. Goldman, Geoffrey F. Joyce, and Pinar Karaca-Mandic, "Varying Pharmacy Benefits with Clinical Status: The Case of Cholesterol-Lowering Therapy," *American Journal of Managed Care* 12, no. 1 (January 2006): 21–28.

55. Niteesh K. Choudhry et al., "At Pitney Bowes, Value-Based Insurance Design Cut Copayments and Increased Drug Adherence." *Health Affairs* 29, no. 11 (November 2010): 1995–2001.

56. See M. E. Chernew, A. M. Fendrick, and B. Kachniarz, "Value-Based Insurance Design," in *Encyclopedia of Health Economics, Volume 3,* ed. Anthony J. Culyer (Amsterdam: Elsevier, 2014), 446–453.

57. Chernew et al., 449.

58. Chernew et al., 449.

59. "2017 Employer Health Benefits Survey, Section 9: Prescription Drug Benefits," Henry J. Kaiser Family Foundation (September 19, 2017), https://www.kff.org/report-section/ehbs-2017-section-9-prescription-drug-benefits/.

60. Sarah Thomas et al., "Dig Deep: Impacts and Implications of Rising Out-of-Pocket Health Care Costs," Deloitte Center for Health Solutions, https://www2.deloitte.com/content/dam/Deloitte/us/Documents/life-sciences-health-care/us-lchs-dig-deep-hidden-costs-112414.pdf.

61. David Orentlicher, "Controlling Health Care Spending: More Patient Skin in the Game," *Indiana Health Law Review* 13 (2016): 355.

62. Harald Schmidt and Ezekiel J. Emanuel, "Lowering Medical Costs through the Sharing of Savings by Physicians and Patients: Inclusive Shared Savings," *JAMA Internal Medicine* 174, no. 12 (December 2014): 2012.

63. Christopher M. Whaley, Chaoran Guo, and Timothy T. Brown, "The Moral Hazard Effects of Consumer Responses to Targeted Cost-Sharing," *Journal of Health Economics* 56 (2017): 201–221.

64. The National Academies of Sciences, Engineering, and Medicine, *Making Medicines Affordable, A National Imperative,* ed. Norman R. Augustine, Guru Madhavan, and Sharyl Nass (Washington, DC: The National Academies Press, 2018).

65. Keith L. Davis, Sean D. Candrilli, and Heather M. Edin, "Prevalence and Cost of Nonadherence with Antiepileptic Drugs in an Adult Managed Care Population," *Epilepsia* 49, no. 3 (2008): 446–454.

66. Ignacio Aznar-Lou, Anton Pottegård, Ana Fernández, María Teresa Peñarrubia-María, Antoni Serrano-Blanco, Ramón Sabés-Figuera, Montserrat Gil-Girbau, Marta Fajó-Pascual, Patricia Moreno-Peral, and Maria Rubio-Valera. "Effect of Copayment Policies on Initial Medication Non-Adherence According to

Income: A Population-Based Study." *BMJ Quality and Safety* 27, no. 11 (2018): 878–891.

67. "Grade Definitions," U.S. Preventive Services Task Force, https://www .uspreventiveservicestaskforce.org/Page/Name/grade-definitions.

68. "Health Reform: Preventive Services Covered by Private Health Plans under the Affordable Care Act," Henry J. Kaiser Family Foundation, https://www .kff.org/health-reform/fact-sheet/preventive-services-covered-by-private-health -plans/.

69. "Breast Cancer: Screening, Recommendation Summary," U.S. Preventive Services Task Force, https://www.uspreventiveservicestaskforce.org/Page /Document/UpdateSummaryFinal/breast-cancer-screening1.

70. Frank J. Wharam, Fang Zhang, Jamie Wallace, Christine Lu, Craig Earle, Stephen B. Soumerai, Larissa Nekhlyudov, and Dennis Ross-Degnan, "Vulnerable and Less Vulnerable Women in High-Deductible Health Plans Experienced Delayed Breast Cancer Care," *Health Affairs* 38, no. 3 (2019): 408–415.

71. R. Scott Braithwaite and Allison B. Rosen, "Linking Cost Sharing to Value: An Unrivaled Yet Unrealized Public Health Opportunity," *Annals Internal Medicine* 146, no. 8 (April 2007): 602–605.

72. Roger Chou et al., "Diagnosis and Treatment of Low Back Pain: A Joint Clinical Practice Guideline from the American College of Physicians and the American Pain Society," *Annals of Internal Medicine* 147, no. 7 (October 2007): 478–491.

73. Paul G. Shekelle et al., "Developing Clinical Guidelines," *Western Journal of Medicine* 170, no. 6 (June 1999): 348–351.

74. Pierluigi Tricoci, Joseph M. Allen, Judith M. Kramer, Robert M. Califf, and Sidney C. Smith, "Scientific Evidence Underlying the ACC / AHA Clinical Practice Guidelines," *JAMA* 301, no. 8 (2009): 831–841.

75. See Zarek C. Brot-Goldberg, Amitabh Chandra, Benjamin R. Handel, and Jonathan T. Kolstad, "What Does a Deductible Do? The Impact of Cost-Sharing on Health Care Prices, Quantities, and Spending Dynamics," *The Quarterly Journal of Economics* 132, no. 3 (2017): 1261–1318; and Michael Chernew, Zack Cooper, Eugene Larsen-Hallock, and Fiona Scott Morton, "Are Health Care Services Shoppable? Evidence from the Consumption of Lower-Limb MRI Scans," NBER Working Paper No. 24869 (January 2019).

76. Anna Staver, "Colorado Becomes First State in Nation to Cap Price of Insulin," *Denver Post* (May 23, 2019), https://www.denverpost.com/2019/05/23 /colorado-insulin-price-cap/.

77. Ashish K. Jha, Ronald E. Aubert, Jianying Yao, J. Russell Teagarden, and Robert S. Epstein. "Greater Adherence to Diabetes Drugs Is Linked to Less Hospital Use and Could Save Nearly $5 Billion Annually," *Health Affairs* 31, no. 8 (2012): 1836–1846.

78. Rachelle Louise Cutler, Fernando Fernandez-Llimos, Michael Frommer, Charlie Benrimoj, and Victoria Garcia-Cardenas, "Economic Impact of Medication Non-Adherence by Disease Groups: A Systematic Review," *BMJ Open* 8, no. 1 (2018): e016982.

79. Lowell E. Schnipper, Thomas J. Smith, Derek Raghavan, Douglas W. Blayney, Patricia A. Ganz, Therese Marie Mulvey, and Dana S. Wollins, "American Society of Clinical Oncology Identifies Five Key Opportunities to Improve Care and Reduce Costs: The Top Five List for Oncology," *Journal of Clinical Oncology* 30, no. 14 (2012): 1715–1724.

80. American Board of Internal Medicine, "Our Mission," Choosing Wisely, accessed June 10, 2019, https://www.choosingwisely.org/our-mission/.

81. Steven A. Edwards, "Paracelsus, the Man Who Brought Chemistry to Medicine," American Association for the Advancement of Science (March 1, 2012), https://www.aaas.org/blog/scientia/paracelsus-man-who-brought-chemistry -medicine.

82. Elias Mossialos, Ana Djordjevic, Robin Osborn, and Dana Sarnak, eds., *International Profiles of Health Care Systems* (New York, NY: The Commonwealth Fund, 2017).

83. Mossialos, *Health Care Systems*.

84. Charles Silver and David A. Hyman, *Overcharged: Why Americans Pay Too Much for Health Care* (Washington, DC: Cato Institute, 2018), 314 (quoting Michael Tanner).

85. Mossialos, "Health Care Systems."

86. Sean Altekruse, Anita Das, Hyunsoon Cho, Valentina Petkov, and Mandi Yu. "Do US Thyroid Cancer Incidence Rates Increase with Socioeconomic Status among People with Health Insurance? An Observational Study Using SEER Population-Based Data," *BMJ Open* 5, no. 12 (2015): 7.

87. Mark A. Hall and Carl E. Schneider. "Patients as Consumers: Courts, Contracts, and the New Medical Marketplace," *Michigan Law Review* 106, no. 4 (March 2008): 660.

88. See, e.g., *Kennedy v. Conn. Gen. Life Ins. Co.*, 924 F.2d 698 (7th Cir. 1991) (explaining the behavior-modification function, and upholding an insurer's refusal to pay a provider of medical services that waived a copayment).

89. Martin S. Feldstein, "A New Approach to National Health Insurance," *Public Interest* 23 (Spring 1971): 99. See also Martin S. Feldstein, "The High Cost of Hospitals and What to Do about It," *Public Interest* 48 (Summer 1977).

90. Martin Feldstein and Jonathan Gruber, "A Major Risk Approach to Health Insurance Reform," in *Tax Policy and the Economy,* vol. 9, ed. James M. Poterba (Cambridge, MA: MIT Press, 1995), 103–104.

91. See, generally, Jonathan Gruber, "The Role of Consumer Copayments for Health Care: Lessons from the RAND Health Insurance Experiment and Beyond," Henry J. Kaiser Family Foundation (October 2006), 11.

92. See *Newhouse & Ins. Experiment Grp.*, at 6, 401–402.

93. 42 U.S.C.A. § 18071(c)(1)(A) (West 2014).

94. Michael Hiltzik, "Courts Hammer Trump For Sabotaging Obamacare, in Rulings That Could Cost the Treasury Billions," *LA Times,* February 19, 2019, https://www.latimes.com/business/hiltzik/la-fi-hiltzik-trump-csr-20190219-story .html.

95. "Health Insurance Exchanges 2018 Open Enrollment Period Final Report," Newsroom, CMS (April 3, 2018), https://www.cms.gov/Newsroom /MediaReleaseDatabase/Fact-sheets/2018-Fact-sheets-items/2018-04-03.html.

96. For an overview of these programs, see "Medicare Savings Programs," Medicaid.gov, http://www.medicare.gov/your-medicare-costs/help-paying-costs /medicare-savings-program/medicare-savings-programs.html. Similarly, some states pay deductibles for qualified (low-income) Medicare beneficiaries. See 42 U.S.C. § 1396a(a)(10)(E) (2006); *New York City Health & Hosp. Corp. v. Perales*, 954 F.2d 854, 859 (2nd Cir. 1992) (discussing that provision).

97. See Mark V. Pauly, "Means-Testing in Medicare," *Health Affairs* 33 (July–December 2004): 546–547.

98. "Health Insurance Coverage of the Total Population," State Health Facts, Henry J. Kaiser Family Foundation (2016), https://www.kff.org/other/state -indicator/total-population/.

99. Ed Silverman, "A Growing Number of States Are Eyeing Laws to Prohibit a Controversial Cost-Sharing Tool," *STAT* (April 4, 2019), https://www.statnews .com/pharmalot/2019/04/04/copay-accumulators-legislation-states/.

100. Christopher T. Robertson, "Scaling Cost-Sharing to Wages: How Employers Can Reduce Health Spending and Provide Greater Economic Security," *Yale Journal of Health Policy Law and Ethics* 14, no. 2 (2014): 239–295 (illustrating the applicable caps using such a median-scaling approach).

101. "Addressing the Increasing Burden of Health Insurance Cost Sharing," American College of Physicians (2016), https://www.acponline.org/acp_policy /policies/insurance_cost_sharing_2016.pdf.

102. Tami Luhby, "Would Clinton or Trump Make Health Care More Affordable?," CNN Money (October 27, 2016), https://money.cnn.com/2016/10/27/news /economy/obamacare-health-care-trump-clinton/index.html.

103. Deborah Thorne et al., "Graying of U.S. Bankruptcy: Fallout from Life in a Risk Society," Indiana Legal Studies Research Paper no. 406 (August 18, 2018), https://papers.ssrn.com/sol3/papers.cfm?abstract_id=3226574.

104. See Katherine Swartz, "Expert Reflection—Easier Said than Done," *Journal of Health Policy and Law* 36, no. 5 (October 2011): 855, 857.

105. Robertson, "Scaling Cost-Sharing to Wages," 270, table 1.

106. Paul Krugman and Robin Wells, "The Health Care Crisis and What to Do about It," *New York Review of Books* (March 23, 2006).

107. Krugman and Wells, "Health Care Crisis."

108. Regina E. Herzlinger and Jeffrey Schwartz, "How Companies Tackle Health Care Costs: Part I," *Harvard Business Review* 63, no. 4 (1985): 69–81.

109. Thomas Rice and Kenneth E. Thorpe, "Income-Related Cost Sharing in Health Insurance," *Health Affairs* 12, no. 1 (Spring 1993): 21–39.

110. Rice and Thorpe, "Income-Related Cost Sharing."

111. See, e.g., Michelle Andrews, "Employers Consider Cutting Health Insurance Premiums for Lower Paid Workers," *Washington Post* (December 5, 2011).

112. "2018 Benefits Enrollment Guide," Harvard Human Resources, p. 10, https://hr.harvard.edu/files/humanresources/files/benefitsenrollmentguide_facultynonunionstaff.pdf.

113. 26 U.S.C.A. § 105(h)(2)(B) (West 2014); 26 U.S.C.A. § 401(a)(4) (West 2014); 42 U.S.C.A. § 300gg-16 (West 2014). Note that the latter statute, which applies to non-self-insured plans, is currently being challenged as part of the broader Affordable Care Act. See *Texas v. United States*, 340 F. Supp. 3d 579 (N.D. Tex. 2018).

114. Robertson, "Scaling Cost-Sharing to Wages," 239–295.

115. 26 C.F.R. § 1.105–11(c)(3)(ii) (2013).

116. Clark C. Havighurst and Barak D. Richman, "Distributive Injustices in American Health Care," *Law and Contemporary Problems* 69, no. 4 (Autumn 2006): 42.

117. 29 U.S.C. § 1132(a)(3) (2012). See also *I.R.S. Notice* 2010–63, 2010–41 I.R.B. 420.

118. 401 U.S. 424, 425 (1971).

119. See 42 U.S.C. § 2000e–2(k) (2006) (enacting the disparate impact theory).

120. Lawrence, "Social Consequences Problem."

121. Katherine Baicker and Dana Goldman, "Patient Cost-Sharing and Healthcare Spending Growth," *Journal of Economic Perspectives* 25, no. 2 (2011): 47–68.

122. Christopher Robertson, "The Split Benefit: The Painless Way to Put Skin Back in the Health Care Game," *Cornell Law Review* 98 (2012): 921; Christopher Robertson et al., "A Randomized Experiment of the Split Benefit Health Insurance Reform to Reduce High-Cost, Low-Value Consumption," *Innovation and Entrepreneurship in Health* 1 (2014): 5–11.

123. Michelle Andrews, "Some Insurers Paying Patients Who Agree to Get Cheaper Care," Kaiser Health News (March 26, 2012), http://www.kaiserhealthnews.org/Features/Insuring-Your-Health/2012/Cash-Rewards-For-Cheaper-Care-Michelle-Andrews-032712.aspx.

124. Govind Persad, "Paying Patients: Legal and Ethical Dimensions," *Yale Journal of Law and Technology* 20 (2018): 177–233.

125. Robertson et al., "Randomized Experiment," 5–11.

## 6. WHAT WE MUST DO

1. Omri Ben-Shahar and Carl E. Schneider. *More than You Wanted to Know: The Failure of Mandated Disclosure* (Princeton, NJ: Princeton University Press, 2014).

2. Drayton A. Hammond, Tiffany Chiu, Jacob T. Painter, and Nikhil Meena, "Nonpharmacist Health Care Providers' Knowledge of and Opinions Regarding Medication Costs in Critically Ill Patients," *Hospital Pharmacy* 53, no. 3 (2018): 188–193.

3. James Surowiecki, "How Doctors Could Thwart Health-Care Reform," *New Yorker* (December 19 and 26, 2006).

4. Jonathan Oberlander and Steven B. Spivack, "Technocratic Dreams, Political Realities: The Rise and Demise of Medicare's Independent Payment Advisory Board," *Journal of Health Politics, Policy and Law* 43, no. 3 (2018): 483–510.

5. "Research on the Comparative Effectiveness of Medical Treatments: Issues and Options for an Expanded Federal Role," Congressional Budget Office (December 2007), p. 11, http://www.cbo.gov/sites/default/files/110th-congress-2007-2008/reports/12-18-comparativeeffectiveness.pdf.

6. Catherine Caruso, "Robert Califf: 'The Clinical Trials Enterprise Has Gone Awry,'" *STAT* (June 21, 2017), https://www.statnews.com/2017/06/21/robert-califfs-clinical-trials/.

7. Ismail Jatoi and Sunita Sah, "Clinical Practice Guidelines and the Overuse of Health Care Services: Need For Reform," *CMAJ: Canadian Medical Association journal/Journal de l'Association Medicale Canadienne* 191, no. 11 (2019): E297.

8. Allison K. Hoffman, "Cost-Sharing Reductions, Technocrat Tinkering, and Market-Based Health Policy," *The Journal of Law, Medicine & Ethics* 46, no. 4 (2018): 873–876.

9. Bruce W. Sherman, Teresa B. Gibson, Wendy D. Lynch, and Carol Addy, "Health Care Use and Spending Patterns Vary by Wage Level in Employer-Sponsored Plans," *Health Affairs* 36, no. 2 (2017): 250–257.

10. Joyce Rogers, "Medicare Is Not a Welfare Program—AARP to President Obama," *Disabled World* (July 17, 2011), https://www.disabled-world.com/disability/insurance/aarp/not-welfare.php.

11. Editorial, "Candid Advice from a Health Care Visionary," *New York Times* (December 14, 2011), p. A34.

12. Robert Pear, "Health Official Takes Parting Shot at 'Waste,'" *New York Times* (December 4, 2011), p. A23.

13. Gerard F. Anderson, Uwe E. Reinhardt, Peter S. Hussey, and Varduhi Petrosyan, "It's the Prices, Stupid: Why the United States Is So Different from Other Countries," *Health Affairs* 22, no. 3 (2003): 103.

14. David Squires, "U.S. Health Care from a Global Perspective Spending, Use of Services, Prices, and Health in 13 Countries," Commonwealth Fund (October 8, 2015), https://www.commonwealthfund.org/publications/issue-briefs/2015/oct/us-health-care-global-perspective.

15. Gerard F. Anderson, Peter Hussey, and Varduhi Petrosyan, "It's Still the Prices, Stupid: Why the US Spends So Much on Health Care, and a Tribute to Uwe Reinhardt," *Health Affairs* 38, no. 1 (2019): 87–95.

16. Brent D. Fulton, "Health Care Market Concentration Trends in the United States: Evidence and Policy Responses," *Health Affairs* 36, no. 9 (2017): 1530–1538.

17. Christopher T. Robertson, "Will Courts Allow States to Regulate Drug Prices?," *New England Journal of Medicine Perspective* (August 2018): 1000–1002.

18. *N.C. State Bd. of Dental Examiners v. FTC,* 135 S. Ct. 1101, 1112 (2015).

19. Squires, "U.S. Health Care."

20. Sebastian Salas-Vega, Othon Iliopoulos, and Elias Mossialos, "Assessment of Overall Survival, Quality of Life, and Safety Benefits Associated with New Cancer Medicines," *JAMA Oncology* 3, no. 3 (2017): 382–390, 388.

21. Donald W. Light and Hagop Kantarjian, "Market Spiral Pricing of Cancer Drugs," *Cancer* 119, no. 22 (November 2013): 3900–3902.

22. Camille Abboud et al., "The Price of Drugs for Chronic Myeloid Leukemia (CML) Is a Reflection of the Unsustainable Prices of Cancer Drugs: From the Perspective of a Large Group of CML Experts," *Blood* 121, no. 22 (May 30, 2013): 4439–4442.

23. David H. Howard, Peter B. Bach, Ernst R. Berndt, and Rena M. Conti, "Pricing in the Market for Anticancer Drugs," *Journal of Economic Perspectives* 29, no. 1 (2015): 139–62.

24. See, generally, Nancy Devlin and David Parkin, "Does NICE Have a Cost-Effectiveness Threshold and What Other Factors Influence Its Decisions? A Binary Choice Analysis," *Health Economics* 13, no. 5 (May 2004): 437–452.

25. Anna Staver, "Colorado Becomes First State in Nation to Cap Price of Insulin," *Denver Post* (May 23, 2019), https://www.denverpost.com/2019/05/23/colorado-insulin-price-cap/.

26. Staver, "Colorado Becomes First State."

27. "Technological Change and the Growth of Health Care Spending," Congressional Budget Office (January 31, 2008), pp. 8 and 10, https://www.cbo.gov/publication/41665; Joseph L. Dielman et al., "Factors Associated with

Increases in US Health Care Spending, 1996–2013," *JAMA* 318, no. 17 (November 2017): 1668–1678.

28. Kenneth J. Arrow, "Economic Welfare and the Allocation of Resources for Inventions," in *The Rate and Direction of Inventive Activity: Economic and Social Factors,* ed. R. R. Nelson (Princeton, NJ: Princeton University Press, 1962).

29. George A. Akerlof, "The Market for 'Lemons': Quality Uncertainty and the Market Mechanism," *Quarterly Journal of Economics* 84, no.3 (1970): 488–500.

30. Christopher Robertson, "When Truth Cannot Be Presumed: The Regulation of Drug Promotion under an Expanding First Amendment," *Boston University Law Review* 94 (2014): 545–574; Christopher Robertson, "The Tip of the Iceberg: A First Amendment Right to Promote Drugs Off-Label," *Ohio State Law Journal* 78, no. 4 (2017): 1019–1052; Christopher Robertson and Victor Laurion, "Tip of the Iceberg II: How the Intended-Uses Principle Produces Medical Knowledge and Protects Liberty," *New York University Journal of Law and Liberty* 11, no. 2 (2017): 770–802.

31. Rebecca S. Eisenberg, "The Role of the FDA in Innovation Policy," *Michigan Telecommunication and Technology Law Review* 13 (2006): 347.

32. Nicholas S. Downing et al., "Clinical Trial Evidence Supporting FDA Approval of Novel Therapeutic Agents, 2005–2012," *JAMA* 311, no. 4 (January 2014): 368–377.

33. Sanket S. Dhruva, Lisa A. Bero, and Rita F. Redberg, "Strength of Study Evidence Examined by the FDA in Premarket Approval of Cardiovascular Devices," *JAMA* 302, no. 24 (December 2009): 2679–2685.

34. Benjamin N. Rome, Daniel B. Kramer, and Aaron S. Kesselheim, "FDA Approval of Cardiac Implantable Electronic Devices via Original and Supplement Premarket Approval Pathways, 1979–2012," *JAMA* 311, no. 4 (January 2014): 385–391.

35. Sarah Y. Zheng, Sanket S. Dhruva, and Rita F. Redberg, "Characteristics Of Clinical Studies Used For US Food And Drug Administration Approval Of High-Risk Medical Device Supplements," *JAMA* 318, no. 7 (2017): 619–625.

36. Zheng, Dhruva, and Redberg, 619–625.

37. Andrew M. Ibrahim, Jyothi R. Thumma, and Justin B. Dimick, "Reoperation and Medicare Expenditures after Laparoscopic Gastric Band Surgery," *JAMA Surgery* 152, no. 9 (2017): 835–842.

38. Scott H. Podolsky, David S. Jones, and Ted J. Kaptchuk, "From Trials to Trials: Blinding, Medicine, and Honest Adjudication," in *Blinding as a Solution to Bias: Strengthening Biomedical Science, Forensic Science, and Law*, ed. Christopher Robertson and Aaron S. Kesselheim (Amsterdam: Elsevier, 2016), 45–58.

39. Asbjørn Hróbjartsson et al., "Observer Bias in Randomized Clinical Trials with Binary Outcomes: Systematic Review of Trials with Both Blinded and Non-Blinded Assessors," *British Medical Journal* 344, no. e1119 (February 2012): 1–11.

40. Deborah Grady and Rita F. Redberg, "Less Is More: How Less Health Care Can Result in Better Health," *Archives of Internal Medicine* 170, no. 9 (2010): 749–750.

41. M. H. J. Voormolen et al., "Percutaneous Vertebroplasty Compared with Optimal Pain Medication Treatment: Short-Term Clinical Outcome of Patients with Subacute or Chronic Painful Osteoporotic Vertebral Compression Fractures: The VERTOS Study," *American Journal of Neuroradiology* 28, no. 3 (March 2007): 555–560; see also James N. Weinstein, "Balancing Science and Informed Choice in Decisions about Vertebroplasty," *New England Journal of Medicine* 361, no. 6 (August 2009): 619–621 (discussing these articles).

42. David F. Kallmes et al., "A Randomized Trial of Vertebroplasty for Osteoporotic Spinal Fractures," *New England Journal of Medicine* 361, no. 6 (August 2009): 569–579; Rachelle Buchbinder et al., "A Randomized Trial of Vertebroplasty for Painful Osteoporotic Vertebral Fractures," *New England Journal of Medicine* 361, no. 6 (August 2009): 557–568.

43. Downing et al., "Clinical Trial Evidence."

44. Zheng, Dhruva, and Redberg, "Characteristics of Clinical Studies," 619–625.

45. Robert M. Califf, "Balancing the need for access with the imperative for empirical evidence of benefit and risk," *JAMA* 318, no. 7 (2017): 614–616.

46. Bruno Kovic, Xuejing Jin, Sean Alexander Kennedy et al., "Evaluating Progression-Free Survival as a Surrogate Outcome for Health-Related Quality of Life in Oncology: a Systematic Review and Quantitative Analysis," *JAMA Internal Medicine* 178, no. 12 (2018): 1586–1596.

47. "FDA Grants Accelerated Approval to First Drug for Duchenne Muscular Dystrophy," U.S. Food and Drug Administration, news release (September 19, 2016), https://www.fda.gov/newsevents/newsroom/pressannouncements /ucm521263.htm.

48. Ed Silverman, "Sarepta to Charge $300K for Duchenne Drug. 'We Tried to Be Reasonable,' CEO Says," *STAT* (September 19, 2016), https://www.statnews .com/pharmalot/2016/09/19/sarepta-duchenne-drug-prices/.

49. Tewodros Eguale et al., "Association of Off-Label Drug Use and Adverse Drug Events in an Adult Population," *JAMA Internal Medicine* 176, no. 1 (January 2016): 58.

50. David C. Radley, Stan N. Finkelstein, and Randall S. Stafford, "Off-Label Prescribing among Office-Based Physicians," *Archives Internal Medicine* 166, no. 9 (May 2006): 1021–1026.

51. Jeffrey Bien and Vinay Prasad, "Future Jobs of FDA's Haematology-Oncology Reviewers," *British Medical Journal* 354 (September 2016): i5055.

52. Sheila Kaplan, "From FDA Expert to Biotech Insider: The Drug Industry Thrives on the Revolving Door," *STAT* (September 27, 2016), https://www.statnews .com/2016/09/27/fda-biopharma-revolving-door-study/.

53. See Donald W. Light, Joel Lexchin, and Jonathan J. Darrow, "Institutional Corruption of Pharmaceuticals and the Myth of Safe and Effective Drugs," *Journal of Law, Medicine, and Ethics* 41, no. 3 (Fall 2013): 590–600 (discussing institutional corruption and applying to this domain).

54. John Jenkins, "CDER New Drug Review: 2016 Update," U.S. Food and Drug Administration, (December 14, 2016), p. 20, https://www.fda.gov /downloads/aboutfda/centersoffices/officeofmedicalproductsandtobacco/cder /ucm533192.pdf.

55. Cassie Frank et al., "Era of Faster FDA Drug Approval Has Also Seen Increased Black-Box Warnings and Market Withdrawals," *Health Affairs* 33, no. 8 (August 2014): 1453–1459.

56. Daniel Carpenter et al., "The Complications of Controlling Agency Time Discretion: FDA Review Deadlines and Postmarket Drug Safety," *American Journal of Political Science* 56, no. 1 (January 2012): 98–114.

57. Christopher Robertson and Marc Rodwin, "'Money Blinding' as a Solution to Biased Design and Conduct of Scientific Research," in *Blinding as a Solution to Bias: Strengthening Biomedical Science, Forensic Science, and Law*, ed. Christopher Robertson and Aaron S. Kesselheim (Amsterdam: Elsevier, 2016), 115.

58. Bernard Lo and Marilyn J. Field, eds., *Conflict of Interest in Medical Research, Education, and Practice* (Washington, DC: National Academies Press, 2009), 104.

59. Aaron S. Kesselheim et al., "A Randomized Study of How Physicians Interpret Research Funding Disclosures," *New England Journal of Medicine* 367, no. 12 (2012): 1119–1127.

60. John P. A. Ioannidis, "Why Most Published Research Findings Are False," *PLoS Medicine* 2, no. 8 (August 2005): 696–701.

61. Ioannidis, 696.

62. David H. Freeman, "Lies, Damned Lies, and Medical Science," *Atlantic Monthly* (November 2010), http://www.theatlantic.com/magazine/archive/2010/11 /liesdamned-lies-and-medical-science/8269/ (quoting Ioannidis).

63. Peter J. Hammer and William M. Sage, "Critical Issues in Hospital Antitrust Law," *Health Affairs* 22, no. 6 (2003): 88–100.

64. Anna D. Sinaiko and Meredith B. Rosenthal, "Increased Price Transparency in Health Care—Challenges and Potential Effects," *New England Journal of Medicine* 364, no. 10 (2011): 892.

65. Carrie H. Colla et al., "Interventions Aimed at Reducing Use of Low-Value Health Services: A Systematic Review," *Medical Care Research and Review* 75, no. 5 (October 2017): 507–550.

66. Michael Chernew, Zack Cooper, Eugene Larsen-Hallock, and Fiona Scott Morton, "Are Health Care Services Shoppable? Evidence from the Consumption of Lower-Limb MRI Scans," NBER Working Paper No. 24869 (January 2019), 1.

67. Joseph P. Newhouse and Alan M. Garber, "Geographic Variation in Health Care Spending in the United States: Insights from an Institute of Medicine Report," *JAMA* 310, no. 12 (September 2013): 1227–1228.

68. Elias S. Hyams et al., "Variation in the Care of Surgical Conditions: Prostate Cancer," *A Dartmouth Atlas of Health Care Series* (2014), 15, http://www .dartmouthatlas.org/downloads/reports/Prostate_cancer_report_12_03_14.pdf.

69. Hyams et al., 22 (this statistic is based on Medicare enrollees under age seventy-five).

70. "Supply-Sensitive Care," Dartmouth Atlas of Health Care, http://www .dartmouthatlas.org/keyissues/issue.aspx?con=2937.

71. Katy Backes Kozhimannil, Michael R. Law, and Beth A. Virnig, "Cesarean Delivery Rates Vary Tenfold among US Hospitals; Reducing Variation May Address Quality and Cost Issues," *Health Affairs* 32, no. 3 (March 2013): 527–535.

72. Ilir Hoxha et al., "Caesarean Sections and For-Profit Status of Hospitals: Systematic Review and Meta-Analysis," *British Medical Journal Open* 7, no. 2 (February 2017): e013670.

73. David Orentlicher, "Controlling Health Care Costs through Public, Transparent Processes: the Conflict between the Morally Right and the Socially Feasible," *The Journal of Corporation Law*. 36, no. 4 (Summer 2011): 807–821, 818.

74. Aaron S. Kesselheim et al., "Distributions of Industry Payments to Massachusetts Physicians," *New England Journal of Medicine* 368, no. 22 (May 2013): 2049–2052.

75. Ryann Grochowski Jones and Charles Ornstein, "Matching Industry Payments to Medicare Prescribing Patterns: An Analysis" (March 2016), https:// static.propublica.org/projects/d4d/20160317-matching-industry-payments.pdf?22.

76. Christopher Robertson, Susannah Rose, and Aaron S. Kesselheim, "Effect of Financial Relationships," *Journal of Law, Medicine and Ethics* 40, no. 3 (Fall 2012): 452–466.

77. Mireille Jacobson et al., "How Medicare's Payment Cuts for Cancer Chemotherapy Drugs Changed Patterns of Treatment," *Health Affairs* 29, no. 7 (July 2010): 1391–1399.

78. Jean M. Mitchell, "Do Financial Incentives Linked to Ownership of Specialty Hospitals Affect Physicians' Practice Patterns?," *Medical Care* 46, no. 7 (July 2008): 732–737.

79. Cam Donaldson and Karen Gerard, "Countering Moral Hazard in Public and Private Health Care Systems: A Review of Recent Evidence," *Journal of Social Policy* 18, no. 2 (1989): 235–251.

80. Amitabh Chandra and Jonathan Skinner, "Technology Growth and Expenditure Growth in Health Care," *Journal of Economic Literature* 50, no. 3 (2012): 652.

81. Gautam Gowrisankaran, Aviv Nevo, and Robert Town, "Mergers When Prices Are Negotiated: Evidence from the Hospital Industry," *American Economic Review* 105, no. 1 (2015): 172–203.

82. National Academies of Sciences, Engineering, and Medicine, *Making Medicines Affordable: A National Imperative* (Washington, DC: National Academies Press, 2018), xx.

83. Reed Abelson, "The Last Company You Would Expect Is Reinventing Health Benefits," *New York Times* (August 31, 2018).

84. Elias Mossialos et al., "International Profiles of Health Care Systems," Commonwealth Fund (May 2017), https://www.commonwealthfund.org/sites /default/files/documents/___media_files_publications_fund_report_2017_may _mossialos_intl_profiles_v5.pdf.

85. Mossialos et al., "International Profiles of Health Care Systems."

86. Mossialos et al., "International Profiles of Health Care Systems."

87. Mossialos et al., "International Profiles of Health Care Systems."

88. Cam Donaldson, *Credit Crunch Health Care* (Chicago: University of Chicago Press, 2011), 20, 26.

89. Scott Gottlieb, "Capturing the Benefits of Competition for Patients," U.S. Food and Drug Administration (March 7, 2018), https://www.fda.gov/NewsEvents /Speeches/ucm599833.htm.

90. "Medicare for All: Leaving No One Behind," Issues, Bernie Sanders, https://berniesanders.com/issues/medicare-for-all/.

# ACKNOWLEDGMENTS

Many years ago, when Elizabeth Warren was a professor and I her student, she opened my eyes to the problem of healthcare cost exposure for the middle class. She encouraged and supported my initial work in this domain.

The University of Arizona supported this work immeasurably, including during research leaves, summer break, and a sabbatical. Librarians Leah Sandwell-Weis and Maureen Garmon, and their team of research fellows, provided excellent assistance. The faculty support team, and especially Bert Skye, have been invaluable. The project has benefited from innumerable research assistants, but most notably Amy Brown, Kelleen Rae Mull, and Ibrahim Garba. The Arizona Health Sciences Center has been a valuable partner in a range of related projects as well. My thanks go especially to Law Dean Marc Miller, who sustained such a supportive and thoughtful environment to produce this sort of work.

Kathi Hanna was an invaluable partner in her role as developmental editor on the book. She brought both health policy expertise and a thoughtful reader's eye to the project as a whole. My editors at Harvard University Press, Thomas LeBien and Janice Audet, have provided initial enthusiasm and then a steady hand as the project came to fruition.

New York University School of Law hosted a year that included work on the book. The Policy Lab at Brown University hosted me as a visiting scholar. I also did work on the underlying ideas while visiting at Harvard Law School, and presented at workshops hosted by the Petrie-Flom Center for Health Law Policy, Biotechnology, and Bioethics. Since my days as a student, I have appreciated the Center's constant support. I thank Einer Elhauge, Glenn Cohen, Holly Fernandez-Lynch, Carmel Sachar, and Cristine Hutchison-Jones in particular.

This book has greatly benefited from the feedback of several generous scholars. These include Mark Hall, Bill Sage, Matt Lawrence, David Rosenberg, Toni

Massaro, Robert Glennon, Roy Spece, Victor Laurion, Jamie Ratner, Cathy O'Grady, and Simone Sepe. My friend Matt Blake has been a great sounding board and reader. Steve Robertson proofread the final manuscript.

Much of this book builds on ideas presented in prior papers, and I am greatly indebted to all the publishers, editors, research assistants, symposia chairs, and especially the coauthors of those pieces. In particular, Mark Hall, David Orentlicher, Nick Terry, James Hodge, Bernard Chao, Jane Bambauer, David Yokum, and Nir Eyal have convened important meetings on these questions. I would especially acknowledge my collaborators Tara Sklar, Victor Laurion, Christina Cutshaw, Steffie Woolhandler, David Himmelstein, David Yokum, Andy Yuan, Wendan Zhang, Joseph Miller, and Keith Joiner—who engaged on projects most directly relevant to this book, some not yet otherwise published. My work with them has been truly formative for many of the ideas sketched here.

Jamie Robertson helped me to conceive the project, persuading me that there was a larger coherent story growing out of myriad smaller papers over more than a decade. She encouraged me to pursue the bigger ideas, to remember the real human stories, and to stick with the project at innumerable steps along the way. She was the first reader of every word.

# INDEX